PAN-AMERICANISM

A FORECAST OF THE INEVITABLE CLASH
BETWEEN THE UNITED STATES
AND EUROPE'S VICTOR

BY

ROLAND G. USHER, P<small>H</small>.D.

PROFESSOR OF HISTORY, WASHINGTON UNIVERSITY, ST. LOUIS
AUTHOR OF "PAN-GERMANISM," "THE RISE OF THE AMERICAN PEOPLE," ETC.

NEW YORK
THE CENTURY CO.
1915

Copyright, 1915, by
THE CENTURY CO.

Published, March, 1915

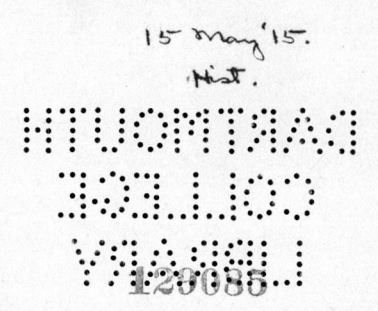

To

THE MEMORY OF

MY GRANDFATHER

WHOSE NAME I BEAR

To

THE LITTLE SON

WHO BEARS MINE

FROM THE LIVING TO THE DEAD
FROM THE PRESENT TO THE FUTURE

PREFACE

I HAVE sought to make as clear as possible within the confines of a brief volume the relation of the United States to the present European situation and to the probable or possible crisis which the end of the war may precipitate. With past history and diplomacy, with strategy and geography, I have dealt where it seemed to me essential to view present factors in their historic relationships; but the major part of the volume has been devoted to the present condition of the United States and of Latin America, with especial attention to Pan-Americanism as a possible solution of American problems. I have not scrupled to examine hypotheses about the future, to compare the probable results of policies, and discuss remote possibilities of war and conquest. The formulation of a national decision in regard to the interests to be furthered and the policies best adapted to that end can result only from an active interchange of opinions between the different sections and interests in the nation and fairly

PREFACE

demands argument about past history and present factors.

To analyze, to discuss, and to examine has therefore been my province and I have left advocacy and proselytizing for those who will draw conclusions from the body of ascertained facts I have done my best to gather. I hold no brief myself for armament or disarmament, for England, Germany, or Latin America, for expansion or imperialism. To treat so vital and controversial a subject objectively and with detachment; to give the reader perspective as well as information, a brief statement of jarring opinions and suggested solutions; this has been my object. Naturally, many of these views set off against each other are contradictory and I beg my readers not to tax me with inconsistency until they are sure that the statements they are comparing are intended to represent my own ideas. I have ventured to suggest in Book IV a reading of the Monroe Doctrine which seems to me to harmonize its apparent inconsistencies and (what is of more consequence) permits us to act to-day in accordance with the dictates of present expediency without doing violence to the true precedent of the past.

To quote evidence and cite authorities was not

PREFACE

possible in a brief book dealing with most of the past and present controversies of American development and not a few of Europe and Asia. Those who will challenge the accuracy of my statements will ask more proof than a few corroborative quotations can afford. For them I have added a short critical bibliography and a few remarks upon the difference in the character of evidence in contemporary history from that in past centuries and its inevitable effect upon the nature of our conclusions.

Though not without definite conclusions about many factors of the situation, I am conscious of no partizanship or interest beyond that of the scholar and observer in search of truth. Yet I am aware that, where notions of impartiality, of patriotism, and of disinterestedness are as various as they are to-day, my own interpretation of these qualities may not be acceptable to all my readers. I can only ask that presumption of honesty and patriotism which each American has a right to expect from another.

WASHINGTON UNIVERSITY, ST. LOUIS.
January, 1915.

CONTENTS

FOREWORD

	PAGES
AMERICAN PROBLEMS AND THE WAR	3–18

Seriousness of the present crisis; clash with Europe's victor inevitable; South America will entice him to Western Hemisphere; the hour for decision here; we must act now; splendid rôle of the United States in history; people anxious to play a noble part in present crisis; knowledge the prerequisite; task of reaching decision made difficult by newness of issue, by varieties of partizanship; we must know—(*a*) whether armament has been essential factor of defense in past, (*b*) the probable victor and his motives, (*c*) whether we are morally bound to defend South America.

BOOK I

THE UNITED STATES

I

FOUNDATIONS OF AMERICAN INDEPENDENCE	21–38

Strategic position of United States the foundation of American independence; first element: the Atlantic Ocean caused isolation in time and space, made European interference in administration impossible, made independence of England a fact; second element: balance of power in Europe, and our lack of geographical relation to Europe important in European quarrels; third element: strategical geography of United States which makes enormous army necessary for invasion or conquest; fourth element: European situation made it impossible for European nations to spare such a force; fifth element: lack of adequate motive for such exertion; —interaction and interplay of these forces during Colonial period and revolution; resultant non-military character of our institutions.

CONTENTS

II

THE SUPREMACY OF THE SEA . . . 39-58

PAGES

The control of the sea by England fundamental fact in our history; to it we owe predominantly English character of American civilization; England's sea-power primarily domestic necessity; other uses seen after control secured; reason for aggressive attitude toward other navies; limitations of the sea-power; their fortunate effect on America; result on the American Revolution; Revolution cost us all privileges on the sea; quarrel with England over rights of neutrals; probable plans for extorting recognition of rights in 1812; result and policy of cordial relations with the sea-power; England's moderation in use of sea-power; to this we owe our lack of a merchant marine; and the size and character of our navy.

III

SOUTH AMERICA AND THE WEST INDIES . 59-79

Colonial period dominated by existence of West Indies; our dependence upon them for medium of European exchange; our determination to have freedom of trade with them; objection to it in England leads to Revolution; Revolution costs us all privileges in West Indies; necessity of cordial relations with sea-power first seen; difficulty of securing favorable terms; factors behind the Monroe Doctrine—(a) our paramount interest in West India trade; (b) necessity to challenge England's control of it; character of English relations with Latin America; independence of republics gives England Spain's control also; challenged by Holy Alliance; (c) tradition of our cordial relations with sea-power; (d) tradition of protection of our independence by keeping European powers out of Americas:—why Canning's offer of coöperation was declined; complex of ideas in Monroe Doctrine of 1823.

IV

THE SUPREMACY OF THE WESTERN HEMISPHERE 80-97

England retains supremacy of Western Hemisphere in 1823; her relations to new Latin-American republics; our interest in West Indies disappeared with downfall of prosperity in sugar islands; cotton changes whole situation by making territorial expansion our immediate interest; resulted in new phase of Monroe Doctrine; England's opposition led to Clayton-Bulwer Treaty; English moderation in use of their supremacy; revolution of situation by rise of German navy; England passed supremacy to United States; results of our attainment of supremacy; nature of our supremacy.

CONTENTS

V

PAGES

OUR PRESENT STRATEGIC POSITION . . 98–108

Developments of nineteenth century rob us of invulnerability; America no longer isolated from Europe; feasibility of administrative or military interference from Europe; United States also able to take offensive; change in character of warfare alters prerequisites of defense; military factors no longer permissive; end of war will probably destroy our remaining defenses.

BOOK II

THE VICTOR

I

EUROPEAN POLICIES AND MOTIVES . . 111–123

The war will not decide economic problems of future; but will place solution in the victor's hands; rapidity of recent economic development and its benefits; determination to provide for its continuance; doctrine of defense for the future and of business at a continued profit; need for expanding markets; all European nations affected by crisis; feasibility of projecting part of some European nation across the Atlantic; economic situation provides the victor with a motive for interference in Western Hemisphere.

II

THE REDISCOVERY OF SOUTH AMERICA . 124–134

South America fitted to solve the victor's problems; reasons why it has played so little part in history—(a) character of early colonization; (b) existence of North America;—its rediscovery mainly due to modern science, and to modern medicine; also to decline in rate of profit obtainable elsewhere.

III

PROBABILITIES OF GERMAN AGGRESSION . 135–150

Character of a German victory; Pan-Germanism will send victorious Germany to Latin America not to United States; suitability of Latin America for German needs; size of the market;

xiii

CONTENTS

extent of resources for development; opportunity for emigration; importance of high development of certain areas; South America most feasible solution for Germany; the easiest for the Allies to concede; the only one Germany can afford to accept; economic and military advantages.

IV

POSSIBILITIES OF ENGLISH AGGRESSION . 151–165

England the probable victor; victory will restore her supremacy in Western Hemisphere; desirable for her to extend her authority in Latin America; she will probably put an end to our supremacy; Alaska can easily be seized; quarrel over relations of United States and Canada imminent; victory will lead to an attempt to limit our trade with Latin America; fundamental domestic economic needs will make extension of English trade with Latin America essential; desire to accelerate pace of England's development probable; and will require increased trade with Latin America.

V

RIGHTS OF NEUTRALS 166–183

United States already at odds with England; English attitude toward neutral trade; character of claims advanced by neutral nations; reasons for English refusal to accept them as valid; specific objections of the United States; why England will accord these serious attention; reasons urging the United States to press the demands; probable results of so doing: ruin of American trade.

VI

JAPANESE EXPANSION AND THE PACIFIC . 184–200

Japan's opportunity; character of Japanese civilization; strategic position of Japan; building of fleet changes strategic situation in Pacific; object of Japanese ambition; growth of German navy robs England of supremacy in the Pacific; she hands it to Japan with conditions; importance of the Philippines to Japan; our opposition to Japanese colonization in Western Hemisphere a source of discord; the European war gives Japan an opportunity to further her ambitions.

CONTENTS

BOOK III

PAN-AMERICANISM

I

PAGES

PREREQUISITES OF PAN-AMERICANISM . 203–217

Meaning of the term; its possible significance in the future; premises of an administrative union or Confederation; prerequisites of such a Confederation—(*a*) federal executive and legislature; (*b*) regular intercourse between the republics; (*c*) legal and social equality of citizens;—probable results of such a Confederation; past history of Pan-Americanism; character of past association; Pan-Americanism not now a reality.

II

FALLACIES OF PAN-AMERICANISM . . 218–231

Assumptions underlying Pan-Americanism; fallacy of a closer geographical relationship of North and South America to each other than to Europe; the fallacy of isolation from Europe; the fallacy of mutual interests between the American republics; historical explanation of these fallacies; common dependence of both Americas upon Europe; sensitivity of Latin Americans; the lack of acquaintanceship between the continents; the United States sundered from Latin America by barriers of race, language, and religion.

III

LACK OF ECONOMIC MUTUALITY . . 232–249

Latin Americans claim that economic benefits of Pan-Americanism all favor the United States; inability of United States to take the place of Europe—(*a*) no adequate merchant marine; (*b*) no exchange facilities for direct business; (*c*) no adequate supply of commodities to fill their demand; (*d*) inability to utilize the bulk of their exports; (*e*) American supply of capital inadequate;—difficulty of supplanting the European nations in the trade of Latin America.

IV

THE SHADOW OF THE PAST . . . 250–266

Lack of mutual trust and confidence between the United States and Latin America; greatest obstacle lies in the history of

CONTENTS

PAGES

the past; Latin Americans interpret our utterances by our actions; past aggression of the United States; treatment of Indians and negroes in the United States; modern Latin Americans, conscious of their mixed parentage, fear the whites; general policy of the white man to make others like him; Latin Americans do not wish to be modeled on United States.

V

ADMINISTRATIVE AND LEGAL PROBLEMS . 267–288

Necessity of common administration and courts to make Pan-Americanism real; premises of such a Confederation are lacking; difference in size between the United States and Latin America formidable difficulty; same disparity between Latin-American republics; administrative difficulties of dealing with so large a territory; methods of appointing officials; obstacles in way of making uniform code of law; in way of enforcing it in the courts; problem of providing a sanction for commands of the Confederation; strength of the democratic movement in Latin America for state sovereignty.

VI

SOCIAL OBSTACLES 289–303

Social equality absolute prerequisite; mixed racial character of Latin Americans; individual attainments; obstacles in way of recognition of social equality in United States; continued independence of Latin America depends upon ability of the people; unwillingness of Americans to grant social equality read as intention to interfere with attempt of Latin Americans to solve their own problems; equality for Latin Americans in United States would mean social equality for all Indians and negroes.

VII

DEFENSIVE WEAKNESS 304–316

Can Pan-Americanism defend the Western Hemisphere against Europe's victor? Latin America not threatened by Europe with political conquest; coöperation of Latin America with United States against Europe's victor impossible because Latin Americans fear United States and not Europe; exclusion of Europeans from Western Hemisphere not to interests of Latin Americans; is defense possible from military point of view?

CONTENTS

VIII

PAGES

THE FUTURE OF PAN-AMERICANISM . . 317–323

Pan-Americanism has no future; prerequisites are non-existent; Latin America about to challenge assumption by United States of supremacy; alliances of Latin America likely to be with Latin states of Europe.

BOOK IV

THE FUTURE

I

CONCRETE ISSUES 327–332

Independence of the sea-power; the supremacy of the Western Hemisphere; expansion in the Western Hemisphere; imperialism in the Far East; all these spell armament.

II

THE PREREQUISITES OF INDEPENDENCE . 333–350

Its ethics; economic desirability; independence a prerequisite of aggressive policy in foreign affairs; prerequisites of independence—(a) an adequate merchant marine; (b) American foreign banking and exchange system; (c) an adequate fleet; (d) an adequate army for defense;—adequacy to be determined by the price set by the victor upon our independence; difference between independence and security; we can afford the expense of such armament.

III

THE ECONOMICS OF EXPANSION . . 351–366

Does the economics of European expansion apply to the United States? Causes of rapid growth of United States; causes of its recent retardation; meaning of economic interdependence; tendency of rate of progress in all nations to diminish; the development of the United States solved the economic problems of Europe in the past; future economic problem of United States; from this will come a demand for help from political agencies; identity of American and European interests; extent of present interests of United States.

CONTENTS

IV

THE ETHICS OF EXPANSION . . . 367–389

Definition of word, ethics; pacifist and individualist ethics as applied to expansion; non-ethical character of economic forces; premise of expansion the desirability of gain; pacifist and individualist ethics never used in past by nations; international ethics based on—(a) notion of self-defense; (b) the ethics of business; subtlety of notion of self-defense to-day; (c) the ethics of the Crusader and explorer;—can justify expansion by the past conduct which nations have agreed was justifiable.

V

THE EXPEDIENCY OF THE MONROE DOCTRINE 390–406

Right of United States to political and economic independence real meaning of Monroe Doctrine; expedients for advancing these ends usually stated instead of the principle itself; true principle too fundamental to abandon; previous expedients we are not bound to maintain; all past expedients now obsolete; we are not obligated to defend Latin America; if Monroe Doctrine means Pan-Americanism, Latin Americans will oppose it; if Monroe Doctrine means expansion or imperialism, to realize it spells aggression; and is to be sustained only by extensive armament.

VI

THE ARGUMENT FOR DISARMAMENT . . 407–421

Duty of the United States to set Europe an example; humanitarian motives; will not involve danger to our integrity; will not sacrifice access to foreign markets; idle to attempt independence of European powers on the sea; aggression unnecessary for the United States; war is incapable of creating economic benefits; intensive development of the United States more profitable than aggression; expense of armament is economic waste; alliance with the sea-power will assure the United States all legitimate advantages.

VII

THE PRICE OF DISARMAMENT . . . 422–442

Armament and disarmament both relative; the United States already disarmed in all but name; real issue a continuance of present policy or to develop adequate armament; price of disarma-

CONTENTS

PAGES

ment the impossibility of reversing the decision when the crisis appears; disarmament may cost us our security; it will probably not cost us our access to world market; it will cost us all our national ambitions, present and future; Latin America will become foreign territory; our extra-continental possessions will be sacrificed; disarmament will retard our economic development; it will compel us to develop our own resources at a constantly diminishing rate of profit; it will compel us to trust our privileges to the good will of the other nations of the world; will this sacrifice really benefit the cause of universal peace? Are the moral and ethical qualities of the present nations such that we can safely trust our national future to their interests and mercy?

BIBLIOGRAPHY 443

INDEX 461

PAN-AMERICANISM

PAN-AMERICANISM

FOREWORD

AMERICAN PROBLEMS AND THE WAR

THE United States is facing a crisis without parallel in its history since the signature of the Declaration of Independence. As a nation, we are less concerned with the European war itself, its causes, its course, than with its ending. Whatever the result of this war may be, whoever wins it, whenever it ends, the victor will be able to threaten the United States, and, if he chooses, to challenge our supremacy in the Western Hemisphere. The motive for challenging it is already in existence; the power with which to do so effectively will beyond doubt be in the victor's hands. We have reached, in fact, a time in our national history when a momentous decision is to be made; one now attainable by careful thought and conscious deliberation, advisedly, wisely; one that is sure to be made later in the face of the crisis itself, hastily, hysterically, and regrettably.

Because the state of war in Europe itself protects us at present from military and naval aggression, it is unwise to infer that it will always do so; for the war will probably destroy that close balance of power in Europe upon which our past immunity from European interference has in large measure rested. Because we have given no just cause for aggression, let us not assume that we may not be assailed; the example of Belgium should suffice all nations for at least a century. Because the belligerent nations to-day avow no intention to make war on us and no schemes involving us, we are not necessarily safe; we have only to remember that all of them regard the present war as a war of self-defense on their own part and of unprovoked aggression upon that of their enemy. Whenever the end of the war comes, whatever the result, it will undoubtedly affect our political, military, and naval position in ways which will scarcely be matters of indifference to us. Exactly what the effect will be only the circumstances of the victory itself can show.

The lure which will in all probability entice the victor to the Western Hemisphere will be South America. So far as the United States is concerned, there can be only two victors in this war. With France, Russia, Austria, and the lesser nations, the United States will hardly be concerned. Only England and Germany are in a position to compete for the supremacy of the sea and for the control of the approaches to the Western Hemisphere. The Monroe Doctrine is commonly understood to mean that the United States obligates itself to preserve intact the Western Hemisphere from European aggression. With it the victor will inevitably clash.

Although we need not doubt that the victor will come and that he will be powerful enough to injure us, we need not conclude of necessity that we are in real danger, or that armament is our true recourse. Elaborate armament, undertaken solely to know that no one could hope to attack us with success, would be foolish; but it does not in the least follow that we are in danger because we are not ready to fight. On the other hand, disarmament proceeding from sentimental pleas about the horrors of war would be unwise. There are conceivably real dangers with which we can easily cope, the preparation for which it would be criminal to neglect. Indeed, before we arm or conclude not to arm, let us count as nearly as we may the cost and view the probable consequences of one or the other. Whatever we do let us undertake it only after very general agreement as to its probabilities. If we maintain the Monroe Doctrine or espouse Pan-Americanism, begin building a merchant marine or strengthening the fleet and the army, let us establish beforehand exactly what ends we purpose to subserve by such means. If we decide on the other hand that extensive armament is inexpedient, we must visualize with exceeding clearness before we come to our final conclusion what the exact consequences will be, and what policies, ambitions, or interests the decision will compel us to sacrifice. Obviously, to enounce certain policies and to neglect adequate armament to maintain them can lead to but one result—national humiliation at the victor's hands.

The hour for decision therefore has struck. We must know in the near future what our attitude is to be toward the European situation to be created by the ending of this war, as well as toward those probable developments of the war in the immediate future which may affect this country. To fail to reach a decision at this time will be to compel ourselves to renounce all the interests, policies, and ambitions which any degree of adequate preparation would make it imperative to maintain or secure. Not to decide is to reach a negative decision as effectively as if it had been reached by deliberation. If we fail to grasp the requirements of our present or future position or to comprehend the probable current of international affairs, we shall simply throw away all opportunity of furthering or protecting the interests of the United States. We shall do so blindly, ignorant of what our true interests are.

The United States has played an important and unique part in the history of nations. Dominion is ours, wealth almost beyond estimation, prosperity, cultivation, liberty, and for these inestimable boons we have paid no price in blood or in women's tears. The foundation of our wealth and greatness lies in no sense in aggression, conquest, or spoliation. We owe all to the development of great natural resources by the honest labor of sturdy men and women. Strong differences of opinion about national policy and the great moral issue of slavery compelled our fathers to fight a long civil war; more than once we have been involved in foreign wars, while once or twice we have been hurried by unfortunate counsel into aggression. Such actions have been contrary to popular judgment, and have fortunately contributed little to our national position. We stand therefore in the congress of nations in an almost unique position as the only great nation which does not in large measure owe its present territory and international prominence to a series of aggressive conquests against its neighbors or inferiors.

The majority of the people of the United States are resolved to play a dignified and disinterested part in this world war, to act if possible in accordance with the highest ethical motives upon which national actions can be based. While they are not disposed to sacrifice essentials if once it is shown that they are truly essentials of the national welfare or of the national safety, they clearly deny that the ordinary premises of European political action have any *prima facie* value for us. The people undoubtedly feel that we have to-day a unique opportunity to place in abeyance our own temporal and temporary interests in favor of disinterested action in furtherance of the highest ideals of the race. They would engrave our national name among those most splendid on history's roll.

If they are insistent that the opportunity should not be thrown away, they are anxious not to be misled as to its true character. Even the least intelligent seem to apprehend instinctively that nobility of action is indissolubly united to wisdom and discretion, and that to be sublime an action must be the result of a conscious choice between alternatives, and not merely the outcome of a headlong impetuosity which by good fortune stumbled across the truth. The American people prefer a generous part devoid of gain and even entailing loss to one which they know beforehand spells selfish aggression or selfish conservation. What is now needed is not action, but that knowledge which must form the basis of intelligent action. Yet as a nation our past indifference to foreign relations and international complications has been almost as marked as our disinterestedness and impartiality; the one no doubt has lent strength to the others. To-day these traits make possible a temperance in action and a discretion in judgment not possible in most European countries where primary interests and antipathies appear in the populace in the guise of passion and prejudice. There has never been a time when knowledge was more imperative; there has never been a time when the people at large were more determined to acquire it. A great variety of policies are being waved insistently before their eyes, and immediate action demanded by vehement advocates. Rightly, the people have denied action and have sought adequate information. They will not be frightened into armament by alarmists, nor yet committed to non-resistance without due consideration, despite the importunity and zeal of idealists and pacifists.

How is it possible to adopt a liberal and unselfish policy without endangering the national safety or risking more of its material well-being than the frailty of the majority will endure? The task of reaching a decision upon the present interests of the United States and upon the policy best adapted to advance them is made difficult by the newness of the issue itself, for in reality we are facing a problem which has never before appeared in our history, to which the policies and precedents of the past do not explicitly apply, and to which it may not be possible to adapt them successfully. We have had no primary interest in crystallizing our foreign policies around some great national necessity, comparable to the European need for the defense of the national independence. In the past our interests have been secondary in importance, permissive rather than essential, issues whose desirability or inexpediency were by no means clear. Nor have these varied interests always been consistent with one another, or complementary. No event has ever focused all of them at once before the nation and revealed their lack of coherence and essential relationship. Sometimes we have furthered one, sometimes another; again a third has received our attention. The present situation, therefore, which does focus at once all our interests, has produced a new problem which compels us to comprehend our lack of a primary interest, and, in the European sense, to grasp the diversity of our secondary interests, and, emphasize the importance of deciding between them. They cannot all be subserved at the same time, any more than we can vote for disarmament and in the same breath reaffirm the Monroe Doctrine.

To establish clearly the fundamental facts of the historic past where our interests had origin is imperative, if we care to see in perspective present interests and possible policies. Otherwise we shall never separate the good from the bad, the cogent from the unimportant. Daily we see excellent causes vitiated by bad logic and ignorance of history; we see praiseworthy motives marred by excess of zeal; unimpeachable premises followed by lame conclusions; specious conclusions which appear convincing until their obvious premises are easily demolished; arguments which would be cogent were not the conclusion itself assumed as a premise. Indeed, it is not about the conclusions and policies which we shall quarrel, but about the premises. What we need to establish at present is the fundamental factors and postulates from which any conclusion must proceed, and which must be duly weighed and considered before any wise conclusion can be reached.

We shall soon have as many varieties of patriots as there are shades of opinion, and much ill-feeling and heartburning over their different policies. If only each could remember to ascribe to others the same honesty of intention by which he feels himself strongly moved! Unfortunately, the most ardent and eager friends are not always the wisest counselors; nor has a passionate affection for one's country and readiness for its service been invariably coupled with accurate information and great discretion. We shall need a wise constraint more often than zeal and adequate information more often than enthusiasm.

One of the most peculiar and in some respects one of the most annoying aspects of great crises is the insistence by most of the adherents of irreconcilable opinions that they alone are the true patriots who have their country's welfare at heart. There is a cheap jingoism always waving the "bloody shirt" and shouting for war and armament without in the least comprehending what the demand involves. There is, if anything, a more dangerous enemy of calm and discreet action in the variety of jingo who has robbed the name of patriot of all its finer and loftier connotations. He spurns as an imputation upon the honor of his ancestors the questioning of his country's preparedness; he thrusts scornfully from him as unnecessary any impartial inquiry into its history to discover whether or not the facts correspond with his suppositions. His bluster masks a very real ignorance and an actual intellectual cowardice; for he is afraid his assumptions might not stand the test of examination and he fears to surrender them because he is not capable of imagining anything to substitute for them. Such "patriots" are not satisfied that our history should be glorious; they insist that it should be glorious according to certain preconceived notions about glory. The search for actual knowledge, the endeavor to reach a clear and wise decision after thoughtful consideration, should be recognized as the duty of patriotism, for by it alone can the true welfare of the country be advanced.

When we stand as a nation face to face with a crisis of undoubted gravity which may imperil in the near future the national safety and which certainly will leave deep traces upon the national structure, we have a right to ask ourselves in all seriousness and with all reverence what have been the props beneath our independence, the foundation of our immunity from European aggression during the last century; the basis of the respect in which we are clearly held by all the great nations of Europe. We are making no sentimental inquiry; we are abroad upon no indifferent quest. We need to know and have a right to know how far our history is the work of military and naval prowess and how far our independence and our proud position in the family of nations are due to factors less evanescent and perishable than the genius of generals and the valor of armies. It may be vital for us to know the truth. If our nation has been built by the fruits of war, there will be at least a presumption raised that we shall need to defend in arms what our ancestors have built by arms. If we find that our independence and security rest, in part at least, on other than military factors, if we can show that the aggression of Europe has been checked in the past by stronger and less personal forces than armies and fleets, we shall raise a very strong presumption that extensive armament will not be indispensable to insure the safety of a rich and powerful nation, intrenched by Nature in a continent, and her loins girt on each side by a thousand miles of ocean.

The cheap enthusiasm of the so-called "Fourth-of-July patriot" eagerly assumes that military prowess must be the basis of national glory, because it is easily understood and furnishes the sort of explanation for independence which the blood-soaked history of Europe has taught him to expect. The United States has the unique distinction among nations of owing its independence and its safety to its geographical situation, and to the arts of peace. To fail to grasp this fact and all it implies is to veil the reality of our ancestors' achievement, and to gloss over its real difficulties and vital significance. To win revolutions and protect nations with conquering armies and victorious fleets is simple and comparatively inglorious; rascals have been good generals; much stupidity and blundering have had to be retrieved by the use of violence, while much iniquity has been exalted by victory. Intelligence, organization, a careful study of the realities of life are indispensable for the achievement of great results without armies. They are a thousandfold nobler and their victories a thousandfold more permanent than those attained to the sound of cannons and to the shrieks of the dying. No true patriot would insist in the face of the horrors of this present war upon believing that the independence of his country had necessarily been won, and necessarily must be preserved, by military and naval prowess. The true patriot will rather rejoice if he can convince himself that no such heavy price was paid to redeem his liberty or to insure his comfortable fireside, and he will look into the future with real confidence and a clear conscience, calm in his belief that we are not necessarily in danger of conquest because unprepared. To the consideration of the past and present position and interests of the United States the first part of this volume will be devoted.

The situation in Europe, the probable victor and his interests and ambitions, will also be of such consequence in reaching a final conclusion that the second book will be given over to their elucidation. We must know who is likely to appear, what circumstances will make possible, probable, or profitable his appearance.

The belief is common in the United States that the Monroe Doctrine has protected South America from European aggression since 1823. If this be true, we have a strong moral obligation to maintain that doctrine in the interests of the weaker American republics, should they be actually threatened by Europe's victor; nor will the United States shirk or abandon this moral obligation because it may involve expenditure and require armament. If such a moral obligation does exist, if the Southern Continent is actually and literally dependent upon our protection, those facts will be extremely cogent. If they shall not prove to be true on investigation, equally material premises will have been established.

The issue is indeed perplexing and immediate. Perhaps the most vital fact in American history is the non-military character of the American people, their disinclination to arm except for the gravest reason, their entire lack of present interest in conquest. In obvious conflict with these national characteristics is the assertion of our paramount interest in the Western Hemisphere and of our right to exclude European nations from it; for if our traditions argue against the use of force, the Monroe Doctrine assumes our willingness to exert it if need should arise. The two are irreconcilable, and the day has now come when the test is about to be made to discover which of the two is the stronger current of our national life.

In reaching some wise conclusion, we shall be much assisted by knowing whether the United States and South America are vitally related to one another, whether they possess mutual interests and sympathies, and really desire to act in concert for the exclusion of European nations from this hemisphere. The variety of notions called Pan-Americanism will require close investigation, for upon the result of that inquiry will depend in large measure the expediency of maintaining the Monroe Doctrine. If our interests and those of South America are mutual and strong, and are based upon fundamental principles of political and economic association, the maintenance of the Monroe Doctrine, even under arms, may conceivably be expedient. But if our interests are not of that nature, it will obviously be unwise for us to base our foreign policy with Europe and South America upon facts which are not existent.

We shall then be in possession of sufficient information about fundamental forces, factors, and policies to discuss in some detail the pros and cons of armament and disarmament and to envisage clearly the probable consequences of the adoption or abandonment of policies. The alternatives should then be clear; the decision between them is for the American people.

BOOK I
THE UNITED STATES

The United States

CHAPTER I

FOUNDATIONS OF AMERICAN INDEPENDENCE

THE strategic position of the United States is peculiar and unique, created by the interplay between our geographical location and great natural forces, economic factors, and conditions in Europe. It has been throughout our history the foundation of American[1] independence. The first and most important element in it is the

[1] The Latin Americans protest against the use of the word "America" to denote the United States of America and of "American" to denote its citizens as contrary to the geographical facts. While an accurate terminology is desirable, the purpose of language is to convey ideas and not to create distinctions, and popular usage in the United States as well as the State Department has so definitely established such a meaning that it has seemed pedantic to object to it. "Central America" and "South America" are used to denote those geographical districts, while "Latin America" and "Latin Americans" denote the twenty republics south of the Rio Grande and their peoples.

Atlantic Ocean, a barrier between us and Europe three thousand miles broad, the existence of which meant for us, in the seventeenth and eighteenth centuries, practical isolation in space and time. Men forget with readiness the commonest facts about life in the past when only sailing-ships were available, and when, too, the ships were small. Then the voyage across the Atlantic was no mere pleasure trip, but an adventure fraught with some peril and accompanied by a great deal of hardship. Storms were not less frequent than they are now; food was bad at the best; scurvy was prevalent; while the sea and wind effectively prevented anything like promptness or regularity of arrival. Swift vessels under good conditions made the voyage in a month. Six weeks was considered a fast trip, and two months was very common. Under such conditions the Atlantic was in point of time wider than it now is long. The regular mail steamers plying between England and Australia travel a distance approaching one half of the circumference of the globe in about the same time that a fast ship under favorable conditions needed in the eighteenth century to go from London to New York.

This general slowness of communication made literally impossible any active interference in

AMERICAN INDEPENDENCE

America by European nations. About three months was necessary under the best conditions to get an answer or to learn of some crisis and to send directions as to what should be done about it. A defeat in America was therefore not really known in England, France, or Spain until the victor had had ample time to make the best use of its results. Before an army could be actually gotten together, embarked, and landed, news of its preparation would have preceded it by a sufficient number of weeks to have permitted preparations for defense by no means as inadequate as the disparity in potential strength between the various settlements in America and the European nations would seem to indicate. Military interference in America was made extremely difficult by the Atlantic Ocean, which until about 1840 placed us as far from Europe in point of time and space as Australia is to-day from New York or London. This is the fundamental fact of our location, this, the fundamental barrier upon which our independence rests. Other factors, potent indeed, have greatly assisted at one time and another this primary geographical position, but it was unquestionably for two centuries and a half the great formative fact in American history.

It created a separation in point of time between

us and England which made anything approaching the government of the colonies from England a literal impossibility. Actual directions could not be received from England soon or constantly enough to be of the slightest avail, even if the colonists had been anxious to obtain them; while to have waited for actual assistance or even for advice would at many crises have invited destruction. Nor could the English find out what was happening in America with either promptitude or regularity. American democracy grew up in the wilderness, to furnish the government and direction which the mother country, for geographical reasons, was incapable of affording. We never were dependent upon England or any other European country. The Atlantic Ocean made us independent from the first.

Independence was necessarily an accomplished fact that no fiat could create, and which was in 1776 a condition resulting from the operation of forces in the decades just passed. The Revolution by no means created the thirteen States. It declared the already accomplished fact that those thirteen States were independent entities distinct from England in ideals and interests, strong enough to maintain themselves against the rest of the world, experienced in self-government, and imbued with the spirit of liberty.[1]

[1] Usher, *Rise of the American People*, 31.

AMERICAN INDEPENDENCE

As a matter of fact, we did not fight for independence; it was thrust upon us. We were separated from the very first so far in point of time from Europe that all their armies and all their fleets were incapable of robbing us of administrative independence. Conceivably, they might have set up a government in America by force, but in no possible way could they have governed us from Europe.

The Declaration of Independence was a statement of the evident fact that the American Colonies were in reality, and long had been, independent of England; that they had governed themselves in the past without assistance, and could do so in the future; that their interests were too different from those of the mother country for them to accept her decisions in regard to policy.[1]

The second factor in our strategic position one might almost call a corollary of our location beyond the Atlantic. For some centuries at least the really vital fact in European politics has been the formation of a series of alliances among the stronger countries for the preservation of what has been called the *balance of power*. The geographical structure of Europe is peculiar, and has juxtaposed a number of strong countries in a relatively

[1] *Ibid.*, 118–119.

PAN-AMERICANISM

small space without erecting between them effective barriers, although leaving at the same time a sufficient geographical hindrance to their complete union. They are separated without being isolated. With no love for one another, they are not able to free themselves entirely from one another's presence. All the nations in Europe, therefore, are potential allies of one another and potential enemies. Very few of them could regard as incredible war with any other nation on the continent; their independence, therefore, and their economic strength and development, are of significance to all other possible enemies and allies. The control of territory obtained by political domination resulting from military conquest would put several nations in a far more advantageous position and enable them to further their own ambitions and antipathies. For instance, the possession of Belgium has been at times of great military advantage to both France and Germany, and has enabled either to attack the other much more effectively. The possession of Denmark or Sweden would be of vast consequence to Russia, and would enable her to threaten Germany's naval position and perhaps insure her the control of the Baltic. Every nation affected by the strengthening of France, Germany, or

AMERICAN INDEPENDENCE

Russia would be vitally interested in either of these happenings.

The United States lacks a geographical relation to Europe of importance in European quarrels. No nation or group of nations could find its independence or integrity threatened by our existence. Our economic development, therefore, produced in Europe no alarms, while the economic development of Germany produced many. As we threaten nobody, the control of our territory would be of no advantage to any European nation for defense or for aggression; indeed, from a military point of view our political independence or dependence is almost a matter of indifference to Europe. To overestimate the importance of this lack of relation to the European situation is impossible. The primary motive for conquest as it appears in Europe is lacking; the primary purpose of an assault upon our political independence is absent. Legions numerous enough to shake the land with their tread, navies great enough to burden the sea with their weight, have not erected in the way of the aggressor in Europe barriers one half as formidable. Our political independence is as secure from Germany or Russia as it is from England or France. The sea is absolutely impartial. We are not a part of Europe. We never can be a part of

Europe. We are independent and free by the accident of geography, a fact which armies and navies are powerless to change and scarcely able to strengthen.

The third factor in our strategic position is the strategical geography of the United States itself. Continental United States[1] is divided into three districts, the Atlantic coast, the Mississippi valley, and the Pacific coast. From a military point of view the three are unrelated, for, while there are certain roads between them, certain strategic points controlling the communications between them along these roads, the enemy might control one of the three without in any way insuring his military possession of the others. The country is so vast, the area necessarily covered by operations would be so stupendous, that its military control in the European fashion by the capture of two or three points is out of the question. The Civil War demonstrated the impossibility of expecting the conquest of the Mississippi valley to insure the control of the Atlantic slope; the Revolution showed the complete fallacy of supposing that any part of the Atlantic slope insured its possessor

[1] Throughout this book, in geographical statements or comparisons, "the United States," or "America," mean continental United States, excluding Alaska and our island possessions.

military control of any sort over other parts of it. If the campaign were being conducted by two or three millions of men, the very magnitude of the operations might conceivably develop something resembling strategic relationship between various parts of the country, but nothing short of the simultaneous invasion of the Atlantic coast at a variety of points could possibly give the aggressor control or allow him even to knock at the gateways leading into the interior.

Fortunately, too, the Atlantic and Pacific coast districts are both comparatively narrow and are separated from the great bulk of the continent by high mountain chains which can be easily passed by an army only at the extremities. Through New York and through Georgia are broad roads leading into the Mississippi valley. If the invader chose one and neglected the other, the United States army could successfully cut his communications with his fleet and leave him at our mercy somewhere in the interior. He would be compelled to operate in force through both, and to guard in addition approaches like the Cumberland Gap, in order to protect his rear. In fact, the Mississippi valley is a great natural fortress, separated from the sea on both sides by mountains whose passes are neither numerous nor difficult of defense. In this vast territory live the majority of the American people and in it are all the essentials for equipping an army and for its indefinite maintenance. The loss of New York as a seaport and commercial center could be easily remedied by using some other excellent harbor. Effectively to blockade the United States would be a colossal task for the English fleet; to take military possession and hold it would be a colossal task for the German army. The strategic character of the Atlantic coast and of the Mississippi valley is such as to require the full strength of any European power for conquest and perhaps even for invasion.

This makes truly significant the delicate balance of the European situation. Any nation sending enough ships and men to insure success in operations against the United States would so weaken its forces in Europe as to invite annihilation at the hands of its potential enemies who have been waiting for centuries for it to commit some such capital blunder. There are several armies in Europe and three fleets which could undertake hostile operations against the United States with definite prospects of success. There is no doubt about it: the United States can be invaded, it might even be conquered; but success would not

AMERICAN INDEPENDENCE

be of the slightest conceivable importance to any European state, and would involve operations of such magnitude that the aggressor would risk his national independence in Europe. The delicate balance between the various European nations, their rivalries and hatreds, their determination to prevent any one state from becoming too strong, have been therefore a cardinal factor in our strategic position. So long as this balance endures, it will so aid the Atlantic Ocean and the strategic character of the United States itself as to make us virtually invulnerable.

Assuming, however, that no European nation had anything to gain by the political control of the United States or by its military conquest, were there not economic reasons rendering such operations desirable? That there have never been such economic motives in the past has also been an important factor in our strategic position. For upwards of two centuries the Western Hemisphere was easy prey for several of the European nations, and had there been a strong economic motive counseling possession, the present territory of the United States might well have been the scene of a battle royal or have experienced at least the vicissitudes of Central America and the West Indies. But while the United States has had the greatest attraction for individuals, it has never furnished nations with an adequate incentive for political conquest. Here men and women have sought homes on a fertile soil, blest by climate and nature, but where the products which interested European nations were lacking. The Spaniard conquered Mexico and Peru for their gold and silver; the English fought and bled to monopolize the importation of negroes to the West Indies and to Central America; kings and princes risked the investment of money in the Hudson Bay Company for the exploitation of the fur trade in northern Canada; and such was the value of the sugar trade of the West Indies in the eighteenth century that European nations fairly jostled against one another in their haste to acquire islands. But tobacco, codfish, grain, lumber, lacked speculative attraction.

Indeed, we had nothing which the Europeans would accept after importunity, and were obliged to sell our own produce in the West India Islands, the Azores, or Africa, where products could be had which possessed exchange value in Europe. Clearly continental America possessed nothing which any European nation thought a fair reward for the expense and difficulty of conquest. The English never had to fight to retain possession of their continental colonies; the French and Indian wars

AMERICAN INDEPENDENCE

were nothing more than raids. The real object of the Seven Years' War was the conquest of the French colonies. In fact, the English themselves did not regard their continental colonies as of any particular consequence until 1763, for the attention of the Government and of individuals was riveted upon the West India Islands. Thus, during the decades when the continental colonies were in the making, the economic interests of Europe lay elsewhere, and the general routes of trade left them to one side. They occupied, indeed, as far as Europe was concerned, for many, many decades the invulnerable, though undesirable position of the poor man who has nothing which the thieves value, and who therefore goes his way in peace.

Our strategic position is really the result of the interaction and interdependence of these factors. None of them alone would be quite so potent. When the width of the Atlantic and the distance in space and time from Europe add themselves to the fact that our location has no strategic relationship, advantageous or disadvantageous, for warring European powers, and then join to themselves the large force needed to undertake operations against the United States plus the extreme danger to which the despatch of such a force from Europe would expose the aggressor, a position somewhat approaching invulnerability is the result. When in addition we literally possess nothing here which would warrant any European nation in conquering us, we may breathe with considerable freedom and calmly regard statements that we are in immediate danger. As long as these strategic factors exist, continental United States will never be in danger of European invasion or conquest. The question whether they are about to change must be reserved for another chapter.

How admirably these forces have protected us in the past centuries appears in our history. In the early sixteenth century the Spanish explored the United States with some pertinacity and saw nothing that they cared for. The victory of the English fleet over the Spanish Armada in 1588 and the revolt of the Dutch effectually occupied the efforts of Spain's greatest ruler. Then during the long years when the weak and struggling English colonies might have been wiped out by assault, the English fleet protected us from other nations. The Atlantic Ocean and the separation in distance and time saved us from English administrative interference and enabled us to develop an indigenous, democratic, independent administration. During the seventeenth century English kings and ministers were much preoccupied with the Civil War,

AMERICAN INDEPENDENCE

the Restoration, and the Revolution of 1689. Scarcely had these been settled when a series of European wars consumed most of the money and much of the energy of the mother country. Then there were the West India Islands, from which came a great income.

In the time of George III, the mother country first realized the strength and importance of the colonies which had grown up on the mainland, and the attempt of ministers to erect an efficient administration of officials resident in America opened the eyes of the colonists to the reality of their political and administrative independence of the English Government, and proved to them the very simple thesis that, if they had wrought so well in the past unaided, they were abundantly able to govern themselves in the future without assistance. The Atlantic Ocean was the true basis of this independence, and the English army and the English fleet could not in any conceivable manner remove it. There was in reality nothing to defend. We must eventually have won the Revolution, even if we lost every battle. In fact, Washington soon saw that he had merely to fight a defensive war and wear out the English; that the one thing he had to fear was a serious defeat in the open field, an eventuality easily evaded by not accepting battle unless the conditions were unusually favorable or the political situation made some sort of a stand advisable.

The English, too, soon learned the truth. They found that there were no strategic points on the Atlantic Coast. They tried Boston, New York, Philadelphia, and learned, to their great disgust, that marching and countermarching had been of no avail; when in force they had marched pretty much where they wished, but were no better off than if they had stayed where they were in the first place. Conquest would require a very large army, would compel them to hold a great variety of widely severed districts, and would make essential subsequently the garrisoning of the country by an army almost as large as the one needed to conquer it in order to keep it in subjection. The Americans had not the slightest doubt that they could resist any effort the English could bring to bear and could continue the war indefinitely. The English were no less confident that they possessed enough force to win the war, but they had no doubt whatever that conquest involved an operation of greater magnitude than was worth while. They weakened their position in Europe more than was safe, and gained nothing commensurate from a military and naval point of view. The continental

AMERICAN INDEPENDENCE

colonies were worthless possessions upon which to expend effort and resources when the same amount of exertion could be directed easily enough toward possessions in the Mediterranean and India of indubitable value. The Revolutionary army was not actually called upon to expel the British; the strategic factors were too powerful to require more than assistance. The army, in fact, merely hastened a result which time alone and passive resistance could not have failed in the end to secure.

The formative effect of our strategic position upon our policy has been deep and fundamental. So well was the operation of these factors understood by the Revolutionary leaders that they firmly impressed upon the country the obvious conclusion that our political independence would not require elaborate military dispositions to maintain. For us wars would be abnormal and in violation of the true interests of the aggressor, since no European power would possess a motive for assailing us or for challenging our independence.

It should be laid down, therefore, as a fundamental tenet of American policy that we need not anticipate war or prepare for it as a probable contingency. Our organization should be fundamentally non-military. What had not needed armies to create could not normally require armies to maintain. If wars did come, if they were, so to speak, thrust upon us, we should meet them as best we could, and depend upon the peculiar structure of our country to delay the invader's progress while we were making adequate preparations. Civil war, if such an unfortunate eventuality should arise, would find both parties equally unprepared and therefore equally matched; but civil war was almost entirely abnormal, unexpected, accidental, and obviously not a thing to be prepared for in a healthy political community. The necessity, therefore, of the defense of the country by a large army was not regarded as likely by the men who won our independence, and to whom indeed we owe the fundamentally non-military character of our organization and the established conviction that for the United States armies are abnormal. Whether or not the time has come to reconsider this decision will appear in its proper place for discussion.

CHAPTER II

THE SUPREMACY OF THE SEA

THE undisputed supremacy of the continent of North America in our own hands, the undisputed control of the seas by England—these two have been fundamental formative influences in the development of the United States, and have left deep marks upon its foreign policy. Even before the germs of English colonies existed in the present United States, this sea-power was a reality, and to-day it still endures. We have adjusted ourselves to this fact during the long centuries of growth, and have so accustomed ourselves to it that we regard it almost as one of the world's axioms, to be accepted accordingly. Yet we cannot omit from consideration the sea-power in England's hands and explain or understand the history of the United States.

To it we owe the predominantly English character of American civilization. Many races arriving here at different epochs have somehow or other become fused and amalgamated into a different nation from any of them, a nation perhaps of mixed blood, but whose characteristics are predominantly English. The English language has conquered all other tongues, as English literature for the vast majority has conquered all other literary traditions. Few other races preserve either their identity or their language into the third generation, and in most it disappears in the second generation. Our laws, courts, and institutions are as clearly descendants of the English institutions of the seventeenth century as are the present practices in England. While tolerant of all religions, the United States is reckoned a Protestant nation, drawing its religious inspiration in the main from characteristic forms of English Protestantism. So much was assured on that summer day when the English fleet wrested the supremacy of the sea from the Spanish Armada in the English Channel; the part of the Western Hemisphere not already occupied by the Spanish fell into the hands of the nation whose fleet controlled its approaches; for better or for worse that nation was to play the leading part in colonizing and developing the Northern Continent. The supremacy of the sea made this inevitable. For this same reason the

THE SUPREMACY OF THE SEA

English nation is the only nation which has played a part as a nation in the upbuilding of the United States. From other nations have come persons of ability, sincerity, and intelligence, whose coöperation has been vital to the result; but the only European nation to play a part in shaping the United States is England. This is a legacy of the supremacy of the sea to the United States, and there is in our history hardly another fact to be compared with it in significance.

The exact nature of England's supremacy of the sea is extremely subtle and complex, and from an international point of view is composed as much of the things which the English refrain from doing as of those which they do; indeed, so far as the United States is concerned, what the English fleet could do if it chose has scarcely entered into the problem. The English supremacy of the sea fundamentally was and is a domestic necessity maintained rather as a part of England's defensive position on the channel than for the purpose of exerting influence in different parts of the world. It is this fact which we must firmly grasp if we are to understand the relation of the English sea-power to-day to international alliances in general and to the United States in particular.

Many centuries ago the English saw that the

control by a fleet of the waters surrounding their island would make it invulnerable. Armies had to be conveyed across the channel by fleets, and could be more easily defeated before they started than after they arrived. From the first they developed their fleet, became in time a nation of sailors, and developed a new type of ship and a variety of naval strategy and tactics which in 1588 vanquished by their own inherent excellence the former possessor of the supremacy of the sea.

Originally intended for defense against invasion, the fleet was promptly seen to be an instrument capable of a variety of uses. When England realized decades later that she could no longer maintain her population from produce raised in the British Isles, she began to import the necessary food, and soon the raw materials required to keep her factories at work, secure in the conviction that the fleet would keep open the highways over which her own merchant marine brought her these necessities of life from distant lands. To-day the industrial fabric of England is built upon the seapower. The very food and clothes of her swelling millions depend upon it. It is still the premise of continued existence, the essential prerequisite of prosperity. Yet although to-day more than ever the prime factor in England's policy, it is still not an international, but primarily a domestic, factor. It was not created to threaten or rule other nations, and exerts an influence in international affairs only as a result of its necessary existence for the maintenance of domestic peace and prosperity. It is to-day so vital for defense that it could not possibly be used for aggression alone; to risk in an offensive war, undertaken purely for aggression, the very bulwark of the national existence would be folly of the worst description, a fact of the utmost consequence in the study of international affairs.

As soon as the English discovered how indispensable the fleet was to their own welfare, they viewed in a different light the existence of other navies. The latter were by no means rivals of an English fleet engaged in aggressive attempts to broaden the English domain and thus to extend her authority and power; they were possible assailants of England, possible protectors of an invading army, and were, first and foremost, capable of taking the bread from the mouths of Englishmen and of stripping their clothes from their backs. Such a possibility could not be coolly contemplated. The very life of England depended upon the control of the sea, not merely upon the prevention of armed invasion. She did not therefore believe it expedient to countenance rival navies or rival merchant fleets, for in the days of wooden sailing-ships a large merchant marine could be readily transformed into a navy quite capable of fighting with deadly effect. To her hostility of navies and merchant marines she joined a disinclination to leave the strategic points controlling the ocean roads in the hands of other nations. They were in fact of no great importance for the defense of England from invasion and of no vital assistance in aggression against other nations; they did insure England's firm control of the ocean highways along which came her food supplies.

Until 1776 the American colonies were a part of the British Empire, and were protected from the aggression of other nations by the English fleet. Our colonial trade and shipping were fostered by the Navigation Acts, and were together the basis of the wealth which made the colonies strong enough in 1776 to claim and to make good their independence. If our independence is primarily due to our own strategic position, it is almost as fundamentally the work of the supremacy of the sea.

The English have understood the limitations of the fleet as well as they have its uses. It could control the approaches to various countries; it

THE SUPREMACY OF THE SEA

could insure access to English ships and restrict the access of other nations; it could always secure for the English commercial privileges. In this sense it could control the land, but never could it insure or even make possible political domination. With the coöperation of an army transported and maintained by the fleet, conquest was possible; without it, impossible. While the fleet controlled the sea, England at home was invulnerable, an army was unnecessary, and the English grew to look upon the creation of an army as an extraordinary measure of so unusual and indeed of so unessential a nature as to require the most extraordinary justification. To send an army away from England could be expedient in few circumstances. Were there any benefits likely to accrue to England from conquest and political domination which the fleet could not secure unaided by the simple fact of its ability to close the seas? The tradition grew firm that any object which could not be attained by the fleet with the aid of a relatively small army was *prima facie* something certain to cost for its achievement out of all proportion to its value. England's island position, the defensive character of her sea-power, made her a non-military nation whose fundamental position made essential an offensive policy on the sea only when her control was threatened, and made inexpedient attempts at the political domination of distant countries the moment large military forces became necessary to establish or maintain it.

For the United States there could scarcely have been a decision of greater importance. The supremacy of the sea has been for three centuries, throughout the whole of our history, in the hands of a nation whose own position made inexpedient an attempt to expand its political authority outside its own borders. The question of force, naturally, was not raised until the American Revolution. We were until then willing subjects of England, valuing the connection and admiring the mother country. With the issue over which the war broke out we are not here concerned. A dispute did arise; subjects of England declined flatly to obey administrative orders and statutes passed by the mother country; they declared in words and made good in arms their determination to resist. They created promptly a situation to which this fundamental English policy applied. Was the political domination in the colonies worth maintaining by an army?

The nature of the trouble was the all-important factor to establish. The English learned from all their officers and officials as well as from many Americans that there was no revolution, but simply an armed outbreak led by a few gentlemen of excellent character, but misguided notions, whose following consisted of men without property and aiming at their own personal aggrandizement and without sympathy with the lofty ideals held by the leaders. The movement possessed, so the English were told, neither strength, coherence, nor support. A little show of force,—and it would be quite essential to show it and not to exert it,—a little pressure on exactly the right persons, the hanging of a few and the exiling of a few more, and the whole would be over. Some years were needed to convince George III and his advisers that their informants in America had been badly mistaken as to the size and character of the movement. Force had been shown, and had not terrified the "rebels" in the least; several attempts to apply it had been met with a firmness which proved that the new movement was by no means the work of a low-spirited rabble; the character of the men who had come forward all over the country to lend it countenance and support demonstrated beyond doubt that the wealth and intelligence of the country had by no means rallied unanimously in support of English authority.

PAN-AMERICANISM

The moment the truth became clear in London the whole situation took on a vitally different aspect. There had been little hesitation about dealing promptly with disorderly conduct in the colonies. There was much hesitation about undertaking the conquest of thirteen colonies which believed themselves independent and whose willing and efficient coöperation in the future was a matter of grave doubt. That they could subdue the colonies they were quite sure, but they were not by any means sure it was worth doing. That it could not be done by the English forces then in America five years of campaigning had abundantly demonstrated. Many thousands of men, and elaborate equipment would be needed to conquer the colonies in the first place, and the English generals who had seen service in America insisted that it would afterward be necessary, in order to maintain English authority, to garrison the country with almost as large an army as was needed to conquer it. Was there anything to gain from the conquest of the Americans which the fleet and the supremacy of the sea did not absolutely insure England? The game was not worth while. The support of armies at a distance for the maintenance of political domination was contrary to England's best interests.

THE SUPREMACY OF THE SEA

Adam Smith had pointed out before the Revolution that American trade did not flow to England because of the political connection, but for economic reasons, and some dim appreciation of this fact had dawned upon English statesmen by 1783. They saw clearly that our trade was the only thing really valuable for England, and that no other nation could get it without England's permission; and they believed that we would trade with England rather than not trade at all. Let us not say that we owe our independence to England's forbearance or to her decision that conquest was inexpedient. We owe our independence to the Atlantic Ocean and to our strategic position, which must in the long run have given us the victory, even if we assume so incredible a notion as the entire worthlessness of the Revolutionary army. But the English decision undoubtedly gave us our independence at a much lower cost than we should otherwise have had to pay for it, and established forever in the relations of the two countries the principle that political domination of the United States was from an English point of view entirely inexpedient. Ever since 1783 this has been a cornerstone of English foreign policy.

There could scarcely be a more important factor in the history of the United States than the control of the sea and, therefore, of all the approaches to this country by a power whose own interests led her to prevent other nations' access with hostile intent, and whose interests also led her to consider inexpedient the use of her power for conquest or political domination.

The true nature of the sea-power and of its benefits to us were appreciated by a few of the leaders in America, but by none of the rank and file. The Revolution cost us all our privileges on the sea and in British possessions and resulted in a commercial crisis of the first magnitude. For the first time we were in opposition to the sea-power, and the cause of our difficulties was less clear than the practical effects upon shipping and trade. The feeling in America was in the main one of acute indignation that the tyrant's hand should still be able to interfere with our destinies. In general, the people were hostile to England as the oppressor from whom we had just been freed, and extremely friendly to France, whose assistance had materially hastened the end of the war. There was on the whole a disposition to defy England and bid her do her worst. We therefore proceeded to quarrel with the sea-power about things in general and presently about things more specific.

The outbreak of the French Revolution led to the

creation of a demand in Europe for the food staples which the colonies raised in large quantities, but the bulk of which had hitherto made the freights too costly to permit export to the Continent or to England. With the outbreak of the war, prices soared to a height which made exportation from America not only possible, but highly profitable. A brisk trade sprang up, the bulk of which tended to drift to France, where the need was greatest and the prices highest, and to a people, moreover, for whom most Americans had the liveliest admiration and whom they were glad to supply with the materials needed to fight our own old enemy. Friction with England was inevitable. We were breaking the English statutes; we were creating a merchant marine; we were supplying England's enemy; English deserters were obtaining protection in our merchant fleet and even in our navy, so they claimed; we were carrying contraband of war in vessels built in America, but manned by cosmopolitan crews. In short, we were doing all the things which the English had deemed from the earliest times peculiarly inimical to their supremacy of the sea in its defensive aspect, and they therefore enforced strictly their rules regarding the right of search, the seizure of English deserters upon American vessels, and the confiscation of contraband in American ships. We protested in vain. We also fought in vain. We could not hope by direct attack to damage the victor of Trafalgar, the possessor of the greatest fleet known to history. Our strategic position, defensively invulnerable, was without offensive strength against a European power.

The statesmen who began the War of 1812 do not seem to have expected to extort anything from England by aggression. They thought indeed that our privateers and frigates might prey upon her commerce and do enough damage to make it worth her while to concede us something; but they knew that our ships were swift rather than large, our sailors gallant rather than numerous, and that pitched battles with English fleets were out of the question. With the destruction of merchantmen and the capture or destruction now and then of some frigate or sloop of war, they were well satisfied. The real pawn in the game upon which they counted was Canada. There was little doubt in Washington that it could be easily conquered, and less doubt that it would give us a decidedly valuable possession to offer the English in exchange for commercial rights of various sorts. They thought they could buy with it what they could not take. As for Canada, they knew the Canadians to be fewer in number than the Americans, and probably no better prepared for war. Troops from England would, at any rate, not appear in considerable numbers while the crisis abroad was so serious. This would enable them, they believed, to conquer Canada in the first place, and, once in our hands, the same forces which had prevented England from conquering America in the Revolution would effectively stand in the way of reconquering Canada without paying an enormously heavier price than the commercial concessions the United States demanded. The endeavor failed, however, and proved the complete futility of attempting to challenge the English supremacy on the sea with obviously inadequate resources. It proved also our inability to extort terms from England by other methods.

The end of the War of 1812 brought once more into prominence the policy earlier espoused by the more moderate leaders, Washington, Madison, Hamilton, Jay, as soon as the Revolution had made clear the importance of the British sea-power. The United States, they had maintained, must have cordial relations and, if possible, an alliance with the power controlling the sea. That England had been the mother country from whom we had just won our independence was regrettable, but it must not stand in the way of our interest in fostering cordial relations with the power controlling all the approaches to our country and all our intercourse and foreign trade. Access to the West Indies and to Europe we must have; only with England's consent and on England's terms could we have it; we must therefore get such terms as we could, and hope in time for better. The Anti-Federalists had always considered hostility toward England as the late mother country more important than our commercial association with England as the sea-power. That the two were irreconcilable they declined to admit till after the War of 1812. There was then something approaching an agreement that our own interests required us to ally with the supremacy of the sea, and to make that alliance a fundamental factor of our foreign policy to the exclusion of all other interests, antipathies, or friendships.[1] Since then such has in fact been our policy, although it has rarely been openly avowed and has often been threatened with rupture by the rise of other interests upon which we clashed with England.

[1] "Great Britain is the nation which can do us the most harm of any one or all on earth; and with her on our side we need not fear the whole world. With her then we should most sedulously cherish a cordial friendship."—Jefferson to Monroe, Oct. 24, 1823. *Writings of Monroe*, Hamilton's ed., vi., 391.

THE SUPREMACY OF THE SEA

England on her part has seen the wisdom of using her sea-power with moderation, and of performing with scrupulous exactitude the various duties it imposed upon her in the interest of other nations. So long as she insisted that her defense and the protection of the imports of food and raw materials made it necessary for her to hold the absolute, unquestioned supremacy on the sea, so long she must pay due heed to the necessities of the nations dependent upon her for their communication with one another. To hamper their freedom of trade, to charge extortionate rates because of her monopoly, to fail to provide enough ships, would infallibly lead to discontent, to the creation of powerful merchant marines by various nations to render the service which the supremacy of the sea imposed upon her. An excellent merchant marine, affording other nations dependent upon her prompt, adequate, reasonable service, with low freight rates, low insurance, and brokerage, has been and still is essential to the continuance of her authority. She must freely and without compulsion do for them what they would otherwise have to do for themselves, and be satisfied with the normal profits which their own merchants might have expected to pay to a merchant marine of their own. So much was obvious.

Never to abuse her power was equally important. It should never be stained by aggression, and the line between defense and aggression must be strictly drawn and never exceeded. At any time a general alliance of the maritime nations against her might shake or even destroy the supremacy which her own domestic needs made more essential to her than to other nations. As long as she recognized and willingly furthered the just and legitimate interests of other nations on the sea, so long would they in all probability recognize her own paramount interest in holding its supremacy. Forbearance, tact, wisdom, generosity even, in her relations with other countries, would be as vital as the strength of the fleet itself in the maintenance of her supremacy. She must prove that her sea-power was primarily defensive by refraining from using it for purposes of aggression. What was necessary to her must never become intolerable to others. In reality the moderation and wisdom with which England has used her authority is more responsible than the strength of her fleets for the length of time that she has been supreme, and for the relatively few times in the past when her control has been really threatened or indeed advisedly questioned.

To the English control of the sea, to their policy

of regarding it primarily as defensive, to the moderation and fairness which they have displayed in their use of it, we owe our lack of a strong merchant marine intended for international oceanic trade and the postulates upon which our navy has been built. Our contact with the rest of the world has been in English hands, and it is really astonishing that we have found so few grounds for serious complaint in the past. Since the War of 1812 harmonious relations have been the rule with England; the mutual interests of both in reaching agreement and in hearty coöperation have been recognized, and such a cordial understanding with England is one of the few settled facts in American diplomacy. To this sea-power and all that goes with it our whole economic fabric has been adjusted. Upon it nearly everything depends. We have never known any other condition, and have had no serious reasons since 1815 to desire to change it.

Our army is based upon our strategic position and the improbability of the need of military strength for the maintenance of our political independence. It has been a police force rather than a military organization in the European sense. It is highly important at this time to realize that our navy has never been based at any time upon the assumption of challenging England's supremacy of the sea. That has become almost an axiom of our policy. We have attempted rather to build a supplementary force, sufficient to police our own waters and to deal adequately with the minor European navies which might conceivably attempt an assault upon us at a time when the situation in Europe might make the English hesitate to send a fleet to American waters on their own account. The recent growth of foreign navies has caused a concentration of English ships in European waters, and has made us feel it desirable to strengthen our navy so as to be able to protect ourselves against any other power than England. There could scarcely be a more striking testimonial to our confidence in the fairness of England, of our belief in the strength of her friendship for us, and in the firmness with which she means to maintain her policy of defense.

CHAPTER III

SOUTH AMERICA AND THE WEST INDIES

SCARCELY less fundamental in its formative influence upon our history than our strategic position and the control of the seas by England has been the existence of the West Indies and of South America. If the first period of our history, a period of growth, was dominated by the Atlantic, the second, a period of commercial expansion, was dominated by the West Indian trade. From its vital importance to our well-being sprang that fundamental concept of American policy that the economic interests of the United States in the West Indies and South America are necessarily paramount to those of any European nation, and are so essential to our welfare and to the welfare of those countries that we should do great violence to the interests of the Western Hemisphere if we should allow any nation to interfere with our freedom of trade. As against

European nations, we must be supreme in the Western Hemisphere, for the mutual interests of the United States and Latin America demand it. We must not forget to-day how far back in the past this tradition has its roots, nor fail to understand that it represents conditions which were at one time significant for the national welfare.

Throughout the first two centuries of our existence the trade of the continent was entirely dependent upon the existence of the West Indian islands. In those times there were few or no manufactures in America, and American merchants imported from England nearly every conceivable commodity from pins and hats to laces and broadcloths. For these we had little to exchange which the Europeans valued: of tobacco, Virginia and Maryland produced sufficient for their own needs of exchange, but unquestionably not enough for the needs of the colonies as a whole; the staples of New England, fish and lumber, the staples of the middle colonies, wheat, corn, and live stock, were too bulky to send to England, and commanded too small prices in a market already overstocked with such produce to make their export profitable. The colonies needed a market in which the produce they did raise could be sold at profit and in which they could purchase something for which Europeans would exchange manufactured goods.

Such a market existed in the West Indian islands, where the sugar colonies of the various European nations had grown to considerable size by the middle of the seventeenth century. They found it too expensive to produce food when land and labor brought in much greater returns if devoted to cane, and they therefore raised few of the necessities of life. To bring from Europe adequate supplies of such bulky produce was more expensive, even had not the length of the voyage to Europe and the uncertainty of arrival made supplies from such a source precarious. The food products of the Atlantic coast were as absolutely essential to the West India colonists as the market was to the continental colonists. The round of colonial trade thus assured the needed exchange. The New England merchants carried to Africa a cargo of rum, which was exchanged for slaves, who were carried in turn to the West Indian islands for molasses or sugar, which, when taken back to New England, was converted into more rum with which to continue the process. The food products of the coast, salt fish and the various grains, lumber in all its forms, were also exported to the West Indies, where they found ready sale in exchange for sugar or molasses, products which commanded a great market in England and the Continent, and which were easily turned into manufactured goods, to be brought back to America and sold by the merchants for more of the food products with which to continue the trade. We furnished the West Indies with a merchant marine; they furnished us with a market; they bought from us their food; they sold us the wherewithal to buy manufactured goods in Europe. The relationship was mutual in the best and strictest sense, for it was absolutely essential to the continued economic prosperity of both. From it the colonists drew the conclusion that the interests of the Atlantic Coast in the West Indies were paramount to any interest which any European country could have, and that freedom of access to the West Indies lay at the root of our prosperity as well as of theirs. It was at this time completely true. From that trade we obtained the wealth which made us strong enough to stand alone, and with it we paid the price of independence.

The result of this situation and of the conclusions which the colonists drew from it was a complete and frank disregard of European claims and regulations intended to fetter or limit in any way this intercourse. With equal nonchalance they violated the British Navigation Acts, the French Regulations, and the Spanish Rules. As all the sugar colonies of whatever nationality needed American products and were ready to pay for them, the colonists sold to all without regard to nationality. To this they were urged by the rapid growth of the coast colonies during the eighteenth century, a growth stupendous in percentage of population and in the increase of the volume of produce, and which made markets more essential than ever. If the producers at home were to continue to sell at profit, expanding markets were essential to ward off the commercial ruin which a glut of produce in home markets would inevitably cause. Soon the English colonies on the continent outgrew the market furnished them by the English sugar colonies, produced more than the latter could possibly use, and required more goods for European exchange than the latter produced. They therefore extended the smuggling trade with the foreign possessions in the West Indies, and drew into their own hands something approaching a monopoly of the West Indian trade, with such results that the year 1764 showed them with perfect clearness that nothing less than a monopoly of the whole West Indian market would suffice to absorb the volume of commodities annually produced by the thirteen colonies. Unless they could sell to this expanding market, production at home must be retarded, and the economic progress of America proceed at a less rapid pace.

This monopoly of the West Indian trade was not received in England with favor. So long as the English islands had been fully supplied from the continent they had maintained a certain natural advantage over the foreign sugar colonies, whose supplies perforce had to be raised on the island or brought from a great distance. When the coast colonies sold produce to all, the English colonies lost their important advantage, and their degree of profit was in consequence seriously reduced. The agreements entered into between England and France as to privileges and restrictions in the cod fisheries off Newfoundland the colonists declined to obey. Salt fish was the great staple food for the slaves in the West Indies; absolute freedom of access to the supply of fish was as necessary to them as access to the market in which to sell it; they demanded both, and both with very little ceremony they meant to take, regulations or no regulations. To compel them to obey these regulations and the Navigation Acts was the intention of much of the English legisla-

SOUTH AMERICA AND THE WEST INDIES

tion which led to the American Revolution. We were no longer to trade with the foreign sugar colonies. That much was clear in London. The moment it became clear in America the merchants saw it would ruin the prosperity of the colonies, since there was no other market in which the surplus products could be sold.

They diagnosed the difficulty as the political bond which bound the colonies to England and made them liable to administrative regulations made in English interests rather than in their own. To admit now that this political bond also compelled them to contribute taxes for the creation and maintenance of a resident administration strong enough to compel the observance of those noxious regulations was to concede the right of the mother country to ruin the colonies. If the political bond was the difficulty, political freedom was the cure. Once obtained, it would insure a freedom of trade with the West Indies and consequently a monopoly of the West Indian trade, for the natives would be forced to trade with the coast colonies as long as the latter alone produced the desired supplies. Interference by European nations could result only in stopping the stream of suplies which their own colonists demanded, and in checking our production of the commodities which they could obtain only from us. The connection between the colonies and the West Indian islands was natural and normal, with which interference was artificial, unnatural, oppressive, and tyrannical. It was not to be expected that freemen would endure such conditions or recognize a political bond which imposed them.

To secure freedom of access to the West Indian and South American trade we fought the Revolution. Administrative independence it was scarcely necessary to struggle for; our strategic position had already taken it from England's hands and fairly thrust it into our own; it was a privilege they could not hope to retain, a burden of which we could not rid ourselves. Our economic position was not thus assured, and a struggle was thought well worth while to remove a captious and arbitrary interference based upon whims and ignorance, and contrary to all normal rights and interests of both the principal parties.

But the results of the Revolution were hardly those expected. Hitherto the English fleet had protected the colonists, assured them access to the West Indies, and looked on more or less indifferently while they broke the regulations of other countries. Under no circumstances were the English accustomed to allow foreign ships to

SOUTH AMERICA AND THE WEST INDIES

capture or interfere with their own. The importance of this protection was not realized in America, because the aid of the English war-ships was rarely needed, and their presence not invariably known. As soon as the Revolution was over and the political bond broken, the English fleet was promptly put into action against the American vessels, and the new republic found that operations which had been wholly feasible with the connivance of the British navy were entirely impossible when that navy was arrayed against it. As a matter of fact, the Revolution robbed us of the rights we had had in all the West Indian colonies, because the American navy was not strong enough to maintain the smuggling trade in the face of the united opposition of all the European owners. We had no rights at all and were not strong enough to defy even the weakest powers in the West Indies, while the British colonies were wholly closed against us.

It was a terrible blow. The leaders saw for the first time the importance of the supremacy of the sea: all our approaches were in England's hands, all our intercourse with the outside world at her mercy. The dilemma was extraordinary. Having defied England as the mother country, roused feeling against her as a tyrant, and won our independence with the aid of her worst enemy, the leaders now found that harmonious relations had to be established with this same country because intercourse with the outside world was absolutely essential for us and was to be had only on her terms. Her double rôle had not been entirely appreciated before the Revolution, and, in the face of the popular hostility to England after the war, it was a difficult fact to make clear to the people. The majority found it hard to understand the necessity of any relations with England. Had not the war been fought for the purpose of severing relations? Had we not fought to obtain an extension of privileges, and should we now humiliate ourselves by begging England to grant us as favors those same rights which we had just thrust from us with contumely and scorn? Nor were the English inclined to forget the Revolution and restore to us, now that we were independent, what we had so vehemently insisted was entirely insufficient while we had been parts of the British Empire. However, there was nothing for it, so the majority of the leaders thought, but to make the best terms we could. Throughout the critical period and the three Federalist administrations negotiations were prosecuted with vigor, but without success. One treaty was agreed upon which granted some of our requests, but which the Senate refused to approve because it did not grant them all.

By 1800 the scene had shifted in Europe. The French Revolution and general European war had created a market on the Continent for American provisions and furnished us for the time being with a direct medium of exchange. This relief from the intensity of the distress felt at the close of the Revolution caused a distinct drawing away from England, lent support to the natural antipathy that Jefferson and the Anti-Federalists had always cherished, and brought negotiations to an end. Above all, it seemed to justify the claim that amicable relations with England were less essential to our prosperity than the Federalists had believed. From the growth of an American merchant marine and a trade with the Continent which broke many of the English war regulations came disputes; from the bickering came disagreements, and out of the quarrels grew in time the War of 1812. If the war stopped all trade with Europe and rendered the whole situation worse than it had been before, its ending brought little relief, because the European markets were now irrevocably lost with the beginning anew of production in Europe. Moreover, England still stood in the way, and prevented our getting across the Atlantic except on her terms.

The situation after the War of 1812, out of which grew the Monroe Doctrine, reveals a complex tangle of interests in which the past and future jostled each other in the minds of American statesmen. The first and most fundamental interest which they seem to have had in mind was the tradition of our necessary connection with the West Indian trade and the consequent belief that as our interests in it were paramount to those which any European nation could have, so the interests of the colonists in the West Indies and in South America were identical with ours, and were consequently contrary to those of European nations. To establish such a fact the Revolution had been fought, and American statesmen were by no means minded to yield the point in 1823, even had they believed it within their power to renounce so fundamental a principle of our polity. It was our primary interest, to be subserved at all costs. The next great outstanding fact was that borne in upon us by the War of 1812—the supremacy of England on the sea and the impossibility of its dispute by the United States. Its corollary was, they realized with considerable anxiety, the supremacy of England in the Western Hemisphere, since the absence of adequate communication overland between the various countries and colonies made intercourse inevitably by water, and accordingly placed its control in England's hands. Such a supremacy was, however, a physical fact which American statesmen, with the War of 1812 fresh in mind, were not inclined to dispute, though by no means one they stood ready to countenance.

Beside these two facts stood the control by England of the trade with South America and the West Indies. For long years England had been interested in South American trade, and even in the seventeenth century had begun to draw a considerable portion of it into her hands. She had taken pains to secure a certain technical sanction for it in the Treaty of Utrecht at the beginning of the eighteenth century, and under this ægis the trade had grown in importance. When English merchants were compelled during the Napoleonic wars to look for a market in which to dispose of the produce they could no longer sell to Europe because of Napoleon's Continental System, they turned to the West Indies and South America. There a certain artificial and technical obstacle—Spanish ownership—stood in the way of their monopolizing the trade in the guise of regulations which denied them freedom of intercourse. Firm in their traditional policy of not acquiring political domination of distant countries which force might be needed to maintain, England seems to have suggested to the South Americans—or at any rate to have encouraged an idea of their own—independence. This would remove all obstacles, and the English control of the sea would enable them to regulate conditions under which other nations should share the trade, for an exclusive monopoly does not seem to have been contemplated or deemed advisable. Independence, it was seen, would be easy to win. The resident governments were weak and incompetent, and the necessary munitions of war the English stood ready to furnish, and would not be inclined to insist upon payment, although the transaction would outwardly be commercial. The operation was perfectly safe, because the English fleet would hold Spain and the rest of Europe on the other side of the Atlantic, and not permit interference. Whether or not these suppositions are true, the fact remains that the Spanish American colonies did revolt and did claim their independence at various times after 1810; by 1823 the process was complete.

To the European nations it was peculiarly

evident that England was about to succeed in the Gulf of Mexico and in South America to the position which Spain had previously held, and it seemed inadvisable to allow her to make so considerable an acquisition of territory under cover of the thin fiction of political independence for the natives. That it meant unusual commercial privileges for England no one doubted. For some years the European powers were too busy arranging the domestic affairs of Europe to be able to turn their attention to the Western Hemisphere, but in due course of time the Holy Alliance of France, Russia, Prussia, and Austria, moved ostensibly by the request of Spain, issued a protest against the loss of the Spanish colonies and intimated the desirability of their restoration to Spain. The blow was of course aimed at England who held the actual control, so far as the outside world was concerned, but the fiction of political independence made it necessary to protest technically against the independence of the republics and to direct any coercion against them and not against England. This would give England the alternative of avowing her control and of defending it or of declining battle and so sacrificing her new allies and her new dominion. France and Russia indeed were moved by no strong desire to hand the colonies back to Spain, but by a great desire to keep them out of England's hands.

The issue was thoroughly well understood in England. Her power on the sea was believed to be the decisive factor, and an assault upon South America was not feared; but she was by no means sure the Holy Alliance would not force the issue. Though not doubting eventual success, England dreaded war, for she wished to control the Western Hemisphere without fighting for it. In any case she was anxious to prevent the United States from joining her enemies, because in the event of a war the location of the United States would be important, and its strength would compel England to increase the force despatched. Canning, the Foreign Minister, made therefore to the United States an offer of the utmost subtlety. He suggested a joint protest of the United States and Great Britain, directed to the Holy Alliance, against the reconquest in favor of Spain of her late colonies, and also suggested that the note should recognize the equality of interests which England and the United States possessed in the Western Hemisphere. Its purpose was apparently to secure from the United States an official recognition of England's new dominion in the Gulf of Mexico and South America.

SOUTH AMERICA AND THE WEST INDIES

If the situation was thoroughly well understood in England and on the Continent, it was none the less well understood in the United States. There were two traditions which influenced American statesmen. The first was that of the necessity of cordial relations between the United States and the power controlling the sea, which had been enunciated so often as to be commonplace. Negotiations however had failed so often as to be disappointing in the extreme, and made so fair an offer as this recognition of equality of interests promising and important. Monroe, the President, and several important public men were in favor of the acceptance of the offer upon these grounds.

There was, however, a second precedent of no less consequence and antiquity. It had early been seen that our strategic situation made us clearly independent of European powers acting from Europe, and that neither invasion nor aggression was to be feared from that source. Our real danger would arise from European powers located in America. The existence of the French colonies since the earliest times, the difficulties of the French and Indian Wars, the fear common during the Revolution that the English meant to build up in the Mississippi valley a great state which would in time absorb the coast states, had demonstrated our danger from resident European colonies and shown that European nations were anxious to establish dominion in North America. While the cession of the district between the Alleghenies and the Mississippi to the United States by the Peace of 1783 ended the danger for the time, it appeared again with greater insistence in the fear of the erection by France or England of a state to the west of the Mississippi. This was ended by the purchase of Louisiana, but the location of the threatened European aggression was merely shifted, first to Florida, then successively to the West Indies, Texas, Mexico, and Central America. Any of them obviously could have been used as a basis for a great European state whose existence in such a locality might very well throw the United States upon the defensive and impose a more serious burden upon the young and struggling community than it was capable of bearing. Declaration after declaration had been made with additional earnestness and upon public and increasingly solemn occasions that we could not see such an establishment of European authority in the Western Hemisphere without grave anxiety and fear for our independence.

To this tradition Adams, the Secretary of State, and those who thought with him, appealed. If

England's offer was likely to further our traditional policy of cordial relations with the sea-power and seemed about to confer upon us some of the commercial privileges in the West Indies we had long sought, was it not also diametrically contrary to our policy of defense? England was suddenly offering the United States valuable privileges which she had long denied us and was asking in return apparently no concessions. To Adams this proved that she was subserving some interests of her own, obtaining from us something which she valued, and it was his duty to find out what that was. Surely it was not our assistance in the protection of the South American republics, for if the English fleet could not save them, we had not enough strength to add to turn the tide. Nor did our moral assistance seem to him sufficiently regarded in Europe to have influenced Canning. The truth was, he pointed out, the protection of the new republics by the English sea-power meant simply their transfer from Spain to England, and before Monroe's message was read, Adams's prescience was demonstrated correct by an agreement between France and England to prevent the re-conquest of the republics. This settled the question of their independence and it really made the joint protest of the United States and England virtually worthless. The deed was done.

In the suggestion that the United States and England jointly declare their mutual interests in the Western Hemisphere, Adams saw the concession that was desired, and that it was a concession which we ought never to make. It was contrary, in the first place, to the known facts; our natural and normal interest in the West Indian trade was greater than that of England could be, and in all probability our interest in the South American trade was of much the same significance. For those people, the ability to secure food-stuffs was more important than the purchase of European manufactured goods. The interests of the United States were paramount to those of England, and the proposed English relationship intended to erect an artificial barrier in the way of a trade indispensable to the welfare of the United States, of the West Indies, and of South America. It was also vitally contrary to our first principle of defense not to recognize the erection of a strong European state in the Western Hemisphere. If any white nation were to control the Gulf of Mexico and Central America, the United States should; our expansion might become essential, and we ought never to recognize any other principle than that of our supremacy in the Western Hemisphere. If for the time the sea-power held us helpless, the situation might change, and meantime we should make our protest against this new English dominion. Such arguments were cogent, and eventually carried the day. As enunciated in Monroe's famous message, they were interpreted both in America and in Europe to denote a defiance of England and an intention at some future time to contest her supremacy in the Western Hemisphere. In reality, the complexity of ideas was much greater. The doctrine comprised our paramount interests in the West Indies and South America as against England or all Europe; the statement that we should consider the erection of a strong European state in the gulf or in Central America as an aggressive act primarily aimed at the independence of the United States; an assertion that such a connection between Latin America and Europe was abnormal and artificial and contrary to the true interests of the Americas; and, lastly, a declaration of our rightful supremacy in the Western Hemisphere as against England or any other European power.

CHAPTER IV

THE SUPREMACY OF THE WESTERN HEMISPHERE

THE supremacy of the Western Hemisphere remained in England's hands because of her continued possession of the supremacy of the sea. It was a physical fact, a result of physical conditions, not in the least to be shaken by diplomatic or military achievements; the intercourse between the various parts of the Western Hemisphere was unavoidably by water, and the water routes were too incontestably in England's hands. The real issue before the American statesmen, as Adams had shown, was not the denial of the existence of such established facts, but the policy of formally recognizing them or of admitting their justice or consonance with the interests of the United States. The doctrine of Monroe's message declared that the United States recognized no paramountcy and accepted no supremacy vested in a European power, and the formal publicity given the statement, to Canning's thinking, attested an American determination to contest the facts at the earliest opportunity.

The South Americans, though torn at first by apprehensions, soon accepted the situation. British statesmen were at some pains to prove to them that they owed their independence to the protection afforded by the British fleet,—a protection which the United States could not furnish,—that England possessed liberal supplies of capital which she would gladly furnish them, while the United States was not able to finance its own development and was seeking large amounts of capital. Manufactured goods the English also had, which the United States did not produce in sufficient quantities for her own consumption and which she was obviously not able to supply for South American needs. South America's crude products could be utilized by the varied industrial demands of England's economic fabric, but did not find and would not for many years find in the United States anything like an adequate market. The fullness of the English hands, the entire adequacy of the English offer to South America, their statesmen were at some pains to make clear. The diplomatic representations of the United States at the Pan-American Congress of 1826, while received with courtesy, were without avail. The physical facts were against us. We could not buy what they had to sell; we could not sell them what they wished to buy; we did not control the approaches to the Western Hemisphere or the trade routes in American waters. Why should they doubt?

In addition the English were ready to recognize and maintain the political independence of the new republics in exchange for a tacit recognition of the English control of the South American trade. The English supremacy in the Western Hemisphere was therefore exceedingly subtle and peculiar: no display of force was made or contemplated; no challenge on the sea was expected; conquest on land was undesirable; the only sanction was to be the potential power of the British fleet. The South American republics were technically sovereign and ostensibly were to be themselves supreme. The English control was almost in the nature of a reserved right to interfere, with the distinct understanding that the interference should in no case touch political or domestic affairs. An open recognition of the English supremacy on the sea was expected in the acceptance of English regulations and restrictions upon trade and in the passage of local regulations to facilitate intercourse with England. No militating regulations against England were to be tolerated. These notions the United States would not accept; the old quarrels over rights in the West Indies were transferred to South America, and were aggravated by the attempts of Congress to impose identical restrictions upon English trade with the United States. Still, on the whole, the English supremacy of the Western Hemisphere was sensed rather than seen, and was subtly concealed in the guise of the supremacy of the sea.

This diplomatic tensity, like that which the Monroe Doctrine, with its defiance of England, had threatened, was relieved by the operation of forces which Canning could not have set in motion, nor Monroe have opposed. The prosperity of the sugar islands disappeared. It had been partly damaged at the outbreak of the Revolution by the interference with the full stream of supplies which had hitherto poured in from the continental colonies, and it was further injured by the falling off of the demand for sugar upon the outbreak of the Napoleonic wars; but the final blow was struck in 1833 by the abolition of slavery in the English West Indian islands. The most valuable of the foreign islands had meanwhile passed into English hands, and the ruin which fell upon the trade embraced nearly all the prominent centers of production. Thus disappeared an extensive market for American products in the West Indies, and our loss of rights in it became no longer of consequence. With it went our paramount interest in the Western Hemisphere and our really vital interest in opposing the English supremacy on the sea. Nor was South America able to take the place of the West India groups. We had little to sell which they were willing to buy, because they themselves produced food-stuffs and lumber and were not engaged in growing staples like sugar and tobacco by gangs of slaves who had to be maintained from imports; nor could they supply us what we needed, an exchange medium adequate for our own purchases of manufactured goods in Europe. There was no longer a mutual economic interest between the Americas to be protected by diplomacy.

An indigenous product, cotton, had appeared in America for which so great a demand developed in Europe that it kept pace with an almost incredible annual increase in production, and began to rouse lively expectations that the eagerly sought medium of direct exchange had at last been found. It would give us, too, a commodity for our European trade of which the sea-power could not rob us and the export of which England would normally facilitate, because she herself demanded the new staple. American statesmen even began to dream of obtaining from her favorable commercial terms in exchange for omnipotent cotton. The potency of cotton was proportionate to the size of the crop, and the development of the industry was a prerequisite of its adequacy as a medium of exchange or as a bribe for other concessions. Immediately great stress was laid upon increasing the rate of its development: we must obtain as soon as possible an amount for export equivalent in value to the sum total of American imports of manufactured goods. For such development land was needed in large amounts and of peculiar quality. The largest crops of the best cotton could be grown at that time only upon the virgin soil of the river bottoms, and even this land afforded the maximum profit only when cultivated by the gangs of slaves, the number of which reduced the expense of oversight and administration to a minimum. Such a degree of return depended as well upon the frequent change of the scene of labor, for the cotton crop soon materially decreased in size on soil lately virgin. The amount of virgin soil in the river bottoms was limited by nature, but the amount of the potential supply available in continental United States was smaller. In the Gulf of Mexico and Central America, however, was a vast area the soil and climate of which were favorable for cotton culture and seemed a legitimate field for its expansion.

New land in large amounts was vehemently demanded and promptly obtained. The expulsion of the Creeks and Cherokees from the Gulf States opened large tracts to settlement and exploitation; large numbers of Americans migrated with their slaves into Texas, a province at that time of the Mexican Republic. The insatiable demand led eventually to the annexation of Texas, to the Mexican War and the annexation of the whole western quarter of the present United States, and to the aggressive assertion of our need for Cuba, the coast provinces of Mexico, and a great many other districts on the gulf. Northern statesmen charged the Southerners with a plan for the establishment of a huge slave empire, embracing all the land bordering on the Gulf of Mexico and all the islands.

In justification of this aggression, certain phases of the Monroe Doctrine were cited. The extension of American authority as a defensive measure

SUPREMACY OF WESTERN HEMISPHERE

was ardently advocated by those who claimed that England purposed to annex Texas or Mexico or Cuba and begin there the erection of a state to contest our position in the Western Hemisphere. Plausibly this compelled us to act in self-defense and forestall so dangerous a neighbor by assuming control ourselves. From it came also plausible claims to interfere in the domestic concerns as well as the foreign relations of the minor countries to assure ourselves that no foreign influence was creeping in or being afforded adequate excuse for aggression. Nor was precedent lacking for such territorial expansion; its inevitability had been predicted by a long line of men eminent in American annals, and its importance to our welfare had been a frequent subject of oratory both in Congress and in the country at large.

To these actual territorial gains and to this presumptive desire for actual possession of the Gulf of Mexico, England raised objections. The intercourse between the various parts of this new empire would necessarily depend upon the sea, which was controlled by England, and she objected to an assumption of sovereignty which ignored the fact of her supremacy and, in particular, to the schemes for the extension of our influence to the exclusion of her own. So insistent were these representations that eventually the United States accepted the Clayton-Bulwer Treaty. The fundamental principle of the document seems to have been that of coöperation between England and the United States in the Gulf of Mexico which had been previously suggested by Canning and rejected by Adams and Monroe. Each recognized the other's active interests in the gulf, agreed not to acquire special interests to the other's detriment or without the other's consent, and explicitly bound itself not to build a canal across the Isthmus of Panama or at any other place without the other's express consent. The treaty was extremely unpopular in America and was assailed as the abrogation of the Monroe Doctrine and an admission that the interests of the United States were no longer paramount in the Western Hemisphere. Neither the treaty nor the principle upon which it was based met with entire approval from subsequent administrations, which again and again declared it without relation to the Monroe Doctrine. Thus matters stood at the close of the century.

Meanwhile the English continued to retain the supremacy of the Western Hemisphere, though they rarely chose to assert it and never demanded its formal recognition by European nations or by the United States. A genuine liberality and tolerance, as well as a sense of expediency, marked their use of it. The economic growth of various nations during the nineteenth century had naturally led to development of their trade with South America; but England viewed it with little apprehension, for she realized that she could not possibly buy the whole of South America's raw products, because she could not use them herself, and that her own interests were furthered more by the development of South America by other nations than by an attempt to monopolize such trade as already existed. The actual volume of English trade and the actual English profits would be larger by sharing with other nations an increased and developed trade than by monopolizing a trade which the circumstances of the monopoly would limit and stunt, even were it not contrary to English policy to interfere with freedom of trade in the markets of the world. She must always refrain from raising issues which might lead to the questioning of her sea-power and hence to an assault upon her means of defending herself. Far from involving a loss of her supremacy or its renunciation, this policy demanded merely a wise employment of it, a recognition of its economic and naval limits and of the essential rights of other nations.

PAN-AMERICANISM

The rise of Pan-Germanism, the creation of the German fleet, the nature of Germany's objection to England's position on the sea, promptly altered the actual facts of England's supremacy. The Germans challenged the rightfulness of the control of the sea by any nation, for it placed in its hands a potential power more detrimental to the interests of all others than any one nation should hold. That the foreign trade and intercourse of any nation should depend upon the good-will, forbearance, or domestic interests of another was intolerable. Nothing short of complete independence could be recognized. Past liberality, present generosity, and assurances for the future were no guaranty of an apparent freedom which ill concealed a very real inferiority. Could not the English close all the avenues of approach to Europe, stop German trade with the rest of the world, and hamper the German development on which her safety depended? The English argument that the control of the seas was an absolutely essential defensive measure for the protection of England's imports of food and raw materials they did not find convincing. Should they admit that the continued prosperity of England was a burden which they were under obligation to further or recognize? Why should they permit England's defensive needs to become paramount to their own?

The building of the German fleet gradually compelled England to concentrate her own ships in the channel and in the North Sea, and thus robbed her of her physical control of the waters of the Western Hemisphere. In reality, so long as she owned the greatest fleet in the world and so long as it remained unbeaten, her control would potentially exist and be implicit in the situation. The actual facts, however, were otherwise. The moment she no longer patrolled American waters in sufficient force to compel obedience to her regulations, her supremacy of the Western Hemisphere became a myth, dissipated by the growth of the German fleet. As long as the existence of the German fleet compelled the retention of English ships in European waters and therefore prevented her despatch to American waters of sufficient naval strength to maintain her old supremacy, the actual control of American waters had passed from England's hands, and would remain a potentiality rather than a fact until the German fleet had been defeated.

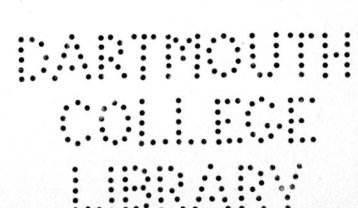

All this the English thoroughly understood, and they were at some pains to explain it to the United States in an attempt to make certain arrangements to insure the exclusion of Germany from the Western Hemisphere in any eventuality. If the supremacy of the seas passed from English hands and the British Empire fell, neither should strengthen Germany. England was not minded to contest the supremacy of all the oceans, of the Western Hemisphere, of the Mediterranean, of Egypt and India at the same time, nor to hand over to her own conqueror, if disaster should be her lot, the plenitude of her own authority. The empire should be broken up, the supremacy of the seas divided, before Germany should fall heir to either. But both would fall into the hands of her successor in the control of European waters, if they were not previously placed in the hands of resident powers capable of defending them and whose normal interests would urge their preservation. The constant reaffirmation of the Monroe Doctrine, and its interpretation in the United States as fairly obliging us to exclude European interests from the Western Hemisphere, gave reasons for hope that the United States would not supinely surrender to a victorious Germany what the English conceived to be our national ambition.

They therefore proposed to hand over to the United States the actual control of American waters and, in particular, of the Gulf of Mexico before the European situation should compel them to renounce their supremacy forever. In the circumstances they were willing to cede it outright, to make the United States supreme, in exchange for an understanding as to the ways in which the United States should use its control of American waters and for an amicable arrangement which would probably lead to close economic relations with the United States that the English saw would be essential to them upon the outbreak of a general European war. The closing of the Black Sea and the Baltic would promptly deprive the English of important sources of food supplies and would necessitate access to adequate supplies elsewhere. The United States alone possessed them. Manufactured goods of all sorts would be highly important for England and her ally, France; certain types of munitions of war could not be produced by the existing English and French factories in sufficient quantities; the United States was the only manufacturing power with a sufficiently large and varied economic fabric to enable her to meet promptly and adequately such demands. Further, a market for English goods during the war would be essential, for, while the rate of production would naturally be reduced, the output would still be more considerable in all probability than could be marketed unless the English should be ready to sell to the United States the amount of manufactured goods which the latter had previously bought from Germany and Austria. The employment of the English merchant marine would be advisable, if not essential; it would find in its trade with the United States a sufficient occupation during hostilities to ward off actual distress. Indeed, the economic structure of the United States, they saw, was complementary to that of England. If the United States could build a canal at Panama, it could also create a great ocean highway to the far East and to the English colonies in the southern Pacific, which might be of supreme importance in case Pan-Germanism was able to close the Mediterranean. If in addition the United States navy could protect the canal and American waters from fleets other than England's, and be able in case of need to patrol effectively the commercial highways across the Atlantic, it could afford England very substantial aid in time of war and further the mutual economic interests of both countries.

The economic development of the nineteenth century had changed the relations of the United States with South America; a close connection between them had become possible, if indeed a

SUPREMACY OF WESTERN HEMISPHERE

certain mutuality of economic interest did not already exist. Varied industries now provided an enormous bulk of manufactured goods for export; the new agriculture furnished vast supplies of food-stuffs which the railroads and steamships were now able to transport cheaply to the European market; modern science had made available for export nearly everything the country produced; nor was the country any longer dependent upon a single staple as a medium of exchange. Changes both in Europe and in America of an unquestionably fundamental nature had revolutionized the whole situation, while the proportionately great development of the United States had freed us from our dependence upon Europe. We were now able to supply the South Americans with manufactured goods; we were able also to use in our own manufactures the staple products of South America; capital for investment was now plentiful in the United States. The close commercial bond which had been impossible because of our economic deficiencies found in its way only the English control of the sea, for the simultaneous development of South America had made those republics able to trade with the United States.

Such reasoning was cogent, the offer was alluring, and was accepted by the United States. The results are familiar enough, but none the less striking and significant. The United States now controls the Gulf of Mexico in actual fact, owns land at Panama on each side of the canal, and exercises a protectorate over the more important islands, Cuba, San Domingo, and Porto Rico; American capital has poured into Central America and, assisted in one way or another by diplomatic agencies, has left the smaller states at present little more than the shadow of political independence and the control of local government subject to suggestion and dictation from Washington. In Mexico, American interests are predominant, but still insistent upon a diplomatic and political support which they have not as yet received. In the Pacific, the United States possesses Hawaii, the Philippines, and various smaller islands, thus effectively controlling the commercial highway across that great ocean and holding a strong strategic position in Chinese waters. The Philippines control on one side the approach to China from Europe and India which Hong-Kong and Shanghai, in England's possession, hold on the other. Strong representations have been made by the United States Government to the European nations with regard to our equality of opportunity

SUPREMACY OF WESTERN HEMISPHERE

in the trade of the far East, and the policy known as the "Open Door" is more or less closely related to these developments.

So far as the Western Hemisphere is concerned, the supremacy of the United States is physically and morally so great that it is not likely to be disputed, even though she should be in no better position than at present to make it good in arms. As against Europe, she is also now supreme. The only fleets at all able to dispute our position are definitely located in Europe until the issue of the war is settled clearly one way or the other. The English and German fleets are in the North Sea and the English Channel, the French fleet is in the Mediterranean, and the three can desert their posts only at the cost of handing over to the others all that they hold dear. While they certainly will not interfere with the United States on any such terms as these, it is well to remember that the situation in Europe rather than our own geographical location or our own naval strength makes us supreme to-day in the Western Hemisphere. Our control as against American powers, our tenure as against European powers, are conditional upon the continuance of something approaching a naval balance of power in European waters, upon a fact which is not within our own control.

CHAPTER V

OUR PRESENT STRATEGIC POSITION

THE vital developments of the nineteenth century in science and in industry have already robbed our strategic position of a part of its former invulnerability, while the European war threatens seriously to alter the more important of its other features, and to make an army no longer a secondary or subsidiary element in our national defense. Our strategic position has been based, as already indicated, upon the existence of the Atlantic Ocean and our separation from Europe in time and space, robbing us of a position influential in military and naval issues in Europe, and giving the rival powers of Europe little or no reason to regard our conquest as desirable. In addition, the strategic character of the country, which requires the continuous use of an enormous army to make conquest practicable or invasion easy, has been of vital importance to us throughout our history, because there has not yet been a time when one of the great nations of Europe has felt itself able to spare so considerable a force from its own domains in Europe. Economic interests to attract a conqueror here, we have had none. In the action and interaction of these peculiar factors, both positive and negative, has lain our practical invulnerability for more than two centuries.

The invention of the locomotive, the steamboat, the telegraph has entirely changed the character of the first and most important of our strategic defenses, the Atlantic Ocean. Indeed, it would be most extraordinary if these changes in communication and transportation had not left an enduring mark upon our position, for they have revolutionized conditions as old as the history of man and have affected greater changes in intercourse than all man's progress since the days of the Pharaohs. Time and space have been annihilated to a degree almost incredible. The land journey even to Philadelphia was during the Revolution an undertaking, almost an adventure, and the arrival of the traveler could not be predicted with any certainty. America is now no farther from London than Newport was from New York by sea in the days of George Washington, while John Adams traveled to New York overland to be inaugurated as Vice-President of the United States in 1789 in more time than it takes to-day to go from Boston to San Francisco or, indeed, from Boston to Paris. In fact, not only is communication more regular and considerably more a matter of course between Europe and America to-day than contact was between the colonies at the time of the Revolution, but incomparably more people in the United States have traveled widely in Europe to-day than had visited in the old times a point one hundred miles from home. The annihilation of time, so far as intercourse is concerned, is even more complete. The telegraph and the wireless place us in instantaneous connection with all parts of the world and give us every morning the world's happenings, to be skimmed through while we take our coffee.

The result upon international politics has been extraordinary. The separation in time and space to which our independence was primarily due has disappeared forever. It would now be possible for a European nation to govern the United States successfully even though severed by the Atlantic. England governs India to-day far easier and better than she was able to govern the continental colonies in the eighteenth century; for, where her administration of the colonies was too slow, too

OUR PRESENT STRATEGIC POSITION

halting and inefficient to be of real consequence, her administration in India is prompt, efficient, and stable. From this inability of European nations to govern distant lands came much of their disinclination for distant political conquests. We are not now protected from conquest by any such factor.

The military situation has been even more strikingly revolutionized. The present war is being fought in Europe by forces of men who have come together from the four corners of the earth. Contingents from Canada, India, and Australia have been established and maintained in the English ranks in France with a readiness and an ease which would have been impossible half a century ago. In the trenches these men are eating food grown in Dakota and in Texas, wrapping themselves in blankets woven from Australian wool by American factories; American mules, driven by Hindus, are drawing English cannon into action, while the Frenchmen who fight beside them are clad in American clothes and wear American shoes. Indeed, the French and English officials regard as perfectly feasible the supplying and provisioning of their armies from the United States, and philanthropists have undertaken to supply the entire Belgian nation with American food and clothes. We shall be blind to the most obvious of facts if we fail to see that a European army can be maintained in the United States as easily as the present European armies can be maintained from the United States. If hundreds of thousands of men can be fed at that distance in Europe, it is at least conceivable that hundreds of thousands of men could be supplied in the United States from European sources. Invasion of the United States is no longer forbidden by the practical difficulty of maintaining at such a distance a force sufficiently large to make an invasion decisive.

On the other hand, for the first time in its history the United States possesses offensive strength, the present to us of the nineteenth century. We might now send a large and efficient army to Europe, which might quite conceivably play a very important part in the actual operations in the field. True, our lack of strategic relation to the European terrain persists; the American army in America is as powerless as before to influence the European situation: but it is now so easy to move the American army and locate it in the precise strategic spot most advantageous that our offensive strength to-day is distinctly to be reckoned with. If our present army is not large

OUR PRESENT STRATEGIC POSITION

enough to arouse apprehension in Europe, our potential strength is enormous, because the number of men and the natural resources on which we have to draw are greater than those of any European nation except Russia, and in point of availability are beyond all doubt vaster than those of Russia. Indeed, our economic strength now makes us of interest to European nations and a potential ally.

These developments that have so much affected our position have worked great changes also in the character of warfare. The premise of unpreparedness which has been the tradition in America assumes of course that the obstacles strewn by nature in the invader's way will be sufficient to delay his progress until we can complete preparations for a reasonably adequate defense. In the days of the Revolution the conditions of warfare made the preparation of defense at the last moment eminently feasible. Nearly every man in the community had a gun and knew how to use it, and an army was assembled by bringing together various men with guns, all of whom brought their own provisions and supplied their own clothes. They were all trained in methods of Indian warfare, which happened to be vastly efficient against the trained troops brought from England, because the nature of the ground in America was so different from that on which their manœuvers originated as almost to erase the difference in efficiency between the trained and the untrained. In such circumstances, aided by the difficulty of supplying an army because of the slowness of transportation, we easily fought a defensive war and won it without having been in the least prepared at the time the war began to cope with trained troops. We have not since that time had to face the question of invasion.

Recent developments in warfare have vitally changed the arrangements necessary for adequate defense. The modern invader arrives equipped with a variety of devices of vast potency, which are to be successfully resisted only by devices of equal potency. The backbone of the modern army has proved to be the artillery, because again and again the infantry has proved available only after this artillery has cleared the way. To create such weapons months are needed; to teach a gun crew how to use one effectively takes longer than it does to make the gun; such cannon fire in a few days an amount of ammunition which as many months may be needed to manufacture. The supply of such materials required to begin a war

OUR PRESENT STRATEGIC POSITION

is vast, the number of men who ought to stand ready trained to step into the shoes of those who fall in the first engagement must be a good deal larger than the uninitiated are inclined to imagine. To produce the supply of ammunition continuously needed requires a plant of enormous size, equipped with highly intricate machinery which can be operated with success only by men who have had long experience in times of peace. It will be obvious to the most ignorant that effective preparation for modern warfare requires foresight and precludes entirely the extemporization of an adequate defense after the arrival of the invader has been signaled.

We have dealt here with only the elements, the tools which the soldiers are to use, and they alone require many months for preparation; but the modern army is really composed of men whose training requires years before they attain a degree of efficiency in manœuvering and in rapid action sufficient to resist successfully a determined assault by a trained army. To-day the men coöperating in an attack ordinarily do not see one another or the enemy, nor do they know his whereabouts or their friends' location. Directions come to them over a wire, information vital to their safety, and the orders upon whose prompt obedience their lives and the very existence of the army as a whole may depend. Under such conditions, a high degree of administrative efficiency and of intelligent coöperation is the prerequisite of the continued existence of the army and demands a sort of training for which ordinary life provides no counterpart or substitute. An efficient modern army can be trained only by actual service in performing the work of defense; to send even a large number of untrained men against modern artillery in the hands of a single army corps is asking them to commit suicide. If preparation is postponed until the invader appears, defeat and conquest will be inevitable.

And the developments of the nineteenth century have thrown down our defensive barriers. Modern inventions in transportation and communication, the new science of warfare based upon them, have definitely and unquestionably rendered us vulnerable from a military point of view. Nor is this all. The war may alter those factors of our defensive position which are still intact. Nothing has yet happened to invest us with a strategic position of itself important for a decision of the issue in Europe; nothing has yet changed our own strategical geography, which makes success depend upon the magnitude of the operations undertaken;

OUR PRESENT STRATEGIC POSITION

nothing has yet made it possible for the European nations to spare so large a number of men from the armies in Europe. Yet we ought not to forget that these factors of our strategic position are those over which we do not exercise control, and that we are in reality defended to-day by the complicated and delicate balance of the European situation. Until that is radically changed, until one side or the other can spare from Europe a sufficiently large army to occupy the United States without imperiling its own safety at home, until the power possessed of the physical strength and the opportunity to use it shall find an adequate motive to cross the Atlantic, we shall still be entirely safe. We need no defense against an invasion which cannot start.

But we can hardly claim that we are without interest as to the outcome of the war in Europe, for it may destroy these remaining features of our defensive position. Our lack of any location which necessarily influences the present tangle of interests in Europe is of consequence merely so long as the tangle of interests persists. The unwillingness of European nations to despatch an army to the Western Hemisphere sufficient in size to endanger us again assumes that the battle in Europe is either not joined or not decided. The decision of the issue in the field in favor of either coalition may finally destroy the delicate balance of power in which lay our security and provide the victor with an adequate force and an adequate motive for aggression. Victory will not necessarily provide him with either, but may provide him with both. To-day we are safe; to-morrow we may be defenseless, except for human agencies.

BOOK II
THE VICTOR

The Victor

CHAPTER I

EUROPEAN POLICIES AND MOTIVES

OUT of past economic and political problems has grown the present war, fought because honest and sincere men of great intelligence and of humane desires saw no other chance of escaping from the dread alternatives which hedged them in. The war will not decide these problems,—economic, political, and moral issues are never decided by fighting,—dispel the difficulties out of which they grew, or remove the specters of economic distress which hover in the background. Victory will merely insure the victors an opportunity to struggle with the very problems out of which the war itself proceeded, with only one change, the elimination of the vanquished. For the right to undertake that settlement, to dictate its terms in their own favor, to impress upon the future their own stamp, are they fighting, and we need not expect that a situation sufficiently tangled to necessitate war for its solution, important enough to all the nations in Europe to make them conclude that this great war was inevitable, and look forward to a victory in it as a solution of their national problems for at least half a century, will not furnish the victor with a grim determination to override any further obstacles which may stand in the way of the solution deemed most desirable for his national future. The victor's interference in the Western Hemisphere, far from proceeding from the whims of kings or emperors, or from the evanescent policies of a militaristic state, will rest upon causes as deep and as far-reaching as history, as complex as modern life in its varied phases, as certain to continue in one aspect or another as the world is to turn on its axis.

Behind the present situation in Europe stands the economic progress of the last half-century,—a progress rapid beyond all previous precedent, beneficial in its results upon nations and individuals beyond the dreams of idealists, marking a more decisive stride in the economic advancement of the race than all the centuries since man began to write the record of his deeds. For the first time in the history of the race the specter of famine and nakedness has been entirely exorcised; there is no longer a doubt that there will be enough to eat and to wear. How stupendous this achievement is we scarcely appreciate. It has made commonplace luxuries for which kings once sighed in vain, and has conferred upon the individual an amount of leisure and an amount of freedom from drudgery unknown since the first Pharaoh began the irrigation of Egypt. With material progress has come an astonishing intellectual advance and the birth of a new corporate soul, of a new nation, of a new individual, who sees with ecstasy the entrancing vision of a great people, imbued with a spirit of self-sacrifice, coöperating in the attempt to advance by conscious effort the temporal and spiritual growth of the future nation. In comparison, the progress of the past seems scarcely worth while; the progress of the present barely sufficient; its continuance so necessary, and its acceleration so obviously desirable as to be beyond question for sane and reasoning men. So keen is the realization of the benefits of this economic growth, so clear the vision of the possibilities if it can be accelerated, that the great nations can scarcely conceive of a sacrifice too great for the attainment of such an object.

For the first time great communities are willing to sacrifice the present to the future; for the first time the patriotism of the present generation is unselfish enough to include the generations yet to be born. We shall ill understand the tendencies of our own time if we fail to appreciate the nobility of this idealism, the splendor of its aim, the marvel of its sacrifice, the fineness of the national spirit which is moved by it, and the strength of its determination to achieve.

The increase of material comforts enormously stimulated the growth of population, a phenomenon which men now realize brought in its train difficulties and perplexities of a nature previously unobserved. It is the determination to insure to the individuals of this greater community all the new economic benefits, to increase their well-being to a point scarcely dreamed of a century ago, and to render certain the possession of at least this degree of comfort by the expanding millions about to be born, which creates the newest, but most characteristic, feature of the present situation. With so much dependent upon the acceleration of the rate of economic progress, the possibility that it is more likely to diminish than to increase is deemed alarming. The astonishing pace at which industry and agriculture have marched has

EUROPEAN POLICIES AND MOTIVES

been the product of factors not likely to be replaced in the future by others of equal potency. The great inventions of the nineteenth century—the steam engine, the railroad, the steamship, the telegraph, machinery of a thousand varieties—have worked marvels which can scarcely be repeated, and which have already exhausted the first great impulse. They were applied in most instances to natural resources almost virgin; the railroad and the steamship opened to settlement and cultivation vast areas of soil untrodden by the white man's foot. The new machinery uncovered and utilized new deposits of coal, copper, silver, and iron of unexampled richness. The last two generations, however, have stripped the earth bare of these first resources, have wasted and despoiled with little thought for the future. The first readjustment of industry to machinery is nearly, if not quite, complete, the frontier gone, unoccupied lands in the temperate zone uncommon, and the profit from agriculture and industry is decreasing while population is increasing.

Most European statesmen cannot predicate the continuance of this abnormal rate of progress while the business of the community and of the state is conducted in the old haphazard and inefficient manner, and they see a solution in the conscious utilization of these great forces and factors by a community willing and able to coöperate as a nation in the promotion of the corporate welfare. The individual must find the mean between his interests and those of the greater aggregate, the majority of whose citizens have yet to be born; the present must not despoil the future, or forget that it must sacrifice a little that the future may reap much. The situation has given birth to a doctrine, which may be termed the defense for the future, predicating policies the results of which will require half a century for achievement, and a second doctrine, which may be dubbed the necessity of business at a continued profit. Each year hundreds of thousands of men are added to the nation's workers by the arrival of a new generation of laborers numerically stronger by hundreds of thousands than the generation which ceases work. For them new work must be found, or the workers already employed will be compelled to share with them. To share means less wages, less work, less comforts, the sting of privation, and soon discontent and emigration to some country promising more comforts. To keep the normal increase of the population at home means that the trade of the nation and its industry must develop at a continued profit; the new hands must have work at a profit that the old hands may also continue to work at a profit, for unless both work at a profit, the wolf will soon appear at the door.

On the other hand, no European nation can view with equanimity the emigration of its citizens as long as the strategic and military situation compels it to defend itself against neighboring countries which cherish antipathies and rivalries reaching back through a mist of traditions into the dim past. The country which loses by emigration loses military strength, and if emigration is the result of economic conditions, it will continue to lose military strength, and to that extent fall into the power of neighboring nations whose population is able to stay at home. In time this disparity in size will make aggression and conquest the preliminaries of national humiliation and absorption. Behind military issues and political or diplomatic policies stands the economic problem.

With the growth of population, the boundaries of European states and their natural resources have not kept pace; there is less territory per capita in Europe to-day than there was half a century ago. If the population continues to grow at the present rate, there will be vastly less half a century hence. The natural resources of every country are less than they were in actuality, and will be proportionately and actually less adequate each succeeding decade. Yet every decade will provide more hands to be employed at a profit that every decade will be less possible of attainment by the utilization of the nation's own natural resources. There are few statesmen in Europe who really believe that the rate of growth of the last half-century can be continued at all unless the nation can secure outside markets capable of absorbing annually by reason of their own internal development the additional produce turned out by the new workers in Europe.

Every nation knows that the volume of its trade with its rivals is greater than with its dependencies, and greater than it is likely to be in such markets as the less developed continents can afford. Not the volume of trade, but the degree to which it can be developed, is of consequence. England will sell Germany more goods, but she will buy more in about the same proportion, the normal increase in England being offset by the normal increase in Germany, in France, and in the United States. The normal, natural development of all communities in Europe should be, and is, reciprocal, and might indeed solve the difficulty were it not for the fact that only England and France are satisfied to continue at the present rate of development. The other nations regard themselves as already behind in an economic race where the loss of place will spell in time national extinction. To them the *status quo* is very unsatisfactory, and a normal growth (in the sense of a growth proportionate to the development of their rivals) they regard as objectionable and detrimental to the national interests. An abnormal growth, disproportionate compared with the development of other nations, that will continue until their economic equality with other nations now more favorably situated is an actuality, is precisely what they deem most essential. From such premises there is no escape. Foreign markets, expanding markets, are necessary for the defense of the future, and the greater good to the greater number yet to be born justifies a war of apparent aggression to insure their welfare.

All European nations feel distinctly the pressure for outside markets, though in different states the problem presents itself in different guises. Germany, Austria-Hungary, and Italy feel that the danger of aggression from their neighbors makes it essential for them to prevent emigration in order to maintain an annual increase of their national strength proportionate to the growth of their enemies. While Russia is growing rapidly, emigration involves peril for Germany and Austria; while Austria is adding hundreds of thousands annually, Italy must increase her strength at all costs. The three nations are so hemmed in by other states that the acquisition of additional territory is impossible, even if the smaller states around them were not experiencing the same difficulty of a rapid growth of population in a limited area the natural resources of which cannot be increased. Russia, an undeveloped country, and therefore anxious to grow at an abnormal rate, finds the problem less acute because of its vast area and the existence of Siberia. In France the difficulty is least because the population has for years been nearly stationary.

Great Britain long ago experienced the difficulty, but for decades was able to view with equanimity the steady stream of emigrants to Australia, to Canada, and to the United States, because she felt confident that her island position and the strength of her fleet made an army less necessary and the retention of the population at home undesirable. From the savings of the past came furthermore an income sufficient to support many thousands of her people at home; from her vast merchant marine, her banking business, and her general services to the world as broker, banker, carrier, insurer, she drew the maintenance of hundreds of thousands of hands; in her dependencies other thousands found occupation and a comfortable livelihood. All these factors, with the steadily increasing output of manufactured goods, have kept England and the English prosperous and contented. But they realize that their prosperity rests upon their access to non-European countries, and that this access depends upon their fleet. The difference between the attitude of England and France and that of Germany and Austria lies not in a fundamental difference in the national problem, but to the fact that their location and their military and naval prowess enabled them to secure the non-European markets that have thus far solved the difficulty. Naturally, they are loath to part with their advantage. The other European nations are grimly determined somehow to solve the same problem, and are willing to contest with force of arms freedom of access to the markets of the world.

Entirely within the bounds of possibility is an attempt to project across the Atlantic into the Western Hemisphere the surplus population inexpedient for the mother country to retain and its establishment in a favorable location where it could develop without losing its identity as an integral part of the nation. Modern transportation and communication have made possible a degree of coöperation between distant groups which might literally erase even as great a difference in space as the Atlantic between the two parts of the same nation, and render possible a real acquaintanceship, a real sympathy in ideals, an essential identity of speech, administration, and methods. Such a state can certainly be founded, and the question of geographical continuity will be relatively unimportant if these other essentials of nationality exist. England has literally and successfully projected herself into Canada. The Germans have long talked of *Das Deutschtum in Ausland* as a reality, as an integral part of the German nation, and there is reason to believe that the migration of large numbers of Germans to Cuba and South America would result in a situation similar to that of Canada and Great Britain. This literal possibility of successfully projecting European nations across three thousand miles of water is a significant consideration for us who live in the Western Hemisphere.

The present situation is only a phase of an economic problem which is permanent, and which will probably influence European policies more

EUROPEAN POLICIES AND MOTIVES

powerfully decade by decade than it does now. We need not doubt the existence of a motive which may lead the victor of this present war to invade the Western Hemisphere. It may be that the only entirely feasible solution of his economic problems will be found there. We must now see to what extent the Western Hemisphere is fitted to assist him.

CHAPTER II

THE REDISCOVERY OF SOUTH AMERICA

THERE is no historical fact more trite than the discovery of South America by Christopher Columbus, and none better attested than its barrenness of wide results for nearly four centuries. Although the first continental land seen in the Western Hemisphere, its real features and possibilities remained unrealized until discovered by our own generation, by whom knowledge about it was first effectively disseminated. This remarkable fact has been thrown into strong relief by the outbreak of the European war, for it is in the undeveloped condition of South America, in its marvelous adaptability for European needs, that the victor will find the motive needed to lure him to the Western Hemisphere. The reasons for this neglect of South America during many centuries are striking; the reasons for its rediscovery by Europe and by the United States are significant; a comprehension of both is essential to a grasp of

THE REDISCOVERY OF SOUTH AMERICA

the potentialities and probabilities rendering a clash between Europe and the Western Hemisphere imminent.

In the early sixteenth century the New World seemed entirely to correspond to the expectations of Europeans. True, many had suffered disappointment; the new land was not the fabled territory of the Great Khan nor yet the location of Quivira and the Seven Cities of Cibola: but the precious metals and jewels were found in Mexico and Peru, and by the middle of the sixteenth century the results of conquest loomed stupendous, rendering Spain apparently the wealthiest of European nations. Then all vanished; the interest in South America of the world in general waned, and men began to forget. We have not far to seek for the reasons. The precious metals and jewels were derived from surface mines, which yielded steadily diminishing returns to the feeble efforts of the conqueror, for the crude methods of mining then understood made it possible to utilize little beyond the surface deposits of comparatively free metal. As always, the question of labor was the most difficult to solve. The Peruvians and Aztecs faded away in the mines and fields, and the other Indian stocks proved scarcely better workers. By the third quarter of the sixteenth century a brisk trade in negro slaves brought from Africa had sprung up, and attempts to develop South and Central America were largely abandoned in favor of the production in the West India Islands of the great staple crops, sugar and tobacco, for which a great demand was appearing in Europe. The interest of Europe in Central and South America was slight in the seventeenth and eighteenth centuries compared with its vital interest in the West Indies, North America, and the East Indies.

We shall probably not be far wrong if we ascribe much of this indifference to the marshy or moist character of the coast regions, strewn with swamps, morasses, and rivers, abounding in insects and malaria, with a soil not often dry enough to make the labor of clearing it worth while. Such a district was not suited for the homes of white men in a new world, and conquered even stern Huguenots, men and women of desirable stock, whose ability and determination failed to found successful colonies. The few Spanish settlements languished, agriculture dwindled, and finally there were left in a semi-somnolent state only trading posts and factories which communicated with the interior by water and furnished a basis for barter with the natives. Around the Isthmus of Panama always clustered a few communities dependent upon the trade with Peru and the western coast. The whole district was ill-fitted to produce the commodities then in demand in Europe, and there were few or no products except dye-woods in which Europeans were much interested or in the development of which they saw possible profit.

In fact, the existence of North America, its superior adaptability for the home-maker, the vast extent of its fertile lands, stood in the way of the utilization of South America by Europeans until the nineteenth century. Much more accessible and much more understandable, admirably adapted for the production of what the European of that day deemed the necessities of life, colonists of all nations sought the United States in preference to lands farther south. For capitalists and merchants the profits of trade with North America and with the West Indies were so great that the probabilities of profit in the development of a less accessible country were not alluring. Indeed, something like the complete settlement of the United States, something like an approximate utilization of the resources of North America, was necessary to render South America an attractive field for enterprise or settlement.

The achievements of modern science and modern

industry, however, are mainly responsible for its rediscovery. They have made South America valuable, desirable to Europeans as never before. The continent itself was inaccessible and was virtually isolated from Europe by time and space in the days of sailing-ships. This, however, was less important than the inaccessibility of the really desirable districts in the interior for the residence of white men and for commercial exploitation. While nearly two thirds of the continent is in the tropics, the prevalence of mountains and high plateaus in its center provides over the bulk of its area conditions by no means tropical, so that much of Peru and Ecuador and the whole of Bolivia are to all intents and purposes in the temperate zone and adapted by soil and climate for the residence of Europeans or Americans. Railroads to carry bulky products to the seaboard, steamships and cheap ocean freights were the prerequisites of the development of the interior of South America. The problem of transportation solved by the nineteenth century opened the whole area to settlement and enterprise. It is now merely a question of time when the whole will be utilized.

Another difficulty, insuperable until the nineteenth century, lay in the inability of European peoples to utilize most of its abounding natural products. It was not merely a question of profit or of transportation; the thing itself had as little conceivable utility when landed in Europe as the famous pocket-handerchiefs intended for the savages in Africa. Like rubber, the market of which is a matter of decades and depends upon the great development of the automobile and the extended use of electricity for a great variety of purposes, a whole class of commodities have been found indispensable to diversified industry which were hitherto useless. Another class the value of which was already known could not have been reached without modern machinery. South America abounds in minerals, the majority of which were non-existent for the Spaniards, partly because it was not profitable to extract the ore unless in large quantities and relatively free, and partly because the valuable metals in low-grade ores could not be separated at all from the foreign substances by the crude methods then employed. Modern drills and dynamite, the steam engine, the new crushers, have been needed to give us access to the mines of the Andes. In the forests are quantities of hardwood suitable for furniture of the finest grades, but too hard to be dealt with profitably by hand and too heavy and bulky to be successfully transported without the railroad.

PAN-AMERICANISM

Not less important has been the growth of the industrial community in Europe and in the United States, the extension of its desires, the multiplication of its wants. As the division of labor became more successful, as thousands of hands were freed from the labor of producing the necessities of life and turned to the task of producing luxuries, a thousand new economic wants clamored for satisfaction for the effectuation of which the community was ready to pay. Nothing short of this rapid expansion of the economic fabric in Europe and the United States, this multiplication of luxuries and new wants, the vital change in the standard of well-being which made the luxuries of the early nineteenth century the necessities of the twentieth, could have provided an adequate market for the South American produce. Laborers now expect to enjoy food and clothes superior to those eaten and worn by royalty not so long ago, and in this extension of the former luxuries of thousands to the millions lay the market for South American produce. The demand must precede the supply, and all the facilities of transportation were unavailing until the demand came into existence.

Access to the coast region has always been easy; residence beyond brief periods has been usually impossible for white men in great districts, while settlements of white men in districts otherwise commercially admirable has been out of the question. For years this barrier of fever-ridden land stood between the settler and the fertile fields and inexhaustible resources of the interior of the northern half of South America. Yet before the interior could be developed on a great scale the coast had to be rendered habitable for white men, because contact with the interior must take place from the coast. We must give due weight to the epoch-making achievements of modern science, which has already worsted malaria and yellow fever, the two dread scourges which closed the coast regions of much of South America to the whites for many generations. It is now merely a question of time when the whole will be conquered by modern sanitation and modern medicine.

The rediscovery of South America has been, and is still, a commercial proposition, and not alone a matter of profit, but of comparative profit, for no merchant normally does business at a loss, and no investor who believes himself entirely sane would dream of putting money into one enterprise so long as a more desirable enterprise was available. On the whole, the rate of profit in the development of a country where crude products must be produced in large quantities and transported great distances will be comparatively small in proportion to the physical bulk of the commodity dealt in. The profit on a pound of sugar, a square foot of timber, a pig of iron, or an ingot of silver is not usually high in percentage, and to make the transaction as a whole really lucrative, the merchant must extend his operations in many directions and produce on a large scale in order that his profit may be certain even if relatively small on each transaction. While rubber companies and mining investors have at times obtained annual profits of fifty or a hundred per cent., and in some cases even larger percentages, such is not the normal profit in South American trade. Before the investor and the merchant would be drawn thither, it was necessary that the rate of profit in ordinary transactions in other countries should fall to a percentage somewhat below that which can be regularly obtained in the production of bulky agricultural staples and natural products. With the profits made in the past in exploiting the United States and the West Indies, South America could scarcely compete, for when opportunities for merchant, investor, or laborer were so great and so near at hand, distant projects were not alluring. Colonial merchants who did not realize at least one hundred per cent. on the year's business thought themselves defrauded. One Baltimore shipowner who lived about the time of the American Revolution purchased a cargo of salt in Bermuda with tobacco, carried it into Baltimore, and cleared a profit of eight hundred per cent. The cotton industry in the South before the war, like the cultivation of virgin soil in the Mississippi valley, produced enormous profits.

Indeed, it might almost be claimed that until very recently Europe and the United States have regarded South America and Central America not as fields for investment and development, but for exploitation and speculation. The attitude of the outside world has changed. Instead of robbing its inhabitants, despoiling the land, and leaving it to its fate, they are now anxious to develop in that continent strong, self-reliant, capable communities which will develop their own resources and with whom ordinary business can be transacted from which the usual rate of profit will be expected and deemed satisfactory. The increase of population in Europe and the United States, the greater keenness of competition, the introduction of machinery, the improvements of transportation, have increased the volume of business and have decreased its rate of profit on individual transactions to a point which makes opportunities for the development of the Southern Continent seem attractive.

The economic independence of South America is at hand; the days of its slavery and degradation are already past; its rediscovery portends the realization of the important part it can and ought to play in the interdependent, international economic fabric. The end of the European war is more than likely to render this fact appallingly clear to the victor.

CHAPTER III

PROBABILITIES OF GERMAN AGGRESSION

THE circumstances in which Germany emerges from the present war as victor will be more significant for the United States than the fact of victory. Should Germany conclusively defeat the Allies on land and sea, she would in all probability carry out the Pan-Germanic schemes for the absorption of Africa and India, and would find in the development of an administration and in the solution of colonial problems abundant occupation for some years for such endeavor as she could spare from the rearrangement of Europe and the reorganization of Germany and Austria. While such a sweeping victory would by no means prevent her from extending her ægis over the Western Hemisphere, it would render an attempt to do so improbable. A victory by Germany and Austria on land and an English victory on the sea will also send the

German armies to India and the far East, and with that eventuality the United States will not be concerned. A naval victory over England and either a stalemate on land or a victory without the annihilation of the French and Russian armies; a qualified victory on land and sea by Germany and Austria not sufficient to humble or crush their enemies, but enough to compel the latter to conclude a peace on terms favorable to Germany—these are the eventualities which the United States ought to view with apprehension. And precisely these circumstances the military and naval probabilities indicate. The English fleet seems likely to retain control of the sea despite diminishing numbers and occasional defeats, and if Germany and Austria win at all on land, it will probably be a victory which will fall far short of the annihilation of the allied armies. This will be the very situation which the United States has most to fear.

In no event is a German army likely to set foot upon the soil of North America to attack the United States, Canada, or Mexico. Though we are told of German plans for the invasion of the United States, no doubt the War Department at Berlin could display in its archives an elaborate scheme for the invasion of every country on the globe, and we shall do well not to deceive ourselves into a belief that the attempt to educate the general staff in various European countries portends an invasion of the United States. Any notion that Germany would even dream of conquering America is based upon a fundamentally incorrect conception of Pan-Germanism.

Economic problems, though not more fundamental than in other European countries, are more pressing in Germany, where the benefits of the economic development of the last decades have been proportionately greater than elsewhere, and where the fear that they may not be durable is based upon a vivid memory of conditions when Germany was less prosperous. Many people now alive in Germany have experienced comparative penury and real prosperity within the span of their own lives, and look upon a possible diminution of the rate of economic progress with something more than a speculative eye. Markets, for the swelling volume of German manufactured goods greater each year by the amount produced by the new generation of efficient hands, Germany is seeking; markets in which she may continue to sell at a profit indefinitely, and so ward off that readjustment of German industry which must involve considerable, even though temporary, suffering to many of her people and probably invite emigration. Rightly or wrongly, she does not feel that the European countries, the United States, and Canada, will offer her such a market. South America and Central America are apparently ideal for her purpose, and she needs merely to remove from her path two technical and artificial obstacles, the English fleet and the Monroe Doctrine. With the one she is at present attempting to deal; to the other she may in due time direct her attention.

Americans who study an atlas but seldom, and who see their own country and Europe depicted on large scale maps, so that Russia, Massachusetts, and Belgium each occupy a full page, and then chance in turning the leaves to stumble across a map of Latin America also occupying a page, have not the slightest realization of its immense size. Its area approximates nine million square miles, about three times greater than the United States, and it contains one state which alone is as large as the United States. Approximately seventy-five millions of people inhabit the twenty republics stretching between the Rio Grande and Cape Horn, but, though they are collectively numerous, it is vital to remember, when we are speaking of the adaptability of various parts of the world for Germany's purposes, that only three fourths as many people as there are in the United States are scattered over an area three times as great. Probably no country so well fitted for development by Europeans is unappropriated by them.

The natural resources of the country are vast almost beyond relief. The land itself is excessively fertile, and the conditions in various parts of the country permit the profitable cultivation of all tropical staples and of most products of the temperate zone, for somewhere the right conditions of soil, climate, and rainfall will be found in conjunction. Its forests produce such commercial staples as rubber, dye-woods, and hard-woods for cabinet making; its mountains contain minerals in profusion—the precious metals, quantities of iron, lead, and tin, besides many minerals of which relatively small quantities are available in Europe and many of which the supply in Europe proper is steadily diminishing. As a field for enterprise, South America is unsurpassed in the world and without a peer.

Its resources have been scarcely uncovered, and the ground has barely been scratched. While in southern Brazil and in the northern Argentine Republic are highly developed areas, much of the coast is entirely undeveloped, and the greater part of the interior is almost virgin because it has not yet been reached by modern transportation. There are thousands of miles of railroads in South and Central America, but the area to be covered is three times as great as that of the United States, the number of people to be reached is nearly seventy-five millions, and the mileage necessary to meet their needs is enormous. Yet upon adequate railroad facilities depends the profitable development of the interior and the coast, for when the railroads are in operation, the rapidity with which the country can grow will depend solely upon the amount of capital which can be drawn thither. That degree of rapid development which the Germans believe essential for their new market is entirely feasible in South and Central America.

As a field for emigration, South America is unsurpassed by any similar area outside of Europe and North America which is not already crowded to bursting with population. Vast areas await settlement—vast areas with a temperate climate, fertile soil, abundant mineral resources, everything necessary for the comfort of a European population.

The South Americans are naturally zealous to win favorable opinions about their country from foreigners,—quite as anxious as the inhabitants of Chicago, London, and Berlin,—and they resent with perfect justice the representation of South

PROBABILITIES OF GERMAN AGGRESSION

America as an uninhabited country. In all fairness we should emphasize the existence of broad bands of highly developed territory where conditions are essentially the same as in Europe and in the United States. If some towns and districts are unprepossessing, there are tank-towns and mining cities in the United States of America consisting of a few saloons and one-story shacks, and the domestic architecture in the Middle West and even in well-known Eastern States has not yet attracted the commendation of artists. Candor will extort from Americans who see nothing but the pictures the admission that Rio Janeiro and Buenos Aires surpass from an architectural point of view the great majority of American cities, and contain certain districts, finer than anything in America, which compare favorably with the show places of Europe. Travelers insist that the reality far surpasses the pictures, and that the hotels and accommodations in the larger cities are luxurious to a degree unknown in a good many parts of the United States. At the same time that we insist upon these facts, we must also stress the existence of vast areas as yet undeveloped, where the population is ignorant and crude when it is not literally savage. The most vital fact to keep in mind about Latin America as a whole is the juxtaposition of the developed and the undeveloped, of civilization and barbarism. Both exist in Latin America.

Were it not true that millions of these people are highly civilized and accustomed to satisfying a very great variety of economic wants by the importation of European manufactured goods, Latin America would offer a conspicuously less favorable opportunity to German trade; for the German problem is in reality a future problem—to expand her trade as fast as her population can possibly grow, to increase her exports in proportion to the increase of industrial efficiency in production, and to sell all at a profit. Not much consideration is needed to show us that South America is naturally better fitted than most European dependencies to afford an expanding market. The population in Morocco and Egypt, like the population in India, has not been accustomed to a high degree of comfort, judged by European standards, and is not easily and rapidly educated in varieties of new wants that European endeavor and capital are essential to satisfy. The pace at which such markets can be developed is difficult to accelerate, and the more expensive and complicated manufactured products are less easily sold there. A market for pianos is more difficult to develop in India than in South America, where European music is a passion with a large part of the native population, where there are opera-houses the architecture of which puts to blush our structures for similar purposes, and performances are usually comparable with our own. The markets for European goods in South America are already developed; the volume of trade is already enormous; it has grown in the last few decades with leaps and bounds, affording proof of the pace at which it will continue to grow under favorable conditions.

The inability of Germany to wait until the day when her navy can beat the English fleet in open battle has compelled her to seek markets outside Europe which can be reached by land and the trade of which cannot be controlled by sea-power, and has aimed Pan-Germanism at Egypt and India, at the fertile valleys of the Tigris and Euphrates. But inasmuch as this assault upon Africa and Asia involves highly unpleasant consequences for other nations, Germany's success may conceivably raise almost as many problems as it will settle. While she has already achieved powerful allies, and in the event of victory may acquire more, her expansion into Africa and Asia has already insured the enmity of two powerful nations, and may probably arouse the apprehension of others. Such a solution of her problem is undesirable as long as another method is available. Such an opportunity is presented in South America. As it is not strategically a part of Europe, its control by Germany would not menace in the least any of the existing coalitions in Europe, Africa, or Asia, and would threaten neither the political welfare nor the independence of European or Asiatic powers. Its possession could not possibly make Germany politically stronger or strategically more dangerous in Europe than she would be without it. This, indeed, may not improbably be the really vital fact which the war will make astoundingly clear. In the event of a sweeping German victory, the occupation of South America will be easier than interference elsewhere; in the event of a victory over the English fleet, whether or not that fleet is annihilated, the control of South America will afford the simplest, readiest, and most expeditious solution of Germany's economic problems.

Above all, in the eventuality which seems most probable,—a German preponderance on land sufficiently clear to compel the granting of concessions by the Allies,—South America will be the easiest thing for them to concede. There is nothing on the globe that would cost the Allies so little without threatening them at all. It is the only thing on the globe, in fact, which they can afford to surrender to a victorious Germany. All the powers except England and France will give away what they never possessed, a sort of giving which most people find easy, and even for England it is a much easier concession from every conceivable point of view than Egypt, India, or South Africa, where the roots of English rule are older, deeper, and better established.

It may not improbably be the only concession which a due regard for the future will enable Germany to accept. If there is one thing more essential for her than another in the preparation of a lasting peace, it is a solution favorable to Germany which does not require concessions involving the honor of other nations. The loss of Morocco, of Egypt, of India, would be serious blows to the pride of the English and French people, and would be so unpopular and lead so inevitably to a demand for reprisal and revenge that German statesmen may well hesitate before demanding or accepting them. No nation's pride would be involved in the cession to Germany of South America, because no European nation has political dominion in South America, outside Guiana, and no control or overlordship of that obvious technical nature the loss of which is so impossible to conceal. All European nations have relations with Latin America of such subtlety, and relations with other parts of the world so public and avowed, that a compromise reached at the expense of South America would surely be agreeable to them all. They cannot, indeed, confer upon Germany privileges of ownership they do not possess, but she will be abundantly satisfied if they covenant not to interfere with her development of the country and with her acquisition of the lion's share of the trade. They can easily come to a tacit agreement to turn their attention elsewhere and leave her unmolested.

From the economic point of view such a solution would be exceedingly advantageous for Germany. South America is so safe from military interference and so easily protected by the victors' fleet from European aggression that it will provide a particularly secure place in which to develop, with German capital in the hands of German merchants, the expanding market on which Germany places her future dependence. No conquest by arms would be desired; no military rule of any sort would be expedient; no army needed to retain the sort of right upon which she would be prepared to insist—a preferential tariff or some sort of trade monopoly or preference which would be as profitable to South Americans as to Germans.

Nor would the acquisition by Germany of England's peculiar supremacy be likely to arouse opposition or even apprehension in South America. The Latin American is well acquainted with the German and finds him personally much to his liking. He is apprehensive not of German merchants, of German fleets, or German commerce, but of German colonists, who would attempt the erection in South America of *das Deutschtum in Ausland*. When he comes to understand that the new Germany will frown upon emigration, he will lose his suspicions of her. The South American, therefore, Germany has not to fear; with Europeans in South America she will be able to deal with maximum ease.

Such a solution would be peculiarly adapted to the maintenance in Germany of an army large enough to hold France and Russia in check. Pan-Germanism is intended to make possible the retention of enough men in Germany to recruit indefinitely an army of sufficient strength to hold in check the swelling hordes of Russia. A victory which compels the vanquished to pay the price in Africa and Asia, will mean the military protection of the new dependencies and their administration by German hands, which, while it will furnish employment for a good many Germans, will draw from Germany a good many men whose loss it may not be easy to replace, and whose number, indeed, may have to be considerably increased as the years elapse. If the day should ever come when a new coalition should rise to wrest from Germany her new empire, the defense of an empire scattered over Europe, Asia, and Africa would in all probability be so difficult as almost to predicate failure. On the contrary, the defense of an empire based upon a German army at home and upon commercial interests with a country like South America, inaccessible to Europeans, making no demands for military protection, and quite capable of administering itself, would be so entirely feasible as to leave almost no ground for hesitation in the contemplation of alternatives.

Quite within the bounds of possibility will be an assault by Germany upon the far East. The Panama Canal, if she can secure it, will afford access to the Pacific by a route eminently safe from European interference. Through it would be feasible, an attempt to free the Eastern nations from English and French domination, to restore to India and China their national independence, free from curtailment or interference, in exchange for that same shadowy commercial supremacy which Germany would like to obtain in South

PROBABILITIES OF GERMAN AGGRESSION

America. She could thus strike a crushing blow at her adversaries' prosperity without herself assuming the sort of burdens which render her enemies vulnerable, and as she would control her own approaches by way of Panama to the far East, dependent upon nobody's consent or permission, she could in the future extend her trade unchecked. Than this no more deadly blow could be struck at England, and it could be dealt with entire safety and without creating future problems. The dream of German statesmen would come true—the disruption of England's artificial and abnormal empire and the restoration of freedom to South America and the far East, with the lion's share of the trade in German hands.

There would remain the United States and the Monroe Doctrine. We have at present the most explicit diplomatic assurances that the Germans intend to regard the integrity of our possessions and do not contemplate an assault on Canada. On the whole, the Germans do not expect opposition from the United States. They realize it would be a gross blunder for them to attempt actually to monopolize the whole South American market, for they cannot supply everything the latter wishes to buy nor consume all the raw produce she must export; but they feel it would also be a sorry blunder to share it with England and France, where the profits of the trade would strengthen Germany's foes and help in the solution of economic problems the insistence and difficulty of which would otherwise weaken them. The United States is different. She neither threatens Germany nor is likely to develop an economic fabric which Germany would need to fear, whatever its size or rate of progress. An alliance with us she would gladly have, and she would willingly purchase it at the price of concessions in South America beyond those dictated by economic prudence. That some such reasoning would influence German statesmen is quite within the bounds of probability.

What, then, would the United States do? Suppose we should decline such a German offer? Shall we not delude ourselves if we suppose that with such interests at stake, such problems to solve, such foes already vanquished, the Germans would hesitate to challenge the Monroe Doctrine?

CHAPTER IV

POSSIBILITIES OF ENGLISH AGGRESSION

FROM present indications most critics conclude that the end of the war will find England still supreme upon the sea. They point to the natural ability of the English as sailors, to the preponderance in size of the English fleet over the German, to the centuries of successful experience behind the English leaders, to the possibility of another Nelson or a new Drake. Victory will not change our fundamental relations to the sea-power nor yet the fundamental premise that the sea-power itself is for England a defensive arm, the use of which for aggression would endanger its own existence. The same considerations which have hitherto made politic England's generous use of her authority would still dictate little if any interference with other nations. Nevertheless, the defeat of the German navy—and in all probability its defeat will mean its destruction—will affect a substantive change in those factors of the situation most essential to the safety and prosperity of the United States.

The restoration of England's supremacy as an actual fact will destroy the balance of power in European waters which has long rendered inexpedient the aggressive use of England's navy and immunized our coast and island possessions from attack. The aftermath of every great European war has found England utilizing the sea-power for the extension of her dominion wherever possible without the coöperation of an extensive military expedition. Without doubt all German colonies will be in England's hands before long, and she will expect to retain the bulk of them at the end of the war; but she will then be able to undertake aggression against others. We must not forget, therefore, that victory will automatically restore to England the supremacy of the Western Hemisphere. Once more her fleet will take physical control of our waters and will be able to exercise in fact the true supremacy which we have had during the last decade and a half. Nor will there be any longer a necessity for generosity; with the defeat of her great rival her imperative reasons for conciliating us will have disappeared. She was anxious for us to hold the sovereignty of American waters because she was anxious to keep it out of

POSSIBILITIES OF ENGLISH AGGRESSION

the hands of Germany; once victorious, she will prefer to retain it herself.

Why, too, should she not extend her present possessions in the Gulf of Mexico? The most desirable possession in the world at the close of this war will be the Panama Canal, the new roadway to the English colonies in Australia, to the English possessions in India, to the marts of trade in China; a new roadway which the fleet alone can control, and one which Pan-Germanism, Pan-Slavism, and Pan-Islam are incapable of threatening. Its approaches are already in England's hands: the Bahama and Bermuda islands, easily controlling the approaches to the gulf from the Atlantic Coast; the really advantageous route through the Windward Islands; the road along the South American coast past Barbados and Trinidad. All these converge upon Jamaica at the very entrance of the canal, commanding its approaches from Europe, from the Atlantic coast of the United States, and from our gulf ports. With the keys of the situation thus in her hands, with an English squadron in active control of the sea, with the notions of expediency dictated by the exigencies of European policy no longer counseling so great a degree of caution, to take possession of the remainder would be a matter of the utmost simplicity and a step clearly advantageous.

At our influence in the Gulf of Mexico she has always looked askance, regarding it from the earliest times as contrary to her interests. Trade with the West Indies she was glad to foster while the continental colonies were subjects of the British crown, but the moment they broke from that allegiance she became hostile to the extension of American trade, and opposed it by means of statutes and regulations which her navy was completely adequate to enforce. The Monroe Doctrine and the diplomatic negotiations which preceded and followed it convinced her statesmen that the United States cherished a desire to extend its authority over the whole of the gulf and the adjacent territory, an impression strengthened and confirmed by the happenings and diplomatic statements of the ensuing decades. We need not suppose that this was forgotten when the understanding was reached which placed the supremacy of the gulf for the time in our hands, nor that the events of the last fifteen years making the United States the dominant power in the Gulf of Mexico have escaped notice. England herself still holds the strategic and naval stations, but the present English possessions are not as commercially valu-

POSSIBILITIES OF ENGLISH AGGRESSION

able in themselves as those of the United States, and the retention of strategic control premises a return to her earlier policy of controlling the gulf as soon as the exigencies of the European situation permit. When the German fleet has been destroyed and the victory of the Allies has shifted the balance of power in Europe and left England free to pursue her earlier policies and recoup her losses, will it not be entirely natural for her to turn once more to the Gulf of Mexico and to expect the United States to surrender a supremacy which she received as a loan, one might almost say, rather than as a gift?

The northwestern extremity of this continent is the province of Alaska, valuable because of its great deposits of gold, coal, and other minerals. Geographically, it is a part of Canada and not a part of the United States; our title to it rests upon purchase rather than upon conquest or discovery, and upon a purchase made at a time when the mineral deposits were scarcely suspected. The simplicity of the operations required to add Alaska to Canada will be apparent to the least informed. Separated as it is from the United States proper, easily approached from any part of western Canada, and inhabited at present by a sparse and cosmopolitan population, it would be difficult indeed for us to defend.

Our relations with Canada have rarely met with English approval. Scarcely had the French been expelled and the American Revolution begun than the thirteen States were negotiating and scheming to add Canada as a fourteenth state, and the project has often been revived since. In 1812 invasion was attempted, with the probable purpose of conquering the province and offering it to England in exchange for the commercial rights for which we had negotiated in vain. Such, at any rate, was the version accepted in England. Further difficulties were occasioned when the present Constitution of Canada was made, while the recent attempts to provide a customs agreement which should give the Canadians greater privileges in the United States than English merchants possessed in England have been thought to be the preliminaries of annexation. To such notions credence has been lent by men in the highest American public offices. Recently a campaign was fought in Canada over the issue of loyalty to England and the rejection of the commercial treaty or its acceptance with the understanding that a closer connection, if not annexation, with the United States was desirable and probable. Rumor is

POSSIBILITIES OF ENGLISH AGGRESSION

once more busy with similar schemes, and is proceeding from quarters whence the news will certainly reach England. Any attempt during the war or at its close to establish a more intimate connection between the United States and Canada will not be viewed with approval in London.

The potential power of England is enormous, and in the present circumstances ought to be better understood. Our whole foreign trade is in her hands, all our approaches are at the mercy of her fleet once that fleet is victorious over its present enemies, and an army could invade the United States from Canada with ease and probably with success. It could not, indeed, hope to hold the country or conquer it, but a dash at New York, Chicago, or Seattle is eminently feasible.

An English victory will also predicate a great change in England's attitude toward the growing trade of the United States with South America. Until comparatively recently, Great Britain paid little attention to the United States or to its assertions of interest in South America because we had neither the manufactured goods nor the capital which the Latin Americans needed, and were unable to use in our own industries any considerable amount of their products. Then from the magic of the industrial inventions of the nineteenth century came the transformation of the United States and of South America. From a power whose commercial influence England might safely disregard, the United States had become a dangerous rival; from a customer whose trade the South Americans need scarcely consider, the United States had become one of their most important buyers. Physically we are able, entirely able, to compete with England in South American markets, and have proved ourselves capable of getting rather more than our share in some of them. During the last fifteen years we have so enormously increased our trade that in Central America nearly seventy per cent. is to-day in American hands, and in parts of South America the United States stands either second or third in volume of trade.

Of these facts, however, the European situation forbade the English to complain. The trade was a necessary consequence of the supremacy of the Western Hemisphere which the building of the German fleet had put into American hands and which, indeed, the English were not at the time in a position actively to dispute, because they were not able to despatch from Europe adequate force to make good their claims. Once the German fleet is destroyed and the supremacy of the sea is again

POSSIBILITIES OF ENGLISH AGGRESSION

incontestably in England's hands, the control of the water routes to the Western Hemisphere hers beyond dispute, will she not take into account the new relationship between the United States and South America, and be driven to ask whether it is to her interest for the United States to possess so large a share of the trade? We shall not need to assume her intention of monopolizing the trade to the total exclusion of the United States and other nations to see that she may well object to the proportion of it which we at present have, and will in particular not view with favor any future increase. She will be able to challenge her new rival's position, and it would not be at all surprising if she objected strongly to sharing with us the trade which Germany has had. During the war American trade with South America will undoubtedly increase in volume, because we may absorb part of England's own market as well as the lion's share of Germany's. When England wishes to resume her normal business at the close of the war, what then? Will American merchants be willing to cede their vantage without a struggle? Will they not fight valiantly for the trade the vanquished have had? Will there not be here ample material for disagreement and dispute, for recrimination and diplomatic difficulties, and, it may be, for arbitrary restrictions and acts leading to war?

In all probability, too, more fundamental factors than these will counsel the extension of English trade with South America. England's home land in the British Isles is not only more restricted than Germany, but utterly incapable of enlargement; additional territory is out of the question. Its natural resources are much smaller than Germany's, for much of its surface is not arable land, and much of its arable land is not naturally fertile, and much of it shows clearly the working of the law of diminishing returns; the mineral resources are neither varied nor inexhaustible, and there are no adequate indigenous supplies of any of the raw products in the manufacture of which England excels. Yet her population is increasing at a rate only somewhat less than Germany's and Austria's, at a rate, although somewhat smaller than in the immediate past, still greater than the resources of the British Isles can possibly support. England does not now feed herself, already imports the great bulk of the materials which keep her factories going, and actually depends to-day upon exporting the greater part of the output. If there is a country in the world entirely dependent upon the possession of foreign markets and of ready access

POSSIBILITIES OF ENGLISH AGGRESSION

to them, it is England. Indeed, it is the English solution of this problem of a rapid increase of population within a restricted area normally too small to support it and impossible of increase that suggested Pan-Germanism to the Germans. The English have encouraged emigration, and have thus kept the population in the British Isles within certain bounds; they have assiduously sought and developed foreign markets in Asia, Africa, and South America; they have taken care of thousands of individuals by means of their merchant marine and their vast exchange business. In these ways they have coped with this problem successfully ever since the time of Elizabeth, when the problem first became clear. But it is to-day exactly as vital for England to *retain* foreign markets large enough to permit her citizens at home to continue manufacturing at a profit in the ratio at which population increases as it is for Germany and Austria to accomplish the same end by the acquisition of markets which they do not now possess; the consequence to England of losing markets will be not less serious than the effect upon Germany of an inability to attain them.

If the war leaves England with the control of the sea, but compels her to hand over to some other nation or nations or to share with other nations some of the markets which she at present virtually monopolizes, it will be imperative for her to replace this loss by the prompt development of a new market elsewhere. It is also conceivable that the growth of her self-governing colonies and dependencies has reached its maximum and will now proceed at a somewhat slower pace. Although the market for manufactured goods in a new country settled by Europeans is at first large, it normally diminishes in the ratio by which the new settlement produces for itself, so that the greater complexity in the economic life of the English self-governing colonies will naturally result in a proportionately smaller demand for English goods. Nor must we forget in this connection the growing sentiment in the English colonies that they ought not to be expected to purchase commodities from the mother country which they can obtain more cheaply from England's rivals; more and more as the decades pass are the self-governing colonies likely to insist upon their economic freedom; more and more will this diminish the demand for English products. The shortage from these varied causes —and let us remember always that a proportionately smaller demand will be fatal even although the actual sum total of goods sold may still show an increase—will compel England to seek new markets in order to maintain the rate of commercial progress essential for the preservation of prosperity in the British Isles.

We may add to these probabilities a quite normal anxiety to increase the pace of England's industrial development considerably beyond the rate of the last few decades in order to replace as soon as possible the capital spent in waging this war. England's comparative inability to maintain her normal rate of production during the war, the comparatively larger number of men taken from industry for the army than in Europe, where standing armies have normally kept large numbers of men outside of the economic fabric, will probably make the drain upon English capital relatively heavier than in the case of other nations. The desirability of replacing it as speedily as possible will be so evident, and the method of doing it by the manufacture in England and the sale elsewhere of increased quantities of goods is so thoroughly well understood, that an English victory almost predicates an attempt to accelerate the development of English industry by the opening of new markets.

Political or international complications may make it impossible to satisfy all these impulses in Africa or Asia, while economic changes in the self-governing colonies may render a solution by a proportionately increased trade with them out of the question. True, we must suppose that Germany's defeat will transfer a certain part of her present foreign markets to the victor, at least until German industry can recover from the war, but it is probable that Central and South America will offer the most favorable opportunity to the English for solving these varied problems and for recouping as soon as possible their losses in the war. If England could sell them, in addition to her present exports, a considerable proportion of what Germany and the United States combined have sold, she would be quite likely to create there the most valuable and dependable market that she has ever had. The geographical isolation of South America both from Europe and from the United States would place the monopoly upon the firm basis of England's supremacy of the sea. If the present war renders English bankers chary of investing capital in Germany, partly because of the possibility of wars in the future, partly by reason of a desire not to help the Germans on their feet too quickly, they will look for some country freed from the possibilities of alarms, unaffected by European complications, not strategically dangerous to other nations or strategically necessary

POSSIBILITIES OF ENGLISH AGGRESSION

to them, a country in which the new economic development based upon that capital would not make it possible to create a new political and military power likely or able to threaten England's own position. There is only one such possibility on the globe sufficient in size, in richness of resources, in the present degree of development attained by its population, to meet this requirement—South America. And there will be on the globe no place where the English can as easily, with as little effort or danger, increase their markets. The war may, therefore, produce a chain of circumstances which may almost force the English to draw into their own hands a considerable proportion of the trade with Latin America which the United States now has, and to resist with determination America's attempt to increase its commercial dealings in that attractive El Dorado of the twentieth century.

CHAPTER V

RIGHTS OF NEUTRALS

THE United States is already seriously at odds with the power which seems likely to be the victor in this war. That the crisis will lead to war with England is not necessarily true; that it may result in war, as it has before, we shall be wise to remember. The interests of the United States as a nation dependent upon the merchant marines of other powers for its intercourse with the rest of the world cannot fail to differ in time of war from those of the power controlling the sea.

In times of peace the actual supremacy of the English fleet has been rarely asserted, and its interference with complete freedom of intercourse between nations has been neither frequent, insistent, nor burdensome; but the outbreak of this present European war has shown the English, as always, the important part which the control of the sea, if rigidly asserted, might play in the campaign upon land, and has led them to change promptly their attitude toward neutral shipping as well as toward that of their enemies. Indeed, it was immediately clear that if the decisive factor should prove eventually to be the possession of the greater resources, the English would win because to their own they could add by means of the sea-power those of neutral nations, and could by the same means limit their enemies' resources to those within their own boundaries. If the German army should demonstrate in actuality any such degree of efficiency as had been claimed for it, a defensive campaign would become essential until vast preparations could be made to bring the superior numbers of the Entente to bear in the field. By preventing exportation to Germany and Austria of anything at all useful, the sea-power could render a military service of the first order, greater in significance beyond all compare than the levy of troops and manufacture of munitions of war in England. If in the end the armies are unable to decide the issue, the sea-power alone, as in other wars, will decide the issue in the Allies' favor.

The English Government, therefore, promptly assumed precisely the position in regard to the use of the sea by other nations which it had hitherto

PAN-AMERICANISM

taken in European wars, and which had invariably proved in the past of the utmost consequence and importance. Napoleon ascribed his failure chiefly to the English control of the sea and their use of it to supply themselves and to interfere with the trade between France and neutral nations. Virtually the English regulations permit complete freedom of trade only with England and her Allies. With her foes all trade is strictly limited, their own ships and those of neutral nations ordinarily being allowed to import only such commodities as are of no possible utility. Upon the trade of neutrals with one another England has always laid certain restrictions intended to prevent the importation of goods by one neutral nation from another which the former could then sell to belligerents. Strict contraband of war, therefore, she has rarely allowed neutral nations to export to one another and within this category she has ordinarily written down everything directly and indirectly essential to the prosecution of war. If the limitation of supplies is to have any effect upon her foes, it must be as complete as possible.

To enforce these provisions and to insure a continued observance of them by all the shipping on the seas, she has invariably insisted upon her right to search any and all vessels of neutral nations, to view their cargoes and papers, to inspect their crews, and to arrest the subjects of belligerents. Contraband of war thus discovered has been promptly seized, and the vessel carrying it has usually been detained until such time as the English prize courts could deal with the case and establish clearly what was contraband and what was not.

Nor have the English ever admitted any right in the neutral nation concerned to interpret their regulations for itself or to interpose any regulations of its own. Their regulations have been enforced invariably by English officials upon English ships or in English courts according to their interpretation of the intention of the English Government and of the interests of England at stake. They have been war measures, pursued for military rather than for naval purposes and have amounted, always to a literal enforcement of the English control of the sea on the basis of English interests.

The complaints brought by the United States Government have ostensibly grown out of specific acts done by English officers and courts in pursuance of these regulations; but these in reality are merely the examples upon which the Government hangs broad general contentions, identical in character and form with those urged by neutral nations against the English claims for upward of three centuries. The fundamental tenet of neutral nations is the freedom of the sea, the contention that no one owns it, advanced by Grotius more than three centuries ago. Outside the immediate waters of any nation, there should be no rules and no interference by one nation with the ships of another unless the two are at war. Neutral ships should have full right of transit, and neutral nations should always have the right to send in one another's ships or in the ships of belligerents goods of all nations, for neutrality ought to place all neutral nations on an equality with both belligerents and confer upon them the right to trade with both upon the same terms. In preparing the list of absolute contraband, defining articles which should be contraband wherever found, neutral nations have included only the absolute essentials of war, while England has invariably insisted upon the broadest possible interpretation of what was useful in time of war. The United States Government accordingly claims that copper, for which there are a thousand uses, is not necessarily contraband of war; the English Government, on the other hand, knows that copper is a most important metal for which there is in many cases literally no substitute in the preparation of munitions of war.

With technicalities, too, the English have had in the past little patience. They have always claimed the right to look at the facts and to form their own conclusions from such evidence as they judged pertinent as to the real destination of the article in question, and as to its real importance for the belligerent for whom it was intended, and, while they have usually listened respectfully to the views of neutral shippers and their governments on these questions, they have never treated them as conclusive. When, therefore, they see a neutral country, like Holland or Denmark, begin as soon as war breaks out to import large amounts of a great variety of commodities which they ordinarily import in small quantities or not at all, they promptly conclude that the commodity in question has not reached its destination when it arrives in the neutral country. The mere technical fact of its consignment to a neutral merchant is not necessarily conclusive, and they wish something more than paper evidence that their foes will not ultimately receive it.

This clash of interests, which is so irreconcilable, is older than the United States, and dates back, indeed, before the days when there were any colonies here. We have no new issue to fight; we occupy upon it a very old position, which neutral nations and their subjects, whether merchants or scholars, have invariably concluded was logical, sound, and just, and one which English statesmen, merchants, and scholars have commonly decided England could not accept. For three hundred years no European war has failed to produce this clash between the English and neutral nations. Never have the English conceded the position and never have the neutrals succeeded in forcing from them a recognition or acknowledgment of their rights. According to the precedents of neutrals, according to the position which we ourselves have previously assumed, we occupy to-day a position logically unassailable, beyond all question equitable and just; but according to past English precedent, our contention is one they cannot grant.

It is not difficult to see the main trend of the English argument that the fundamental demands of the United States are inadmissible. For us to demand freedom of trade with Germany in many of the articles on the English list of contraband is tantamount to a request to allow us to prolong the war in order that we may make profit out of it. England, they will insist, is fighting for her life and is not considering questions of profit or loss; by limiting her foe's supplies from the outside, by cutting off rigorously everything conceivably essential to war, she can strike him a deadly blow. Undoubtedly this means that neutrals are not to send him the things he really wants, the things, therefore, for which he is willing to pay the most and of which he would use the largest quantities, the things obviously for which the English search must be the most active and the confiscation of which must be the most rigid. That this involves a certain amount of inconvenience and probably actual financial loss to a good many American citizens the English readily admit, and they regret it, but they still insist that the measure is a war measure, aimed at Germany and not at us, and that England is willing to pay for such damage to American citizens as can actually be demonstrated. More than this she cannot concede without sacrificing a great military and naval advantage, which may conceivably decide the war in her favor, in order to increase somewhat the profits in business of certain American citizens. The matter is vital to England, they will insist, involving her independence, her integrity, and, it may be, her very existence. It is for Americans a mere matter of profit and loss, affecting only a few Americans and probably only the degree of their profit. How, they ask, can a sane man hesitate between such alternatives?

Yet, the text of the American note of December 26, 1914, made public with the consent of the English Government on January 1, 1915, shows that the difference of opinion between England and the United States virtually amounts to a request to England to admit the validity of our opinion as to the necessity of certain specific things to her safety. Our interpretation of the established rules of international conduct is also emphasized as something which she should regard. Above all, the Government asks that seizure of goods as contraband should take place only after actual evidence has been produced that its technical destination is false and a belligerent destination intended. "Mere suspicion is not evidence"; mere presumption or a likelihood that such goods may eventually reach a belligerent is not sufficient warrant for detention. These issues involve certain very obvious and exceedingly practical difficulties, as the English answer pointed out. To produce evidence which a prize court could recognize might be entirely beyond the power of the English officers, although the main facts of the situation might show that a small neutral nation is entirely unable to utilize in a year in normal ways the amount of certain commodities consigned to it from the United States in a single month. Nor can the English Government verify the correctness of the ship's manifest without bringing the vessel to some port where careful examination can be made by qualified officers, who can weigh bales of cotton for concealed copper, and open boxes marked "machinery" to make sure they do not contain rifles. A certain delay is inevitable unless the inspection and search is to become perfunctory. To attempt in time of war to decide questions of public safety and military expediency by rules of evidence and regulations agreed to beforehand has always seemed inexpedient, because the cases which actually appear defy classification; the ingenuity of merchants is great and the ease of outwitting any technical requirement obvious. A demand by the United States that the English Government should accept the manifest as accurate until clear evidence appears of its falsity, therefore, is asking them to countenance smuggling in defiance of their regulations, unless they can produce a type of evidence which the very nature of the case renders almost impossible.

Certain facts clearly writ in the situation make

it probable that the English will give serious attention to the formulation of a compromise as favorable to the United States as the exigencies of the situation will admit. They are considerations, however, which have nothing to do with the demands, their technicalities, or their justice. The English, French, and Belgian nations are at present dependent for a considerable proportion of the necessities of life upon imports from the United States. They are counting definitely upon equipping Kitchener's army with munitions of war and clothing manufactured in the United States, in pursuance of the practice which permits private persons in neutral nations to sell armament to belligerents. If strained relations between the two countries interfere in any way with the stream of imports or with the fulfilling of these contracts, the consequences to England and France will be exceedingly serious. A cessation of intercourse might prevent the adequate reinforcement and even the maintenance of the armies in France, give the German preparedness an importance which it has not hitherto had by exhausting the supplies of the Allies while the German accumulations are still considerable, and thus weaken and perhaps defeat the Allies. This is quite conceivable. Intercourse with the United

States is indispensable if the Allies are to win. No doubt, too, the English would consider an unfavorable attitude toward them of public opinion in the United States, which has hitherto been favorable, as something to be avoided if possible. To lend countenance in any way to the agitation of the Germans and Irish is undesirable.

Should the difference of opinion come to an open breach and result in war, the United States navy, even if it did not coöperate with the German navy, would at once give the English navy foes to meet so numerous as to deprive it of the preponderance in numbers which the English regard as essential. To send a detachment from the Channel Squadron to keep the American fleet in American waters would effect precisely that division of the English fleet for which the Germans have been praying, and which might result in the annihilation of the British sea-power and the downfall of the British Empire. These are possibilities only, but so eminently possible as to cause reflection in London. They may well stir the minds of the Americans who are anxious for the Allies to win and who might not be quite so anxious for the United States to press its demands if they realized that the logical conclusion might be a victory for Germany. Such are the factors which counsel the English to yield.

Who, now, are those who urge the administration at Washington to remain firm? Great pressure has probably been brought to bear upon the administration by the interests most affected by the new English list of contraband. The copper interests in particular have been injured and have been no doubt proportionately active; but in all probability the political pressure has been greater than that of the business interests, for the war has as conspicuously favored some interests as it has injured others. As a whole, the United States export trade shows growth, and the continuance of the war will lead to a truly astounding development. Something may plausibly be ascribed, therefore, to the lessened majorities of the Democratic party at the November elections, which showed clearly that no votes can be lost if the party is to win in 1916. Already there are powerful interests in important States which have been alienated from the Democratic party by the attitude of the President upon Belgian neutrality and other issues. The Germans and the Irish are exceptionally strong in such important campaign States as New York, Ohio, and Illinois, in which any close election may be won or lost by a few thousand votes. In Wisconsin and in Missouri are great numbers of Germans, and both have been joining the doubtful column. A strict and watchful attitude toward England, therefore, is at present a good political move, and to this supposition the publicity given the American demands before they had been presented to the English Government lends color. So far as the English Government is concerned, the publicity must have had an unfavorable effect, because it precipitated ill feeling in the United States without giving the English Government an opportunity to yield and thus obviate the difficulty. Certain business interests, however, and the Irish and the Germans have so actively assailed the administration's neutrality that the Democratic leaders probably felt some clear and public demonstration was needed to reply to charges which might have adverse political effect if not denied.

When we view the probability of the pressing of these demands by the United States, we become at once aware of results more serious to her than those with which a quarrel would threaten England. In a word, war or even a serious quarrel with England would probably ruin American commerce, foreign and domestic. At present only the markets of the Allies and of neutral nations are open to us, and the inability to export also to Germany is actually serious. If now we quarrel with England, the markets of the Allies will be closed, and we shall feel promptly a lessening demand for American products abroad compared with which the present difficulty is entirely negligible. We are so accustomed to the fact that we constantly forget that American exports are carried at the moment entirely by English and French ships. The shipping of the United States and neutral nations in the Atlantic trade is negligible. Without the use of the English merchant marine, the bulk of our trade would be absolutely unable to reach neutral ports in Europe or in Africa, South America, and the far East. Our own facilities for dealing with any of this trade are utterly inadequate. Furthermore, much of our trade with Asia, Africa, and South America has been consummated by means of exchange on London or Paris, a matter of custom rather than one of necessity, a practice followed because understood and agreeable to our foreign customers. Nor must we forget that all the American firms who have signed large contracts with the English and French governments for every conceivable variety of commodity would be totally ruined by war between England and the United States. The magnitude of the commercial disaster which would immediately ensue is staggering to contemplate.

For England to set in motion factors which would involve such destruction would be simple. She has merely to pass a statute of the character of the old Navigation Acts, requiring English ships to carry all goods of other continents to England and France. The whole English merchant marine would then accept American goods only when consigned to England and France. We should be robbed of our trade with the rest of the world, and if, as a result of the quarrel, we declined to export to England and France, we should be in the same situation in which we found ourselves in 1808—unable to trade at all. It is the English merchant marine we need, and the loss of which we have to fear far more than the encroachments of the English navy. If the quarrel develops into war, all English ships would promptly become belligerent shipping, and would as a matter of course decline to carry our trade anywhere; all American shipping would become lawful prizes of the English commerce-destroyers; American cargoes and consignments on the high seas, in England, or in English ships, would all be subject to confiscation and seizure; and American cargoes found anywhere would be immediately regarded by the English as contraband of war. The commerce of the United States in transit would be a total loss, and all American goods shipped subsequently would be so obviously in danger that no insurance company would take the risk. The only American trade that would remain would be such as the English would permit the small fleets of neutral nations to carry under such conditions as they laid down. The American navy might conceivably protect the few ships we have and possibly, in conjunction with the German navy, defeat the English fleet; but the navy could not take the place of the English merchant marine, and before the English navy was beaten we should be irretrievably ruined.

To count upon the English necessity for American imports and to suppose that their need of our food-stuffs and munitions of war will compel them to grant our demands is to forget the equally obvious fact that we are so entirely dependent upon exporting to them, that we ourselves cannot in our own interest press the issue to a point which threatens to interfere with our trade with them. So serious for the United States will be the results of a quarrel between England and the United States that the Government may not deem it wise to force this issue upon England. The political consequence would be of a nature which the Democratic party can hardly contemplate with calmness. The votes of the business community as a whole are vastly more important than those of the Germans, the Irish, and the few interests at present injured. There should be, in fact, no hesitation in recognizing that the present inconvenience under which American trade suffers, and the losses of a few persons, are far less important than a truly formidable array of consequences extending to the ruin of American business. To secure by diplomacy such adjustment as the English feel able to grant is wise and necessary, but to attempt to force the English beyond diplomatic negotiations can proceed only from a failure to appreciate the gravity of the situation.

CHAPTER VI

JAPANESE EXPANSION AND THE PACIFIC

"THE Pacific will be the storm-center of the future," the Prime Minister of New Zealand recently declared. He gave expression to a belief prevalent in Japan, where an armed conflict with non-Asiatic powers is widely regarded as inevitable, and where popular opinion has singled out the United States as the first foe to be met. Many of the political and economic difficulties experienced by European nations are pressing upon Japan. The rapid growth of population in islands limited in area has raised the question of markets and new territory, the founding of colonies and the issue of emigration, with an insistence almost as great as in Germany. The outbreak of the European war has furnished the Japanese an unexpectedly favorable opportunity for attempting the solution of these pressing economic problems.

The strategic position of Japan is commanding.

JAPANESE EXPANSION AND THE PACIFIC

She occupies an island group which makes her virtually invulnerable as long as Europeans must wage war from a distance and the Chinese army and navy are neither large nor efficient. The area of the islands is not inconsiderable—much larger than Americans suppose. In this invulnerable position lives a population as large as that of the British Isles, nearly half as great as that of the United States, and almost two thirds as extensive as the entire population of Latin America, a people, physically hardy, military in temper, willing to be organized and to submit to authority. They are incredibly energetic and industrious, sustaining life on an amount of food almost unbelievably small, and content with an aggregate of comforts which most Americans would regard as scarcely better than subsistence. To these qualities they add an unusually sensitive and artistic intelligence, a literary taste and appreciation subtle in the extreme, together with a sense of beauty of line, form, and proportion which surpasses beyond much doubt anything Americans or Europeans have to show. They are a powerful people, an industrious people, a highly civilized nation, and have more than once proved themselves to possess the courage, the endurance, the *élan* of conquerors. They are thrilled by the achievements of the last two generations; they believe they stand at the beginning of a great period of prosperity, achievement, and dominion, and are eager to insure their national future by any and all means within their power.

Chance has located this extraordinary people in a very peculiar strategic field. The islands grouped along the Asiatic coast do not seem to have exerted that vital influence upon its trade that England has had upon European development. There is, of course, the passage through the straits at Singapore through which has streamed for centuries the commerce between China, Japan, and India. Its possession, however, has little significance for the defense of either China, Japan, or India, and is certainly of no great assistance in a military or naval sense to a power attempting to take the offensive against any one of them. Nor is it by any means as difficult for shipping to avoid the passage of the straits as it is to evade the passage of the English Channel. Indeed, the geography of Asia, the area and height of its mountain chains, the great size of India and China, the pacific teachings of their religious philosophers, have made naval and military operations rare, and have left Europeans in undisputed possession of what they have deemed the strategic points for the control of the trade between Europe and Asia and between India, China, and Japan. To the English the control of the Red Sea, the Cape of Good Hope, and Cape Horn seems desirable, because they are the approaches to Asia for Europeans and enable their possessor to hold Europeans at a distance. So far as Asia itself is concerned, their possession is of little consequence. The European occupation of the Spice Islands, the possession of the Philippines by the United States, the colonization of Australia and New Zealand by the English, have yet to demonstrate that they placed their possessors in a position of strategic advantage giving them or promising them control of the Pacific. So large an ocean, flanked by such enormous continents, with such large groups of islands on the Asiatic side, and so very few between Asia and America, creates a strategic problem of great peculiarity. The land is so placed that it does not control the water except in so far as it provides a basis of operations for a strong fleet.

Such a fleet the Japanese possess, the only fleet of a resident power in the Pacific, with not merely naval stations, but a true base of supplies, sustained by an industrial fabric capable of building new units and of repairing old. No doubt the Japanese, when they undertook the creation of a really large fleet of European type, were well aware that they would infallibly obtain in time the control of the Pacific, whether or not European nations continued to hold what they believed to be strategic points. While England claimed the supremacy of the seas, they saw very clearly that her control of the Pacific had depended largely upon her ability to keep other European nations at a distance through her control of the passages between Europe and Asia. The supremacy of the Pacific had been won in European waters, had been maintained there, and had never been challenged by an Asiatic power. The English had kept in the Pacific enough vessels to patrol its waters, apprehend pirates, and deal with such stray cruisers as might slip through the cordon in Europe. So long as competitors in the Pacific were limited to Europeans who could be disposed of by the fleet created by England for home defense, such a supremacy was easy to maintain. Such a supremacy it would be easy to overthrow. The Japanese saw correctly that the control of the Pacific rested not with the land, but with the water; and saw with peculiar clarity that upon the control of the water would depend the admission or exclusion of European nations. The building in Japan of a fleet of modern ships, the teaching to the Japanese themselves of methods of

JAPANESE EXPANSION AND THE PACIFIC

European warfare, therefore, would revolutionize the conditions upon which the English supremacy had been based and would promptly put them in a position to control the Pacific. Unless the English could send a fleet into the Pacific sufficiently large to destroy the Japanese, the Japanese would actually control the situation, because they would possess the largest fleet actually afloat in Asiatic waters. Still, they would do well to avoid a clash with the English and would be wise not to risk annihilation.

The fleet would make possible the realization of Japanese ambitions and enable them to cope with the pressing economic problems of rescuing the population from penury and insuring the possession of foreign markets. To the south they saw immensely valuable islands, the Celebes, Java, and others of the great group known as the Spice Islands, from which for generations various European nations had drawn a great revenue, which still produced in profusion natural products much in demand in Europe, and which were still the basis for an immensely profitable trade. The Japanese were quite able to read, and found no difficulty in learning from the commercial history of Europe, as written by Europeans, that the economic progress and strength of the greatest nations in Europe was supposed to be based upon the trade with the far East. They saw the English, the Germans, the French eagerly extending their possessions in Africa and in Asia solely for the purpose of developing markets.

It was not difficult to draw the conclusion that, if the superior economic position of Europe against Asia was due to the trade with Asia, Asiatics might not improbably expect from the development of their own trade with Europe benefits in some measure similar to those already achieved by the Europeans themselves. In Japan the crowding population lived in penury because of the lack of fields to cultivate and of work to perform. Why should not they as well as the Dutch direct the labors of the natives in Java? Why should not they as well as the English carry Asiatic produce to Europeans? Why should not they as well as Germany or the United States be acquiring islands along the China Sea or dependencies on the mainland? They saw in Europeans no qualities they themselves did not possess or could not develop; they knew themselves capable of performing efficiently all the work Europeans did in the far East; they admitted no moral superiority, no artistic supremacy, no intellectual capacity greater than their own. Why should these crude

Westerners sup from their dish, drink from their cup, grow rich from their labors? Why should Asiatics of any race or condition labor through long years to create profits for European merchants?

"The East for Asiatics," became the slogan of a great national movement; the absolute, definitive exclusion of Europe from Asia became its object. They would deny that Europeans possessed interests in Asia of a nature Asiatics were bound to recognize or respect; they would insist that Asiatics had rights in their own country paramount to any possessed by European nations or individuals, and the extent of which was to be judged by Asiatics and not Europeans. To take possession of the Philippines, the Spice Islands, Borneo, Sumatra, Java, and the like, they saw would be easy and profitable. A small expenditure of force, and the thing was done. Its doing would solve all Japan's problems, furnish an outlet for her energetic population in places safe from the aggression of European or American, and permit the upbuilding in the islands fringing the Chinese coast of an empire of Japanese states, governed by Asiatics, developing Asiatic territory in the interests of Asiatics. It was and is a great ideal, a splendid nationalistic vision the achievement of which they deem well worth sacrifice and suffering.

Already they see dawning the day when this vision is to become a reality, in the development of Japan, in the growth of the Japanese navy, and in the exigencies in Europe, forcing the English to recognize and tolerate the growth of the new power. The new development was carefully timed to coincide with the growth of the German fleet and the German army, for the ability of England to protest effectively against the creation of the Japanese fleet was in direct proportion to the size of the fleet which she could spare from European waters for service in the Pacific. The growth of the German navy in very fact robbed the English of their boasted control of the Pacific. To meet the aggression of the Germans and successfully defend England, they were compelled to withdraw the effective English ships from the Pacific as well as from the Gulf of Mexico, and to concentrate them in the North Sea and the English Channel.

Here is the real condition on which is based the Anglo-Japanese entente. The fact that they were no longer really supreme in the Pacific, the English saw it futile to deny, and futile to invite its challenge by the Japanese. They told the latter frankly that while they would prefer to maintain their own control, they were not in the least minded to hand over to the Germans the con-

JAPANESE EXPANSION AND THE PACIFIC

trol of the Pacific as the result of a defeat in the North Sea, and were anxious to arrange affairs in such wise that their own downfall as a world power should not result in the acquisition of their authority by Germany or any other nation. In this way alone could they effectively limit the unfavorable results of a defeat. To facilitate Japanese success in case of their own defeat in European waters, they proposed to hand over the actual physical control of the Pacific without more ado. As their own naval stations and factories were not of naval importance to Japan, these they would expect to retain, but all except a few English ships should be withdrawn from the Pacific. On the other hand, they did not fail to intimate that the continuance of Japanese control would be entirely dependent, in case of their own victory in Europe, upon the manner in which it had been and was about to be exercised. Victorious in the Atlantic, they would no longer be foreclosed sending to the Pacific a fleet easily large enough to defeat the Japanese and extend English sovereignty as far as they desired. Until the issue was decided in Europe, the Japanese should rule; but they should consult the English and act invariably as the mutual interests of both powers dictated. Naturally, they should not use their sea-power to

England's detriment; the punishment for treachery would be condign when the victory in Europe untied England's hands.

If the Germans won, the Japanese were to take possession promptly of the English possessions, and it is just conceivable, though of course upon such questions as this we can simply make plausible conjectures, that they were also to have a reversion to the English tenure in India. The ambitions of Russia have long been viewed with apprehension in London, and the fear has been, and is still great, that should the Germans win in Europe, the Russians would reach India first: they are already a mere few hundred miles from the frontier defenses, while the Germans have great distances to travel. Truth to tell, England is quite determined that neither of them shall have it. An English defeat is to break up the British Empire. The self-governing colonies will of course retain their independence, and the Japanese are to succeed to the English overlordship in the far East, or at least make certain that other European nations do not obtain it. Should England win, her position in the Pacific and perhaps in India will be due to the Japanese, and the debt of gratitude will no doubt be adequately discharged by the cession to them of the Dutch and

JAPANESE EXPANSION AND THE PACIFIC

German possessions in the far East. In reality, the Japanese have undertaken the protection of the English interests for the present, with the clear understanding that everything they do will accrue to their own advantage in case the English are defeated, and will be suitably rewarded in case the latter win. Whatever happens, the Japanese cannot lose.

We may well ask, therefore, what effect this situation is apt to have upon the United States, the Panama Canal, and Central and South America. The strategic position of the Philippines as the next link in the island chain which the Japanese wish to create might almost be said to make them essential to Japan. No doubt the energy and industry of the Japanese can make the Philippines one of the garden spots of the world and a really valuable economic asset. For the development of a Japanese merchant marine and an extensive trade with the United States across the Pacific, as well as for the naval control of the Pacific, the Japanese will need the islands in midocean, particularly Hawaii, which the United States at present possesses. To secure these islands, war is regarded in Japan as inevitable, for they cannot conceive of the voluntary sale or cession of such property by the United States. To occupy all of them is obviously an easy task; the United States fleet in the Pacific and the army in the Philippines are neither of them large enough to cause the Japanese anxiety, while any grief on the part of the Filipinos at our dispossession seems problematical. The real difficulty which the Japanese fear is that of obtaining the formal cession from the United States, and they believe it may be necessary to extort it from us by operations of their fleet against our Western harbors, or perhaps by a timely invasion of the Japanese army which would seize San Francisco and as much land as it deemed essential to create a district for the surrender of which the Philippines and Hawaii would be a worthy ransom. The protestations of the Japanese that they have not the slightest intention of conquering the United States or of waging an aggressive war against us are in all probability sincere and truthful, but the least experienced student of diplomacy can hardly fail to see that they by no means exclude some such program as this. If advices from Japan are reliable, there are considerable portions of her people who regard a nominal war with the United States for the obtaining of these objects as the inevitable first step in Japanese national expansion.

Another question which has attracted far more

JAPANESE EXPANSION AND THE PACIFIC

attention, but which in comparison is scarcely worthy of mention, is the attempt of Japan to colonize in the United States, Mexico, and South America. The opposition in California to the settlement of perfectly respectable and well-conducted Japanese citizens has caused a breach by the State of the United States treaties with Japan, and has led to the formation of a public sentiment which denies the Japanese social equality and the right to own land. This the Japanese resent keenly. They say with truth that we ourselves expect and demand in Japan not only equality, but privileged status, and in return are not willing to accord them in the United States the barest elements of equality. They believe their national honor is involved, that they ought not to accept from us anything less than the fullest and frankest recognition of legal and social equality. On any other basis they feel they must decline to deal with us. So much they have felt sufficiently offensive, but for the United States to interfere on the strength of the Monroe Doctrine with the settlement of Japanese in Latin America they think positively beyond the bounds of international decency. That we should decline to accept them in our own country was at least understandable, but that we should insist upon excluding them from Mexico they felt to be a position which neither logic nor reason, to say nothing of international law, could defend. As the projection across the Pacific into South and Central America of large colonies of Japanese is to-day perfectly feasible, and may indeed be from the point of view of the Japanese and of the South Americans eminently desirable, the Japanese have no intention whatever of recognizing any prerogative in the United States to question or investigate their right to colonize South America or of permitting any interference with it by the United States.

There are in these issues plenty of grounds for a war between Japan and the United States in which all the logical and technical rights would be on the side of Japan. We are distinctly inviting reprisals and armed opposition by persistently advancing claims which the Japanese cannot admit consistently with their national honor as they conceive it. Unless we are prepared to recede from such positions as we have recently taken, a conflict with Japan is only a question of time. Whatever the outcome of the European war, so powerful a nation will scarcely be willing to allow such claims as ours to go long unchallenged.

There are therefore vital interests which may

lead the Japanese to seize the occasion of the present war in Europe as an admirable moment for an attempt to drive Europeans from Asia in the interests of Asiatics. While Europeans are so busy at home, she will have no opposition to meet. Should the war continue several years, an active alliance between Japan, India, and China might put Asia into the hands of Asiatics in such a fashion that Europeans would be unable to regain a foothold. In several years' time adequate military dispositions to deal effectively with Europeans could be completed. It would not, in all probability, be necessary to do more than render the conquest of Asia a hazardous and difficult task to prevent the victors of the European war from undertaking it. So far as Asia has been conquered at all, the work has been done by small bodies of Europeans with the coöperation of large bodies of native troops. To fight a war in Asia which would require an army of European soldiers large enough to meet a determined army of Asiatics, equipped with European guns and officered by men trained in Japan, would be a task the magnitude of which might well cause the victor to hesitate.

Nor should it be forgotten that the financial indebtedness of Japan, which taxes the capacity of that country to meet the interest and principal payments, is all owed in Europe and America. So far as any tangible evidence of that capital is in existence in the world, it is in Japan, where the logic of the Pan-Germanists is just as good as it is in Germany. The Japanese have only to repudiate their entire indebtedness to free the nation from a staggering load and put it at once in the possession of its whole economic development at the price of what they have already paid. The control of the Pacific, the annexation of the Spice Islands and the Philippines, the expulsion of foreigners, the assurance for all time of financial independence—these are indeed things to conjure with. And we who can see clearly so much at so great a distance with so little aid, may well pause to wonder how much more the Japanese themselves can see, and how long caution and prudence will counsel them to wait before attempting the attainment of such desirable ends.

BOOK III
PAN-AMERICANISM

Pan-Americanism

CHAPTER I

PREREQUISITES OF PAN-AMERICANISM

TO some, Pan-Americanism is the Utopia of peace, a demonstration of the superior morality of the Western over the Eastern Hemisphere, of the New World and its Christianity over the Old. To some it is a dream of the monopolization of South American trade by the United States; to others, the Monroe Doctrine and our chivalrous protection of the weak against aggression; to others, a vision of empire in the Western Hemisphere. To many in South America, Pan-Americanism stands for the peculiarly hypocritical fashion in which the elder brother makes known his demands for the deference due to him and for the privilege justly his. Pan-Americanism is not yet a reality. The word still connotes a varied and inconsistent complex of ideas: pacifists, capitalists, imperialists, have built in its name structures framed in the image of their own desires and ambitions.

We are less concerned with what Pan-Americanism has been or has meant than with what it may mean in the future. What should it be; whom should it include; what should be its object; what problems may it solve? Will it protect the Western Hemisphere from Europe's victor or from the aggression of Japan? A knowledge of the position of the United States in its relation to Latin America, of the interests of the United States and those of Latin America, and of the fundamental economic and administrative factors in both, will be important not only for the elucidation of Pan-Americanism, but for a grasp of our future problems. If a closer union between the United States and the Latin American republics is feasible and desirable, it will furnish a premise with which the foreign policy of the United States must reckon. If it is not feasible, we shall perforce ground our conception of the fundamentals of American policy upon different notions.

Let us therefore deal with the possibility of a really close relationship transcending by far the meetings of diplomatic representatives and such general expressions of good-will and sympathy

PREREQUISITES OF PAN-AMERICANISM

as are usual in the correspondence of sovereign nations in Europe. Let us view as an hypothesis an administrative union between the United States and the twenty Latin republics, for Canada is always tacitly excluded from the question of Pan-Americanism, and extend it beyond some vague customs union, vague defensive alliance, or voluntary business court, to a substantive confederation of sovereign states. The word raises at once visions similar to Pan-Germanism, Pan-Slavism, Pan-Islam, which draw their vital meaning and purpose from the assumed necessity of the closest conceivable connection between Germans, Slavs, or Mohammedans. Unless there is a reality existent which will furnish the basis for something more than a temporary and quasi-artificial bond of dubious strength and utility, we shall be forced to admit that Pan-Americanism is a misnomer and the ideas it connotes fictitious and vain imaginings.

While the premise of Pan-Americanism obviously cannot be that of racial unity, as in the case of the European movements similarly designated, it does assume that the geographical proximity of North and South American results in something approaching the isolation of the two from Europe, so that the geographical connection between them is closer than that of either with

Europe or Africa. It also predicates quite clearly the political and economic independence of the Western Hemisphere against the rest of the world. The necessity of a broad basis of mutual economic interest in any organic union has been proved in the past a most important and fundamental factor. Clearly, mutual interests are essential to Pan-Americanism, and must be assumed to exist between the various states in the Western Hemisphere, which must therefore be supposed to have divergent interests from European states, or at the very least to find their fundamental interest in relations with one another rather than with Europe. Not less vital is the obvious assumption of mutual trust and confidence between the various states in the Western Hemisphere, not transcending perhaps their trust and confidence in European nations, but certainly yielding to one another all credence and faith which they themselves could desire in return. A need for mutual aid and protection against Europe, if not against the rest of the world, Pan-Americanism peculiarly assumes and predicates necessarily the ability of these states to make effective use of their combined strength against aggression from without. Indeed, one might almost say that mutual protection should be assumed to furnish the real nexus of the new state, and that the existence of the present war in Europe, and the probable aggression of its victor in the Western Hemisphere, ought to furnish the impelling motive for the creation of this organic union, and remain for a time at least its most important feature.

What, now, are the prerequisites for the erection or creation of a Pan-American confederation or union based upon such fundamental premises? If the foundations of the structure are significant, the structure itself is the visible and tangible evidence of the existence of the new entity, and will be, if anything, more essential to its eventual success than the premises. An organic union would have little strength and possess only a very small quantity of organic nexus, unless it was at least a confederation of sovereign states, with a common executive and legislature in whom were vested definite if, perhaps limited, powers to act, and with discretion to decide upon their own initiative, in a way binding upon all members certain matters of mutual interest explicitly delegated to them. The inequality of the various states in size might be solved by giving them unequal numbers of votes, so graduated as to make it impossible for the large states to be outvoted by the small states on matters vital to them, and to foreclose the possibility of the control of the confederation by the large states. By leaving the large states in the minority, the small would be protected, while by requiring a two-thirds vote upon important issues, the three or four largest states would obtain an effective veto, for they could always prevent the confederation from acting at all. A schedule of issues might be prepared with different percentages graduated according to the importance of the subject. In this way the difficulty might be solved of a confederation in which one state, the United States, would be as large as all the others, and three other states would be larger and wealthier than most of the remainder.

Some common administrative body would be essential. The conduct of foreign affairs by the confederation, the abandoning by all members of their previous policies and independent dealings with other countries, with either the abandonment of the Monroe Doctrine, or its assumption by the confederation, would be highly important. Free trade within the confederation and a uniform tariff against foreign countries, a uniform currency, uniform weights and measures, with uniform banking, bankruptcy, and commercial laws, would be eminently desirable. The courts of the confederation should decide suits between states or between the citizens of various states, as the United States courts now deal with the affairs of individuals and states. There would of course be the taxes for purposes of administration and defense, apportioned among the sovereign states in the same ratio as the votes in the Federal legislature, and collected by the local authorities. All actions of the confederation would necessarily be binding on its members, except for certain limitations indicated by a bill of rights, which of course would be intended for the states rather than for private citizens. Officials and judges could probably be selected impartially and apportioned roughly between the various states, while in the lower ranks of the administration civil-service rules should be applied. The confederation in its relation to its members would recognize freely their complete sovereignty in all domestic affairs, with certain reservations as to the extent to which the confederation could pledge these sovereign states by its action in foreign affairs, war, or peace. With limitations, the confederation might be required to maintain republican government in all the states, to subdue revolutions or riots, and to insist upon changes of government by peaceful methods rather than by revolutions. It might even go so far as to compel the existing government to redress certain classes of wrongs when complained of in certain formal ways by a large number of its own citizens or by other states or their citizens.

Regular intercourse between the states would be a necessary feature in the maintenance of their mutual acquaintance and friendly understanding, and would normally result from their mutual economic interests. The creation of a merchant marine to carry their commerce in ships belonging to members of the confederation and to carry the exports of its members to foreign nations would be indispensable to the establishment and continuance of that economic independence of Europe which it might be readily assumed was in accordance with the normal interests of the confederation. This would be further assured by the development of a system of federal banks, which would provide for direct exchange among the members of the confederation and with Europe, and could control the currency and facilitate the distribution of capital throughout its extensive territory. Each member would supply others with capital and itself obtain capital from others.

Absolutely essential to the development of any strong bond, and to the strengthening of the mutual trust and confidence between the various members, would be an unqualified recognition of the legal and social equality of all its citizens in all states of the confederation. As the acceptance of social equality by the various South American peoples is virtually complete, this phase of the problem would largely depend upon the granting of social equality to South Americans by the citizens of the United States. Without such acquiescence, the assurances of the Government of the United States, its promises and laws, would be futile; but upon the desirability—one might almost say the necessity—of establishing such social equality would depend the strength, if not the very existence, of the confederation.

These do not seem to be excessive demands or prerequisites of a closer Pan-American union. They mean simply that the new confederation should be a state with organs possessed of independent authority; that the political, administrative, and economic aspects of the new state should be realities and not fictions. They demand that the new state should actually possess the political and economic independence, that its assumed isolation and divergent interests from Europe would make desirable, and to preserve which the union itself had presumably been formed.

PAN-AMERICANISM

The results of the formation of such a confederation ought to be vital to the welfare of all its members. It should end revolutions and maintain stable government, forever remove the apprehension in South America of aggression from the United States, and furnish a rapid and simple method for the decision of disputes between sovereign states or their citizens. It should protect the Western Hemisphere from European aggression, isolate it from the wars convulsing that continent, and dedicate it to the peaceful arts. From it should flow mutual economic benefits in the growth of trade and commerce, the development of industry, the fostering of agriculture, the growth of a merchant marine, and perhaps in good time the growth or development of a distinctively American literature, art, and music.

No such extended relationship now exists or is at present seriously discussed. In the past Pan-Americanism has referred to such relations as the American republics have actually had with one another, and has denoted nothing definite in regard to their actual character, although it has connoted invariably something of comity and a desire to extend the friendly relations between them to something approaching an agreement on matters of common policy. As early as 1826 a

Pan-American congress was held; Henry Clay and James G. Blaine both used their wide influence to father the movement; since 1889 a variety of congresses, some of ambassadors and diplomats, some of scientists, have met. Very recently a Pan-American Union was formed, with a governing body consisting of the American Secretary of State and the ambassadors or diplomatic representatives in Washington of the twenty Latin-American republics. As administrative head was appointed an American who had seen diplomatic service in Latin America, and an assistant director who is a Latin American. A building has been erected in Washington, and a staff is at work collecting statistics, general information, and a library regarding Latin America. The publications of the union are intended to furnish accurate information about commercial opportunities in the Southern Continent. Its practical work is economic rather than political and, for the present is apparently aimed more at developing markets in South America for United States merchants than at the general development of South America itself. Some years ago Secretary of State Root made an extended trip in an attempt to draw closer the bonds of the American republics; the three largest republics recently mediated between the United

PAN-AMERICANISM

States and Mexico, both of whom accepted their offices. Within the last weeks the governing board of the Pan-American Union voted to make representations to the European belligerents on the question of neutral trade and shipping in American waters.

Yet none of these efforts has extended beyond the meeting of representatives of the various republics in their character as sovereign states. They have conferred with one another more or less amicably in diplomatic fashion, but have reached few conclusions of particular import. Indeed, they were incapable of acting on any subject with binding effect because they were delegates conveying messages from sovereign states rather than representatives empowered to consider and decide the matters in question through interchange of argument. The meetings were, strictly speaking, the recognition of a relationship forced upon them by the geographical accident of the others' existence rather than evidence of an intention or a desire to make closer the bond. Nor was there at any time a definite pledge of the continuance of the meetings. It is highly important that we should not exaggerate the actual facts; these diplomatic conferences contained no greater pledge of mutual interests, unity, policy, or identity in ideals than conferences between the United States and the representatives of European powers. While they premised the existence of questions upon which some sort of agreement was advisable, we should realize that questions equally practical and of an absolutely similar nature are constantly presenting themselves for decision between the Latin-American republics and European nations.

Not only is Pan-Americanism not a reality, but we have no actual evidence of a desire on the part of the American states to make it real. The Latin-American republics would probably protest that they had given no pledges or promises whatever indicating an intention or a desire to form an organic union to which the United States should be a party, and it is by no means clear that South American statesmen regard a close union of the Latin-American republics alone as feasible or desirable. The more serious thinkers are inclined to feel that the amalgamation of some of the republics into federal states is perhaps possible and that the confederation of others might be arranged; but the most conservative regard seven entities as the smallest number entirely feasible. It is at least worth while remembering in this connection that it is whispered in Latin America that these

Pan-American congresses are useful methods of stimulating a realizing sense among the Latin-American republics of their need for coöperation against the aggression of the United States in South and Central America. In fact, from the recent activities of the Pan-American Union and from the acceptance of the mediation of Argentina, Brazil, and Chile between Mexico and the United States, the conclusion has been drawn that a vital change in the policy of the United States was impending. Instead of treating the Latin-American republics as inferiors, the United States was about to recognize formally their sovereign equality. Far from this being understood as a prelude to the formation of a Pan-American confederation or state, the profound and favorable impression made upon South America by these recent events has been due rather to the hope that they portended the formal and public renunciation by the United States of the Monroe Doctrine and the aggressive schemes for the conquest of Central and South America which they have felt to be the only possible explanation of the past acts of the United States. The recognition of equality would be the necessary diplomatic approach to a formal enunciation of the new policy.

Pan-Americanism is not now a reality, but it is

none the less important for us to consider whether it might become an actuality. If the word is to denote in future no more than it does at present, it stands for nothing of consequence, and least of all for anything peculiarly American. We are dealing with the possible creation of something which never existed and which does not now exist—an organic bond between American republics, founded upon mutual interests and involving mutual benefits and obligations, as contrasted with a merely permissive and essentially temporary relationship of a quasi-diplomatic character. Unless we can demonstrate that Pan-Americanism has behind it deep fundamental concepts and is likely to subserve important American ends, a close connection with the Latin-American republics will scarcely be a policy for the maintenance of which the United States ought to sacrifice anything of substantive value. If such is now the true meaning of the Monroe Doctrine, the expediency of its continuance will then become a matter of grave doubt.

CHAPTER II

FALLACIES OF PAN-AMERICANISM

THE theoretical basis of Pan-Americanism lies in the belief that the geographical proximity of the two continents of the Western Hemisphere has naturally created between their inhabitants mutual interests, and literally predicates different interests in the Western Hemisphere from those of Europe, and a more normal relationship between states located in the Western Hemisphere with one another than with Europe. We shall scarcely need to do more than glance at the map to see that the more developed regions of North America are in actual distance as far from South America as they are from Europe, and that South America is geographically more closely related to Africa and to southern Europe than it is to New York and to New England. The distance between the principal South American ports and London is not much greater than the distance from New York; Spain and Portugal are

FALLACIES OF PAN-AMERICANISM

both relatively near Brazil; both Florida and the Sahara Desert are nearer to South America than the parts of Europe or the United States with which South Americans are most anxious to deal. The Pacific coast of South America has indeed been nearer to the western coast of the United States than to Europe because of the long voyage around Cape Horn, trebling the distance as the crow flies. The Panama Canal will make an important difference in the geographical isolation of the western coast of South America, but there can be no real doubt that there is no necessary geographical proximity or relationship between the North and South American republics that all do not have with Europe. The foundation of a political and social union upon a geographical bond no closer than the bonds which join the United States to Europe and Africa is obviously building upon the sands. It is a fallacy to suppose that the juxtaposition of North and South America necessarily creates political or economic interests in common between the inhabitants of the two continents. We might as well interfere for similar reasons in the domestic politics of the Azores, Morocco, or the Gold Coast. Indeed, the bonds of geographical relationship between the United States and the British Isles are a great deal closer than they are with Brazil. This, however, predicates extremely little.

As a matter of fact, it is also a fallacy to suppose that any part of the Western Hemisphere is isolated from Europe by its location without at the same time being equally isolated from the United States. Real isolation results from a lack of communication and a lack of acquaintance, and is due nowadays almost entirely to the difficulty of communication or to a lack of common interests, neither of which seem to have any necessary relation to geographical distance or location. The railroad and the steamship, the telegraph and the newspaper, have tied together beyond the power of separation in the future places sundered by the length of continents and the width of oceans. Where communication exists, there is neither separation nor isolation; until it exists, even actual contiguity of boundaries will not break that silence and indifference between two countries in which lies complete isolation. Peru and Brazil communicate with each other infrequently and irregularly; both are in constant touch with affairs in London, Paris, and New York. Similarly, the information in New York about Buenos Aires is much more extended, accurate, and contemporaneous than the notions in Maine about Alabama. The great commercial and political centers are inevitably in closer contact with one another than with the parts of their own country; and nearly any part of the United States has more regular contact with New York or Chicago than with any other part of North America. Isolation is more a matter of time than of space, and common interests are due to the ease of transportation and communication more often than to geographical location.

The greatest of fallacies is the assumption that the Western Hemisphere is isolated from Europe. Since the coming of the telegraph and the steamship, the railroad and the newspaper, isolation from Europe is impossible. Indeed, one might almost say that so far as there is any isolation in the world to-day it exists more nearly than anywhere else between the various parts of the Western Hemisphere. In point of time and expense it is quite as easy to travel from London or Hamburg as from New York or Boston, to South American ports on the east coast. The fastest and largest steamers in the South American trade are in the European service; when South Americans travel they do not hesitate to choose Paris instead of New York; and the Americans who have ever traveled in South America are few compared with the multitudes who have made the rounds in Europe. There are thousands of Americans who know London and Paris well who have no conception of the location of the smaller South American countries; there are thousands of South Americans who are in a very similar condition regarding the United States. Ignorance is the greatest of separators; indifference creates the most difficult isolation to overcome. American notions of the Southern Continent resemble those of the Englishman who thought he should sing "Away down South in Michigan" and spend the day mowing cotton and sugar and plucking maize from the savannas.

A glance at the newspapers of the various countries shows more news in a South American newspaper about Europe than there is about the United States, and very often more about the two together than about all the other states in South America combined. There is often more news about South America in the London dailies than there is about the United States, but invariably more news in the New York papers about London than about the twenty Latin American republics. What little there is about them is usually crowded into small type in some inconspicuous corner, unless it so happens that the news concerns the

FALLACIES OF PAN-AMERICANISM

possibility of trouble between them and the United States. Domestic news, as such, regarding both South America and the United States receives on the whole a good deal more attention in Europe than it gets from the newspapers of the other continent. Far from its being true that the location of the United States and South America in the Western Hemisphere has created and fostered a relationship between them, a most elementary study of either will show that the relationship of both to Europe is a thousandfold closer and more vital than their relationship to each other. Indeed, the contact of most South American states with Europe is closer than with the next Latin American state. The only geographical factor really common to the United States and the Latin-American republics is the fact that none of them are located in Europe or Africa.

Pan-Americanism assumes a certain separation of interests between Europe and the Western Hemisphere and a certain identity of interests between the United States and Latin America. Let us not mince matters in questions of such grave importance as these. This is a fiction the falsity of which has been exposed by the European war. It was not apparent sooner because of the lack of keen interest on the part of both Europe and the

United States in South America. The significant interests of the United States, the indispensable interests, the prerequisites of economic well-being, are those with Europe. The significant interests of Latin America, the predominant interests, indispensable to their economic well-being, are those with Europe.

The assumption that this common relationship and interest between the various countries of the Western Hemisphere is the result of their geographical location seems to have been originally based upon the accident of their discovery at about the same moment. Two continents not previously occupied by Europeans were both situated in the same relation to Europe and it might therefore be assumed that things equally related to the same thing would be closely related to each other. Their undeveloped condition and the subsequent growth of communities by exploration, conquest, and settlement not unnaturally raised a presumption that their problems were similar. Would not the attitude of the two continents toward Europe, which held them in subjection, be identical? Was not political independence worth more than a sort of government not much better than the crudest form of exploitation? Independence would naturally carry with it freedom from

FALLACIES OF PAN-AMERICANISM

the obligation to receive such criminals as their own government saw fit to locate in their borders, or to obey such laws and regulations as the mother country saw fit to make in her own interest. The common interest of both in political independence from Europe was so obvious and natural that it promptly became the basis for a series of assumptions regarding a more extended interest between them, and in particular for the notion which lies at the root of the Monroe Doctrine and Pan-Americanism that America was for the Americans.

We shall display as students no great amount of candor in admitting freely and frankly the dependence of the whole Western Hemisphere upon Europe for artistic and intellectual leadership and inspiration. Paris is the Mecca of South Americans. Thither drift, nay, one might almost say *hasten*, in a fashion contrary to the South American temperament, all those who desire to study, to travel, or to celebrate the acquisition of wealth. Dresses designed by Worth and Paquin are as common in the great South American cities as they are in our own large cities; the decoration of homes, the general aspect of municipal architecture and city planning is distinctly that of the recent French school, and most important buildings have been designed by prominent French architects or their pupils. French literature has been the model of the more recent schools of poets and novelists in most South American states; French art and music are those most desired, although Spanish literature, Italian music, and English political philosophy exert a deep influence and are well known. There is in it all very little that is American. Such resemblances as the casual traveler sees between the United States and South America are due entirely to the fact that both have followed the same models. We are both dependent upon Europe, we both reflect Europe—to that extent we are similar. It is truly a fundamental and important fact that all parts of the Western Hemisphere look rather to Europe than to one another for the highest things as well as the baser.

Probably this common dependence upon Europe explains the sensitivity of most South Americans to what they suppose to be the attitude of superiority assumed by the United States over them in purely intellectual achievements and the arts of civilization. Our attempts to police the less orderly republics, to assist in their financial arrangements, seem to them to proceed from a conviction on our part that we are not only bigger, but better; not only older, but wiser; and that we are

FALLACIES OF PAN-AMERICANISM

discharging a moral obligation by giving them the benefit of our superior culture and of our greater wisdom and experience. All South Americans will admit that we are bigger, but there are not many who will sincerely admit that we are better than they are, or more skilled in the essential arts of civilization. They lay great stress upon the fact that we are different, and decline to yield us superiority in literary, artistic, or musical appreciation, in the architectural arrangement of our cities, or the possession of superior conveniences for the cultivation of the arts and sciences. The older South Americans do not admit that there were writers in the United States at the end of the eighteenth century who could rival Bello and Almedo, and not many in the decades before the Civil War who were better than Andradi; while the young men regard Rodo and Ugarte as critics and orators quite as intelligent as our own contemporary writers, and feel that Carillo is a greater master of the technic of the short story than any recent American writer. Indeed, several South American authors have been favorably received by European critics, a fact of which the South Americans are entirely aware; and they are also well aware that the number of American authors who have received similar recognition is not large. In common with most Europeans, they deny that there is any such thing as an American literature or an American art. As they do not claim for their own efforts an equality with Europe, they see no reason why we should claim equality for ours of similar grade. They are very sensitive upon these matters—sensitive to a degree of which most Americans have little conception. We are not likely as Americans to believe our progress no greater than that of South America, but as investigators we need not be surprised to find that the South Americans themselves decline to recognize our superiority, and are nettled by any tacit assertion of it, however delicately and subtlely advanced.

The most serious consequence of the comparative isolation between North and South America and of their common dependence upon Europe is their lack of acquaintance with each other. This is a fundamental and serious obstacle in the way of Pan-Americanism, for knowledge is the indispensable prerequisite of confidence, understanding, and mutuality. Until we know each other, we cannot conceivably form strong bonds of association; intercourse and frequent communication will alone beget acquaintanceship. Unfortunately, all the normal aids to

FALLACIES OF PAN-AMERICANISM

acquaintanceship are lacking, and great fundamental barriers exist in the difference of race, language, and religion. In South America the intermixture of races is common; the white, the red, and the black have intermarried. Although in the United States such intermarriage results in social ostracism, the difficulty of blood might not stand in the way if it were not for the difficulty of language and religion. Men must speak the same tongue in order to become acquainted; real acquaintanceship is not made through interpreters. The prevalence of Spanish or Portuguese in South America coupled with a total ignorance of both in large portions of the United States, forms a barrier between the peoples which only time and a very real desire to become acquainted can remove. The Catholic religion in its Latin-American form tinctures the whole life of the people, but is not ordinarily sympathetic to citizens of the United States; the fundamental religious philosophy of most Americans is widely different. Race, language, and religion,—there could scarcely be three greater barriers in the way of the creation of that degree of acquaintanceship upon which alone firm political association can be built.

From our ignorance of each other proceed

constantly misunderstandings on essential points. The peaceful disposition of the vast majority of American people, one might almost say the strength of their determination not to attempt conquests in Latin America, is not so generally credited as it should be. Our real anxiety to treat them as equals does not convince them. Fundamental words like law, democracy, faith, honor, interest, business efficiency, do not connote to them the same things that they do to us, and our utterances and theirs usually require interpretation even when we speak ostensibly in each other's own language. To speak in words is easy; to express ideas is difficult; and nowhere does the lack of acquaintanceship show itself more prominently than in such matters as these. The difference in racial temperament aggravates all other difficulties, and raises new barriers in the way of explanation and comprehension.

They do not speak our language or think in our terms; their eyes look upon a different universe; and their ideals contemplate a different future. We have no common interests with them, nor are we closely connected with them; we are, in fact, sundered by totally dissimilar interests and by a generally different outlook upon life. If there is any such thing in this world as isolation, separation, divergence, we are isolated from Latin America by the fundamental, impenetrable barriers of race, language, and religion, law, customs, and tradition. Powerful agencies operating with great force and persistence will be needed to create and preserve any relationship between the American republics in the face of these obstacles. Not only are the premises of Pan-Americanism fallacies; their very antitheses are realities.

CHAPTER III

LACK OF ECONOMIC MUTUALITY

"THE people of the United States have always desired a *Zollverein*, a fiscal union of all the republics; they wish to gather into their imperial hands the commerce of the South, the produce of the tropics." They aim at making a trust of the South American republics," Alberdi has said. "They aim, after the Spanish fashion, at isolating the southern continent, becoming its exclusive purveyor of ideas, and industries." Thus does Calderon give expression to the very common belief in South America as to the real aim and purpose of Pan-Americanism. It is merely the Monroe Doctrine in a new guise, the wolf in sheep's clothing. It is the supremacy of the United States in the Western Hemisphere masquerading as amity and friendship. So long as the economic situation is fairly thrust before them and so long as that situation makes so essential to them close and friendly relations with Europe, they cannot fail to appreciate the consequences of "America for Americans." To exclude the European powers, to attempt to raise commercial barriers against them, and to insist upon fostering by diplomatic or political methods the trade of the United States to the detriment of trade with European nations—all these connote infallibly the establishment of a relationship between the United States and South America vastly more favorable to the United States than it can conceivably be to South America. The very principle itself upon which Pan-Americanism is based, the common interest of the people living in the Western Hemisphere and the normal divergence of their interests from those of Europe, is false, fallacious, and dangerous. The South Americans do not have and cannot have, as they view it, the same interest in the development of trade with the United States, to the exclusion of European trade, that the United States obviously has in obtaining a portion at least of that trade which European nations have at present. The profit is all on our side. The South American sees in Pan-Americanism no economic mutuality, but a very definite, if somewhat subtle, selfishness on the part of the larger country.

The proof lies in the fact that the United States

cannot perform for South America those services indispensable to the welfare of South America that European nations render. The case of Central America is somewhat different: the geographical connection is closer and transportation therefore more rapid and less expensive, while the extent to which enterprise in Central America is already in American hands is so considerable that the question of economic mutuality is at least arguable, although the natives are not by any means willing as yet to concede that it is convincing. In the case of South America, however, the facts seem clearly to indicate that the South Americans are right in denying the claim of mutuality. The peculiar character of our economic position in the world makes it impossible for us to play the part of middleman between the South American producer and his customers throughout the world. South American trade at present (except for a quasi-coastwise trade with the United States) is distributed to all parts of the world by English and German ships, a contact insured from interruption during the last century and more by the English fleet and English policy. Most commercial transactions are completed by exchange on London, where the bills of South America are paid and their credits understood,

LACK OF ECONOMIC MUTUALITY

though a similar service is now performed by certain of the great German banks for a part of that trade. It should be obvious that Pan-Americanism cannot become a reality, nor can an organic union independent of Europe be formed in the Western Hemisphere until the union is capable by its united efforts of performing those services indispensable to its continued economic well-being that certain European powers at present render. Neither the United States nor any of the South American republics possess a merchant marine capable of carrying the trade between the United States and South America alone, to say nothing of the trade between South America and the world at large. The combined naval force of the twenty-one republics would be incapable of protecting the roads across the Atlantic against the English fleet. Far from being able to provide South Americans with adequate international exchange facilities, American merchants are not at present able to do business directly with them, because there is no chain of American banks in Latin America through which direct exchange can be had on New York. The United States, like the rest of the world, does business with Latin America to a large extent through London. When we do not carry on our own business by direct exchange, the absurdity of supposing that we could promptly supply Latin America with the necessary exchange facilities for her trade with the rest of the world ought to be so apparent as to prove conclusively that Pan-Americanism could not finance itself. No doubt adequate arrangements could in time be made, but business is extremely conservative, and the obstacles in the way of a movement to substitute New York for London as the exchange center of South American business are fundamental. Few American business houses at present maintain branches of any importance in South America; not a great many houses maintain resident agents, compared with the number generally maintained by English and German firms; the American consuls are only too seldom well enough acquainted with the language and sufficiently adaptable to establish firm friendships with South American merchants and win their confidence; American drummers rarely speak Spanish or Portuguese and are too inexperienced in South American methods of business to approach prospective customers in ways which they approve. The strong foundation of established business acquaintanceship consists in long years of satisfactory dealing with well-known firms, and in long years of

LACK OF ECONOMIC MUTUALITY

relationship with well-known banks; these, the very bricks of commercial exchange, are lacking, and are not to be made in a day. We must not forget that the active interests of American merchants in South America are not much more than two decades old, while the traditions of business with London can show as many centuries.

These are merely the externals of financial relationship, the arrangements necessary to complete the close business connection. Finally, international finance is not a question of currency or yet a question of banks. If it is difficult to make trade flow along channels contrary to the established habits of merchants and the normal route of exchange; it is impossible to create it unless the elementary facts of supply and demand coexist. International exchange, as a matter of fact, is carried on in goods. Though the individual merchant ostensibly sells his goods for money, he really receives the articles which he buys with the money. So far as the nation as a whole is concerned, money, exchange, banks, finance are merely the methods by which the goods received in exchange for its own output are distributed in proper quantities to its own merchants. The nation makes goods and buys goods with them, and in the long run sells goods only where it can buy goods in return, or at least where it can buy commodities which can be sold to some other nation for the goods which it needs at home. All truly profitable commercial association must be based upon the exchange of actual commodities. When, therefore, a proposition is made which involves the sale of the bulk of the goods produced by one nation, it will be economically sound only when the other nation is ready to sell in return the goods which the first needs. To be of mutual advantage, the goods sold must be offset by the goods bought.

Before the United States can take the place of the European nations in the South American trade, it must be prepared to supply South America with the goods which the South Americans desire; it must either produce those goods itself or procure them elsewhere. It will be exceedingly obvious, however, that if the United States takes South American exports, sells them in Europe, purchases European goods with them, and then sells the latter to the South Americans, it has simply compelled the South Americans to pay American merchants an additional profit for handling European goods which the South Americans could have bought more cheaply by trading directly with the European nations that produced them. The producer in Europe has his

LACK OF ECONOMIC MUTUALITY

price, and if he deals with a South American merchant, he will sell at that rate. But if he sells at that rate to an American merchant, who then sells to the South American merchant, it will be clear that the American must charge the South American a profit for himself, in addition to the cost of the article and the charges of transportation; otherwise the American will himself make no profit on the transaction. To be profitable to the South American, the United States must buy goods which South America produces in exchange for goods which the United States itself makes. Any other arrangement will cost one party or the other an additional sum paid simply for the privilege of allowing the other to play the part of the middleman.

These facts are familiar to any one well informed about international trade. The United States does not produce the goods which South American nations demand to any such extent as would be necessary to make the monopolization of the trade by the United States of mutual advantage. The tastes of South American buyers are luxurious and fastidious in the extreme, and they have been accustomed in the past to buy fine clothing, furniture, and the like from France, Belgium, Germany, or that part of the world which produced the finest articles. In most cases they have dealt directly with the producing nations, in other cases they have bought through London; but what they have bought have been for the most part commodities which the United States is not prepared to make. The bulk of American trade seems, in fact, to be in staple articles of a character or quality which they could buy elsewhere, but which they take from us because they must in the long run accept the goods which we make in exchange for the commodities which we buy from them. Because they buy of us, we must not assume a preference on their part for our goods. It may well be that they merely accept them because we are anxious on our own part to obtain what they have to sell.

If we are incapable of supplying the total South American demand, we are even more incapable of absorbing the total supply. It is highly conceivable that we might produce what they wish; it is not at all likely that we could consume an equal value of the sort of goods we should have to accept in exchange. South America exports a great variety of natural and crude products. It is, for instance, the world's chief supply of rubber, one of the great sources of supply for coffee, hides, and dressed meat. The amount of this type of produce which we can actually consume in the United

LACK OF ECONOMIC MUTUALITY

States is very obviously much less than the world can consume. In order to develop a really mutual interest in the trade between the two continents, we must not only increase our ability to produce, but our ability to consume; and while we can certainly expand the one at a rapid rate, the pace at which we can develop the other will be proportionately much less. We should therefore be forced to sell the surplus of South American produce elsewhere. If the South American was receiving and consuming American goods for this surplus produce, we should have to buy with it European goods and consume them ourselves; but we should be unable to quote as good a price as the South American could get for his goods if he sold them direct to Europe, because American merchants could not afford to exchange the commodities without some profit.

This is all as simple as A plus B or 2 and 2. If men deal with each other directly, each will get the other's actual price: he will pay what it cost to make the article plus a reasonable profit. If they deal through a third party, each will have to pay for the other's article what it cost to make it, plus the producer's profit, and in addition something for the middleman's time. It is often necessary for individuals to pay this additional profit, and so enhance the cost to themselves of what they buy; it is not often necessary for nations to pay an additional profit of this kind. It is above all difficult to secure an additional profit, of advantage only to the middleman, by creating a political situation which forces some nation to trade through a middleman where it previously traded direct. The long and short of it is that unless we can sell direct to the South American goods of our own production which he himself wants, we shall compel him to pay us a profit that he would not otherwise have to pay, and shall therefore tax him for the privilege of doing business with the United States. A Pan-American confederation that involved such commercial relations with the United States would not answer the South American's notions of mutuality.

When a nation in the position of South America sells a great volume of crude produce to some nation like England, which occupies the position of distributor rather than middleman, it may well be that the producing nation will wish to deal through the distributing nation with those nations that it is difficult and inconvenient to reach directly, and which are already dealing in a similar way with the distributor. A nation performing the function of an international clearing-house for

LACK OF ECONOMIC MUTUALITY

merchandise saves time and expense for all parties involved, and therefore pays its own commissions. Such a position the English have successfully held for decades, but its usefulness and profitableness to other nations lie in its universality. If we could move to New York the world's clearing-house in exchange and trade, it would then become profitable for the South Americans to buy through us, just as it is at present profitable for us both to buy through London. But for them to deal with us, and for us then to deal with London, would not be advantageous to them. The United States, in fact, is not in an economic position to take the place which Europe holds in the South American economic fabric. We could not supply them with a merchant marine, with the protection of a fleet, with exchange facilities, export from the United States what they wish to buy, or utilize in the United States the bulk of what they have to sell. Until we ourselves are able actually to utilize the bulk of their produce, we cannot monopolize the South American trade without creating an artificial situation the basis of which will be uneconomic and lacking in mutuality, resulting in greater profit to us than it affords them.

There is one more step to take. The rate of future development in South America will depend upon the amount of foreign capital that can be procured at any one time; the continuity of progress will be measured by their ability to borrow in successive years. Inasmuch as South America is an extremely favorable field for the investor, it will be very much to the advantage of the United States to loan them capital; but their interests are furthered only when they obtain as much capital as possible at the most advantageous possible rates. Pan-Americanism, "America for the Americans," the exclusion of Europe and of European interests, means, if interpreted literally, that it ought to be more to the advantage of the South Americans to borrow capital in the United States than to borrow it in Europe. Unfortunately, there is no particular advantage for them in securing capital from the United States, and there would be very distinct disadvantages in limiting their opportunity to borrow European funds. Capital in a rough sense obeys the economic law of supply and demand, and can usually be bought cheaper where there is more of it for sale. Money is usually cheaper in Europe than it is in America, and it is usually easier to obtain it even when the current rates are the same in London and New York. The reason is obvious. The European nations are older and wealthier; their surplus is

LACK OF ECONOMIC MUTUALITY

greater; they have a smaller proportion of the national wealth invested in permanent fixtures; and the surplus available for foreign investment is accordingly greater.

If South America were to be limited to the amount of capital it could obtain in the United States, or were compelled for political and military reasons to borrow in the United States rather than in Europe, its rate of development would certainly be slower than if it were free to borrow in the financial markets of the world. The amount of American capital compared with the total European capital is small; the proportion of it available for South America would normally be smaller than that available in Europe. If new political relationships of the nature of Pan-Americanism were established on a basis which contemplated the exclusion of the European on principle, or placing him in a less favorable position than Americans, European investors would hesitate about loaning to South Americans; South America would speedily see the stream of capital from Europe diminishing, and would be dependent upon the United States for a new supply. This could not in the circumstances be nearly as great in volume as the supply they might have drawn from Europe. Here again is a lack of mutuality. The

United States is able to lend, and South America is not; it could not loan the South Americans as much as they will want, nor in all probability on as favorable conditions as they would like to obtain. The United States is the gainer under any circumstances. It will be advantageous for the South Americans to establish a closer connection with Europe than with the United States.

In any case, a very large proportion of the South American trade must continue to flow to Europe, whatever the demand in the United States for South American produce or the demand for American goods in South America. For years to come the South Americans must pay with exports the interest on the heavy European loans they borrowed in the past. Unless they repudiate their debts, they must pay in time with exports the capital as well as the interest. In the case of undeveloped countries trade is the expression of the basic financial situation. The bulk of the imports is new capital coming in; the bulk of the exports discharge obligations for interest and capital. Trade of necessity flows to the country which has invested money and flows with difficulty to countries which do not invest money. Normally, therefore, the trade of undeveloped countries with the rest of the world bears some rough pro-

LACK OF ECONOMIC MUTUALITY

portion to the investments of the rest of the world within their borders. Hence, the trade of England with the Argentine Republic is enormous because of the vast total of past English investments and the large amount of new capital sent annually. The trade of the United States with South America has recently developed with great rapidity, because we have begun to invest largely in the Southern Continent. If, therefore, we are to supplant England and Germany in the South American trade, we must be prepared to take the place of England and Germany as investors of capital, and be ready not only to quote the South Americans favorable terms, but to provide them now and in the future with the bulk of what they wish to borrow. If we can actually furnish them any such amount, we shall capture their trade as a simple matter of course; they will have to import goods from us equal in value to the capital they borrow, and they will be compelled, if they are honest, to export to us in return commodities equivalent each year to the interest plus the capital payments which fall due. This is the real basis of English and German trade with South America, and something like it must be established before we can achieve a similar economic monopoly.

Nor must we forget that we cannot monopolize

it in reality until our investments exceed the total investments, past and present, of other nations. Even if we should be able to assume such a position, it would still be more advantageous to us than to South America, unless it should also be true that the amount of capital available in the United States for investment should be greater than the amount available in Europe, and obtainable on better terms. Even the most optimistic prophets will scarcely venture to predict such a commercial future for the United States. Yet until some such situation becomes a reality, Pan-Americanism cannot be mutually advantageous to all the American republics. We have yet to learn of the formation of a strong organic bond which has not possessed some strong mutual economic benefit for all its members, nor can we imagine a connection, however weak and shadowy, between the United States and the Latin-American republics, which did not somehow, involve this economic question. A customs union would perhaps be the slightest association which would deserve the name Pan-Americanism, but the mere suggestion is regarded in South America as tantamount to a declaration of the determination of the United States to monopolize South American trade for its own selfish purposes. They

LACK OF ECONOMIC MUTUALITY

cannot conceive of a commercial relation to the United States which would be as favorable to them as their relationship to Europe; and they therefore regard as inexpedient any unions, associations, policies, or connections which predicate a closer connection with the United States than with Europe.

CHAPTER IV

THE SHADOW OF THE PAST

WITH such fundamental obstacles in the road of Pan-Americanism, with such barriers to break down before it can become a reality, its future will be indeed dark unless they can be removed by the common efforts of the states concerned. Here we meet with perhaps the greatest stumbling-block of all, of a character that makes peculiarly difficult the removal of any of the fundamental barriers already enumerated—the lack of mutual trust and confidence between the Latin republics and the United States. Before "America for the Americans" can become a reality, the Americans must possess a thorough belief in one another's disinterestedness and freely accept one another's actions as performed in that perfect good faith which alone can avoid serious disputes, or permit effective compromise between jarring interests. All this the United States is unquestionably ready to accord the Latin-American republics; nay, there can be no reasonable doubt that the United States actually does accord them all this. The difficulty lies in the inability of the Latin-American republics thoroughly to convince themselves of the disinterested motives of the United States. They fear that Pan-Americanism is conquest in some subtle guise; they discount our protestations; they look askance at our actions, and remain unbelievers. The barrier which stands between us and them is the one most difficult to remove—the shadow of the past, their interpretation of our own past acts, the logic of American policy as revealed to them by acts which are beyond our power to change. *Quis custodiet custodem?* asks Calderon.

Mutual confidence must find its roots in mutual understanding and agreement not alone upon the policies of the present, but upon the interpretation attached to the history of the past. It will be surprising to most Americans to learn in these days when we stand aghast at the magnitude of the conception of Pan-Germanism, and censure it as unprovoked aggression, when many of us regard the kaiser as a barbarian and talk about him as a hypocrite, who prepares for war while delivering himself daily of mouthings about peace, that many honest, sincere, and patriotic South Americans regard the United States and Pan-Americanism as cast in this same image, and describe us in terms not less uncomplimentary and even more vigorous. There are few things said recently in the United States about German aggression the counterpart of which cannot easily be found in the influential South American newspapers and the works of serious thinkers. They censure us less for our schemes of aggression than for what they consider our hypocritical, sanctimonious assumption of virtue. To be assured that the rod which they actually feel bruising their flesh is an olive branch extended by the dove of peace is to them the height of absurdity.

It will not be at all necessary for us to accept their version of American history or agree with their strictures upon our diplomatists, to realize that in this misunderstanding between honest and sincere men on both sides as to the meaning of acts now past recall, is one of the most serious barriers which could possibly exist in the way of extending the connection between the American republics. Unfortunately, American foreign policy has not always been consistent, nor have the utterances of our diplomatic Secretaries of State been uniformly discreet. The advocate of the American view has a difficult task before him in meeting the South American charges. It is not to our present purpose to investigate the dispute, and it suffices to point out how easy it is for us to quote Mr. Root and Mr. Wilson, and to have them retort with equally explicit utterances of Mr. Fish, Mr. Olney, and Mr. Roosevelt. Our chief witnesses have not left us an entirely consistent stream of testimony, and it is difficult to convince the South Americans that the pacific utterances which we ourselves believe represent the true current of American policy are more valid than the belligerent statements on which they rely. It would not be nearly so serious if both parties agreed heartily upon something which students knew was actually wrong; it is not necessary that what they believe should be true, but that they should actually agree upon something,—the premise of close union and the basis of energetic action. We need not attempt to discover which view of American history is true; the vital fact is that the South Americans have repeatedly declined to accept our version.

They are inclined to interpret the utterances of our statesmen by the logic of their actions. Like the European, the South American is skeptical as to the importance of pledges, of promises, or intentions, and relies almost entirely upon the logic of facts. We remember many times in the past when we have foreborne to act in the spirit of aggression; they cannot forget the times when we have not foreborne to act. Leaving aside all disputed facts or events susceptible of more than one interpretation, as thoroughly moderate and representative a South American as Calderon states the case against us thus:

The northern Republic has been the beneficiary of an incessant territorial expansion; in 1803 it acquired Louisiana; in 1819, Florida; in 1845 and 1850, Texas; the Mexican provinces in 1848 and 1852, and Alaska in 1858. The annexation of Hawaii took place in 1898. In the same year Porto Rico, the Philippines, Guam, and one of the Marianne Islands, passed by the Treaty of Paris, into the hands of the United States. They obtained the Samoan Islands in 1890, wished to buy the Danish West Indies in 1902, and planted their imperialistic standard at Panama in 1903. Interventions have become more frequent with the expansion of frontiers. The United States have recently intervened in the territory of Acre, there to found a republic of rubber gatherers; at Panama, there to develop a province and construct a canal; in Cuba, under cover of the Platt amendment, to maintain order in the interior; in San Domingo, to support the civilizing revolution and overthrow the tyrants; in Venezuela, and in Central America, to enforce upon these nations, torn by intestine disorders, the political and financial tutelage of the imperial democracy. In Guatemala and Honduras the loans concluded with

THE SHADOW OF THE PAST

the monarchs of North American finance have reduced the people to a new slavery. Supervision of the customs and the dispatch of pacificatory squadrons to defend the interests of the Anglo-Saxon have enforced peace and tranquility; such are the means employed. . . . The Yankee ideal, then, is fatally contrary to Latin-American independence.[1]

Recent events have roused South American apprehensions much more rapidly than the pacific utterances of our statesmen have been able to allay them. Until the present, South America has been protected from European aggression and, as they believe, from American aggression by the English fleet. For more than half a century after the declaration of independence by the South American republics, England interposed a determined resistance to the attempts of the United States to extend its influence in Latin America. This is the view accepted in Europe and in Latin America. When the rise of the German fleet and other circumstances elsewhere described caused the concentration of the English fleet in the North Sea, and the decision to hand over the supremacy of the Western Hemisphere for the time being to the United States, the South Americans became extremely uneasy and apprehensive of the worst. The Spanish-American War had

[1] Calderon, *Latin America*, pp. 303–304; 306.

seemed to them the baldest sort of aggression, but the founding of the Panama Republic, our recent dealings with the small Central American states, and in particular our recent refusal to recognize Huerta as President of Mexico, were in their eyes flagrant, unprovoked aggression, aggravated a thousandfold by statements of pacific intent and the denial of any desire at conquest. As if we had not conquered vast areas of Latin America in the last few years as fully as if we had declared war and waged it! As if we have not robbed many thousands of Latin Americans of everything except the barest shadow of political independence! If this does not spell aggression, they ask us to furnish them with some version of our acts which will be more consistent with the actual events than are our protestations of amity and peace. They know that we are not at present equipped for the conquest of South America, but they know that we can easily prepare. They believe that while we can achieve our purposes by peaceful penetration, spheres of influence, benevolent assimilation, and manifest destiny, we shall not bother to create armies and build fleets; but they ask us to have at least the decency to acknowledge that, by whatever name we call it, this is conquest.

One other issue has risen to prominence, and is

more important than is usually admitted. South American peoples are the result of a mixture of Spanish, Indian, and negro blood, in which usually the Indian or the negro predominates over the Spanish. They are what we are pleased to term in the United States a half-breed nation, and therefore view the attitude of Americans toward the Indian, the negro, and the half-breed with peculiar interest. Our treatment of those three classes is a very ominous shadow, indeed, cast in the path of Pan-Americanism. In our relations with them during the last three centuries, in the present opinion of the American people about all three classes, they see foreshadowed the probable attitude towards them of a nation of this power in the north, whose existence they feel is perilous to them, and whose aggression is dangerous and near. Indeed, it is our attitude on this question which provides them with the uncontrovertible proof of aggression. The mere fact that it is not difficult to demonstrate that few persons in the United States have any such ideas or, perhaps one should say, are even aware of any such notions, makes no vital difference. They are written so plainly upon the past history of the white man in the New World that all the protestations of statesmen and the rhetoric of orators cannot veil them from the eyes of the descendants of the red man and the black man.

When the whites came to the Western Hemisphere they brought with them two premises of action, both of which, to all intents and purposes, were one and the same: only white men and only Christians had rights or could own land. The whites talked about discovery, about the first finding of what the red man and his ancestors for countless generations had known! The assumption was plain: until some white man found it, it had not existed at all. Only the white man could claim title to the land. Strange kings who had never seen the New World granted to favorites and dependents millions of acres of land occupied by Indians who had inherited them from remote ancestors. Occupation, possession, use—all were futile to protect the Indian against dispossession. He owned nothing; he had no title; he possessed no rights which demanded recognition. Two damning facts were proved against him: he was not a white man; he was not a Christian. He could never become a white man, though he might become a Christian; and the whites recognized no rights or privileges of any human being in the New World unless he was white. On the whole, these general premises were strictly followed.

THE SHADOW OF THE PAST

Only white men were citizens for more than three centuries; only white men could govern; and no Indian's consent was asked nor his opposition regarded. Again and again he was pushed from his property without scruple and without apology by white men who did not regard him as existing at all. That he might have rights was not to the majority even a tenable supposition or a speculative possibility. Ever since the white man landed in the Western Hemisphere to the present day the red man and his descendants have been exploited and hounded from place to place.

The negro had still fewer rights; worse yet was his lot. That the Indian could go where he pleased so long as he did not interfere with the white man was generally admitted: but the black man was not free. Year after year white men and Christians went to Africa, seized the black man, carried him from his home, and sold him like live stock or lumber in the Western Hemisphere, in North America, in South America, and in the islands of the sea. He was a heathen; he was not white; he never could be white, neither he nor his descendants. Virtuous and sincere men debated in the eighteenth and even in the nineteenth century whether the negro could have a soul. We ought to blush to record that until a short time ago that question was usually answered in North America in the negative. The Indian's land they took from him, the Indian's property was theirs, and they exploited it. They robbed the black man of his home and often of his family; they denied him his soul; took even the little that he had, his liberty, and only too often his life. It must be remembered that we are dealing here, not alone with negro slavery in the United States, but with negro slavery in the West Indies, in Central and South America. The negro slavery against which the North protested was mild, just, and expedient in comparison with the negro slavery which is still remembered in South and Central America and in the West Indian islands. Their traditions show it at its worst.

The modern South American is proud of his race, proud of his country, aware of personal attainments and a right to life, liberty, and property; but he knows that in all probability there flows in his veins some of the blood of the red man and some of the blood of the black man. He knows that the white man has treated the half-breed precisely as a full-blooded Indian or negro, and that in the United States the slightest tincture of either is likely to create unfortunate distinctions. To-day this is passing. The Indian and the negro are both taking their place in the American community, but it is too recent to remove from the mind of South Americans the haunting suspicion that the United States looks upon Latin America as a half-breed country whose people cannot own their land, who are not entitled to its resources as against white men. They see in Pan-Americanism and in the Monroe Doctrine something still of the old attitude of the Spanish conqueror and the English adventurer, and explicitly compare the United States with both. While so black a shadow remains as the past dealings of white men with the Indian and the negro, mutual confidence between the United States as a white nation and the Latin American republics as half-breed states is difficult to predicate. They cannot forget, nor can they believe that we have forgotten or changed. Our assumption of a tutelage over them, our insistence that we must keep the peace in Latin America, help the erring and unfortunate, contains for them a denial of their own rights, and a degree of interference with them which would be incredible if we really believed them white men. They can credit our acceptance of their economic progress, they can conceive that their increase in strength would make us hesitate in the pursuit of schemes of aggression; but time and time alone can convince them that we no longer regard their ancestry as an indelible stain.

If the nearness of countries to each other is to be the principle of association, why does not the United States seek to dominate Canada? If lack of development and ignorance of the arts of civilization is a criterion, why does not the United States interfere in Africa, and assert a right of tutelage in Morocco and the Congo Free State? They are in point of distance no farther than the majority of South American states from New York. Why do we not spread our protecting ægis over Turkey or Japan, which are neither in the hands of white men nor of Christians? The palpable fact that we do not assert even a shadow of right in any of these countries the Latin Americans explain very simply: it is because some European nation of white Christians is already performing this duty in that territory. We recognize the claims of Christians and white men, and do not interfere even with the most shadowy of their titles. With Latin America we interfere because we do not, they persistently insist, recognize them as possessing rights equal to our own, because we do not actually recognize them as white men in our deeds. If we did think of them as white men, as Christians and as equals, tutelage, protection, interference, exploitation, would be as unthinkable and impossible between the United States and Latin America as between the United States and Bulgaria, Morocco, or Liberia. Was anything heard, they ask, with considerable force, about the policing of Latin America by the United States between 1783 and 1823? The United States obviously recognized Spain as paramount and supreme, because Spain was a white nation, and had equal rights with other white nations. Does not the Monroe Doctrine date from the moment of the Spanish defeat? The instant other white men's hands were removed, did not the United States advance its claims to impose its own white hands, on the assumption, apparently, that some white men must exercise at least a supervision over their weaker brethren?

To over-emphasize this aspect of the situation is easy; to ignore it is fatal. No really close student of Latin America can deny that something of this sort lies behind a good many otherwise inexplicable things. The difficulty lies not in the truth of such charges, but in the fact that they are believed to be true.

The general policy of the white man in his relations toward those whom he chooses to regard as his inferiors has been to insist that they shall become like him. They must learn his language, go to his schools, wear his kind of clothes, think the same ideas, believe in the greatness of the white man. The Spanish brought this policy to South America, as the English brought it to North America, as the United States carried it to the Philippines and Cuba. Is not the complaint of the United States against Mexico fundamentally the objection that its people are not like Americans, and do not govern themselves according to the notions of democracy and law which Americans believe to be right? Does not even the mild policy of President Wilson insist that the Mexicans shall become as Americans, and understand the words, law, order, and democracy as Americans understand them? The Latin Americans passionately resent all insinuations that any of them or all of them need to be changed, developed, educated, or civilized on the American model. They regard themselves as entirely worthy and respectable citizens; they approve of their own ideas; and consider their government no further short of ideal rule than many Americans think the government of the United States is. The burning of negroes, the lynching of thieves, the work of vigilance committees in the far West, the failure to apprehend and punish murderers—all these the South Americans evidence as a lack of civilization in the United States quite as serious as their own particular difficulties. If graft is common in Latin America, does it not flourish north of the Rio Grande? Is it worse for some Latin American official to receive money from an American trust for privileges than it is for American State legislatures to take it from the same hand for a similar object? Is the stealing from the people by officials in Central America different in kind or in purpose from the fleecing of lambs in Wall Street or the operations of certain trusts? Finally, the South Americans do not consider the United States a model according to which they wish to be reformed. If they were to pick out teachers and tutors, they would much prefer the English, the French, or the Germans, all three of whom they regard as their superiors not only in strength, but in the arts of civilization, and from whom they are willing and eager to learn.

These are the obstacles which seem to stand in the way of a mutuality of confidence and faith in the Western Hemisphere. Scarcely anything more fundamental can be conceived than the present lack of these essentials to unity and cooperation. To demonstrate the falsity of these notions, we must prove something more than our own consciousness of innocence and rectitude;

we must convince them of the falsity of their fears and assumptions. How this can be accomplished, and when, it would be rash to predict, but it certainly can be done only by acts and deeds both striking and disinterested. The occasional speeches and protestations of individual statesmen will not avail. Of the good-will of individuals the South Americans are already convinced. It is the nation, the United States as a nation, which must speak, and speak decisively and plainly, before the Latin Americans will believe what we know to be true.

CHAPTER V

ADMINISTRATIVE AND LEGAL PROBLEMS

THE tangible expression of Pan-Americanism would necessarily be the administrative and legal fabric created by the various American republics to cope with those problems common to them all, in the existence of which the new bond of union could alone find justification. The complexity of the administrative fabric would indicate the closeness of the bond and the immediacy of the problems, as well as their variety, number, and fundamental or temporary character. To it all foreign nations would look for an earnest of the reality of the new state, and by its strength and efficiency would they judge the importance and extent of the connection. Pan-Americanism finding its expression solely in infrequent diplomatic congresses, the delegates of which were without power to act, would have no administrative fabric that would deserve the name. A customs' union, with certain agreements in regard to uniform tariffs, currency, weights, measures, and the like, would be a reality, but not a state, and would represent a very limited type of common interest. Until Pan-Americanism can find tangible existence in a strong, independent, efficient state, until it provides at least for a common administration, common courts and law, even though the legislative powers should be quasi-diplomatic in character and of the nature of international treaties, it will be a dream, a vision, a hope, of little influence in international affairs.

Before the dream can be realized and the vision exist, this strong administration must be the very real expression of mutual interests, existing conditions, and popular ideals. A democratic state not closely linked to conditions will be a fiction. In this administrative and legal fabric the mutuality of the economic interests of the various members of the Confederation and their mutual faith and confidence in each other's good intentions should find expression. The uniformity of regulations and laws would necessarily be closely associated with something like a similarity of conditions in the various states. From the general notions already existent in the community, of right, justice, ethics, and expediency, would the new rules and laws draw

ADMINISTRATIVE AND LEGAL PROBLEMS

their breath of life. Unless in fact the administrative and legal fabrics are the actual expression of an approximate agreement among the various peoples of the confederation upon these fundamental notions of right, justice, and expediency, unless they express the mutual confidence of the people in one another and the realization of mutual economic interests, unless they are based upon homogeneity of conditions, the confederation would scarcely be operative. It could not provide effectively for the needs, common to all the states and their citizens, which it was created to solve. An equality between the citizens of the various states would also normally find expression in the laws of the new confederation, while the provisions regarding procedure would necessarily place all duly accredited citizens in one state, whenever absent from home, on a par with the citizens of all other states. The confederation would be an artificial bond, a mere potentiality, until such an administrative and legal fabric had actually come into existence. Until such a fabric gave expression to some such fundamental conceptions as these, it could not itself be a reality. It is scarcely possible to exaggerate the vital significance to Pan-Americanism of these prerequisites.

The foundation, for such an administrative and

legal structure seems to be lacking, however; the facts themselves, as we have already suggested, do not answer to the assumptions. The mutuality of economic interests, the mutual faith and confidence in one another's good intentions are at present only too clearly non-existent. The general lack of acquaintance between the United States and Latin America makes difficult any agreement upon the general postulates of political science. But we are here more particularly concerned with specifically technical difficulties in the way of a strong, stable, and efficient administration.

The difference in size between the United States and Latin America is a formidable bar. The United States contains alone about one-quarter more people than the whole of Latin America, even though these people are located upon an area only one third as large. The economic development of the United States is so much more advanced and complex that the disparity in wealth and resources is still more striking. Stable government, again, is so old in the United States and so comparatively recent in South America as to create a difference in administrative and legal tradition of the most formidable type. Yet it has not been found possible in the United States to administer the Western communities according to

ADMINISTRATIVE AND LEGAL PROBLEMS

the traditions and precepts eminently successful in New England. The difference of economic conditions, of social advancement, the difference in the age alone of the State, has made it necessary to treat the two in radically different ways, even though the problem in general presented striking fundamental similarities. If a community of New Englanders located in Ohio has found expedient different practical methods from those adopted by New Englanders in Oregon or from the New Englanders in New England, the imagination is scarcely capable of depicting the necessary practical adjustments for communities as different in economic development, as unequal in age, and as sundered by race, language, and religion, as are the United States and the Latin-American republics. Common administrative and legal requirements which would meet the approval of all the States and work to the practical satisfaction of all citizens would probably represent the experience of years and be the final product of a long series of experiments, and in all probability of numerous dismal failures. Nothing short of strong mutual ties of interest and confidence could maintain a Pan-American Confederation during this period of administrative and legal experimentation.

If the difficulties and differences between the

United States and the Latin-American republics as a whole were not sufficient, the past has provided a very similar situation in Latin America. We speak in loose fashion of two entities; we write for the sake of convenience about the two Americas; and tend to assume an essential homogeneity of conditions in both, or, at least, extremes no greater than between the various States of our own Federal Union. But as a matter of fact "America" is a fiction, because we tacitly exclude Canada, Alaska, and Central America, while "Latin America" has no reasonable basis for existence. It is a historical and geographic caption used for convenience by historians and scientists to denote the fact that at one time a large territory was nominally subject to Spain and achieved political independence at the same epoch. A few relics of the Spanish occupation —some proportion of Spanish blood in the people, a general adhesion to the Roman Catholic Church, some general notions of law due to Spanish ideas about political science—have lent a certain respectability and a semblance of accuracy to the name. But the phrase denotes no greater uniformity of conditions or of ideas than the word Europe or Asia.

The number of states in Latin America is large, the variety of natural conditions is astounding and

ADMINISTRATIVE AND LEGAL PROBLEMS

creates radically different economic and administrative problems in different parts of the continent. The disparity in development between certain states is almost as great as between the United States and Latin America as a whole, while the antiquity of stable government varies from states whose administrative traditions extend for generations, to those who have to our thinking not yet achieved it. The Argentine Republic and Brazil occupy between them four sevenths of the total area of the Southern Continent, have half of the total population, and more than half of the commerce. They contain two highly developed regions, one in southern Brazil, and the other in the northern part of Argentina. Here the interior has been knit to the coast by an excellent system of railroads; agriculture has been developed; education and the arts have made progress, and find their expression in large and beautiful cities. But northern Brazil and southern Argentine Republic are by no means as advanced, and the great bulk of the enormous area of the former is inhabited only by savages; there are parts of it which the white man's foot has not yet trodden. Indeed, the general uncertainty as to its topography and conditions is so marked that controversy has risen over facts which would in most countries have been established beyond doubt half a century ago. Chile is a large and wealthy state on the western coast, with an ambitious and energetic population and a very large foreign trade. Indeed, the A B C countries, as these three states are called, have about four fifths of the total foreign trade of South America.

Their existence creates an administrative situation, so far as the other states are concerned, not different in kind or degree from that between the United States and Latin America as a whole. The smaller states fear absorption by these large entities almost as much as the Central American states fear absorption by the United States. Between these large states and the smaller South and Central American states there are no mutuality of economic interest, and no faith or confidence in one another's intentions. A uniform administration and law for the whole of Latin America would in all probability antagonize the small states if it satisfied the large, and fail of the support of the large states if it were satisfactory to the smaller. The racial unity, while striking when Latin America is compared with the United States, is not much greater, when the republics are compared with one another, than the racial resemblances of many states in Europe which have maintained their racial differences for centuries. As against the

ADMINISTRATIVE AND LEGAL PROBLEMS

United States, as against Europe, the Latin-American republics are ready to unite, because they find in resistance to foreign aggression a mutual interest of undoubted strength. But if the specter of conquest could be removed, the one common bond between them would disappear, and the probability of agreement upon other points would be not much greater than that of agreement between them and the United States, Germany, or England upon administrative and legal questions. Indeed, Pan-Americanism finds in its way not only physical and economic inequality between the Northern and Southern continents, not only administrative and intellectual inequality between the United States and Latin America, but an inequality in all those directions between the Latin-American republics which is not less striking and significant, and perhaps not less difficult to obviate.

The administrative task of forming a federated state to extend over two such enormous continents, to govern 175,000,000 people and about 12,000,000 square miles of territory, must not be forgotten. Administration depends for efficiency upon rapidity of communication. The distance in space between the extremes of the new confederation would be as great as that between England and

South Africa, which is regarded by many as so great as to preclude governmental connection. The area covered would approach the vastness of European and Asiatic Russia, a state supposedly too large for effective administration, and it would not present the same facilities for transportation that Russia possesses. Contact between the various parts would be slow and therefore difficult.

Such physical conditions would place before a common administration the maximum of administrative difficulties. The number of transactions involving the various countries, to say nothing of their respective citizens, the multitude of possible difficulties for the courts to solve, of administrative disputes to be settled, of officials to be appointed and supervised, of bills to be paid, of accounts to be rendered, would, without any complications at all, even in the most favorable circumstances, provide problems which no single government in the world has hitherto successfully struggled with, and which have disrupted empires smaller in area and less ambitious in scope. The English Empire is not an administrative reality, for the Imperial Government attempts only a very general supervision of the great bulk of the territory involved. The Roman Empire was much smaller in size. Indeed, Pan-Americanism, even

ADMINISTRATIVE AND LEGAL PROBLEMS

if all its premises were realities, might easily fail for lack of ability to solve the elemental problems of efficient and rapid action and of prompt obedience, responsibility, and honesty of officials. It is surely worth remembering in this connection that we are none too well satisfied in the United States with the success of the Federal Government in all these matters, and that the Latin-American republics are in most instances obviously less successful than we are. Neither would be likely to deal efficiently with an administrative problem in its very nature more difficult than any yet solved by a civilized community.

It will perhaps be enough to advert to the difficulties of choosing officials for the confederation satisfactory to all its members. By common consent democracy has been less successful in the choosing and appointing of officers than in any other regard. Yet upon securing capable and efficient men would depend the whole success, and perhaps the very existence, of Pan-Americanism, however weak and nominal the bond might be. Here in particular would appear the influence of the United States and of the three largest South American states. They would normally expect to divide between them the most important posts and the bulk of the smaller posts. This would hardly be agreeable to the seventeen other states. If the general experience in all twenty-one republics is any criterion, there would soon appear undue influence of various kinds, underground wires, and back-stairs influence of the sort which makes government difficult at Washington and in our own States, and which has almost made stable government impossible in several of the small Latin-American republics. Estimate all these influences at a minimum, and they would still aggravate the other administrative difficulties to a point which would perhaps overthrow the whole fabric.

One of the most vital aspects of the possible bond which might be called Pan-Americanism would be the uniformity of commercial law and a criminal code and procedure for all the American republics. This might be perfected without necessarily involving the creation of an administrative fabric and would be of obvious utility, but the difficulties of agreement about the general provisions and the practical details of any kind of legal system are fundamental. Naturally the United States would object to adopting Latin-American ideas as a whole, and the Latin Americans would object to accepting our Federal law as a whole. We should, indeed, have much difficulty in providing a set of principles and practical provisions in the United States which lawyers would uniformly accept as representative or workable. So much of the law of the United States is state law, and so varied are its provisions upon fundamental questions of personal liberty and commercial expediency, that the enactment of a uniform Federal law, obviously desirable and generally agreed to be expedient, has usually presented such practical difficulties in reaching a compromise mutually satisfactory that action has sometimes involved years, and has more often proved impossible. To provide, therefore, a uniform series of principles for the twenty-one American republics would require not only some general agreement upon the broad principles of justice and expediency, but some sort of compromise between the different practical expedients already used in forty-eight States of our Federal Union and twenty South American republics. Yet upon the satisfactory character of the general principles evolved and the practical expedients selected would depend the real usefulness of a system of common courts.

Even greater difficulties would present themselves to the judges of the confederation in an attempt to apply broad principles to individual cases. The law as enforced invariably reflects something of the community's ideals of morals, of ethics, of what is fair, best, and reasonable, while it usually falls to the judge to apply these standards as well as the technicalities of the law to individual cases. It is here that the lack of racial unity, of a common language, of a general agreement upon the postulates of religion would present the most serious practical difficulties that the officers of the confederation would have to solve. A confederated state might satisfactorily adjust itself to the governments of the twenty-one republics, and by the exercise of great tact and discretion might possibly be able to secure harmony. If its budget was not large and its taxes were collected by the governments of the various republics, the people would seldom realize the expense of the confederation or feel called upon to consider its position and pretentions. In the courts, however, individuals would meet individuals, and personal prejudices and passions would find an outlet only too persistently, and would usually present personal, racial, and religious stimuli of such a nature that a settlement of the case satisfactory to both parties would be abnormally difficult to reach. What could be done in murder trials, where the culprit and the murdered were of different race

ADMINISTRATIVE AND LEGAL PROBLEMS

and religion? Would it be possible for public opinion in the United States to view with entire equanimity the trial of a white man and an American citizen by a South American jury composed of Indians, negroes, and half-breeds? Would the South Americans find any less objectionable the trial of a South American citizen by a jury in Texas or Arizona? The burning of negroes and the lynching of "greasers" have made a decided impression in Latin America, and are a good deal more common in the United States than most of us realize. Here the mutual faith and confidence of the various communities would be most essential, and here its absence would do the most harm. As conditions are at present, it would be scarcely possible to convince public sentiment in certain parts of the United States that an American citizen convicted by a South American jury was not hanged on general principles, or to demonstrate to a good many portions of the South American public that a South American criminal was not dealt with harshly in our Southern States because of his race and color.

Commercial cases would be the most common, and would present difficulties less serious in degree, but not less grave in nature. The most valuable service a uniform system of courts might render would be the decision of cases between the citizens of different states and those widely sundered in space. Among the cases which would appear before such tribunals would be naturally those upon the border-line between law and equity, where the adjustment of the interests of the parties could not be effected by the plain interpretation of principles or yet by clearly established precedent. These are always the most difficult types to decide, because they involve the interpretation of principles and precedents in the light of the general notions of lawyers and judges as to what is fair, right, and expedient. Decisions of this sort would be less certain to meet the approval of parties as little acquainted with each other as Latin Americans and citizens of the United States. The interpretation of oral contracts, the definition of equities in property, the decision about the facts in cases arising from the failure specifically to perform contracts—all these would inevitably appear. They would present the maximum difficulties of solution, because of the ease with which one party or the other could plead an insufficient knowledge of the other's language, and therefore a misunderstanding of what he said, or a difference in commercial customs, permitting him to demand certain allowances for a delay in specific performance, which the

ADMINISTRATIVE AND LEGAL PROBLEMS

other would regard as unjust and unnecessary in the light of the business ethics of his own community. The judges would be continually meeting a series of irreconcilable differences, where compromises would be difficult, because both parties were right according to their own customs. The American business temperament furthermore accommodates itself with impatience to the dilatory proceedings in our own courts. It would regard proceedings that we considered normally swift in South America as entirely impossible. Here, again, would be a constant source of friction.

The most difficult issue before the confederation as a whole would be that of some sanction which would enforce obedience to its commands, and insure the payment of its taxes by its own members and their respective citizens. The seventeen smaller states would easily be dealt with; but it is difficult to see what would happen if the confederation decided, after due deliberation, that some rule or statute was vital for the vast majority of its members that the United States or Brazil should declare with equal solemnity and vehemence was destructive of its interests. How could the confederation possibly compel one of its largest states to yield obedience? Would not a confederation dependent upon voluntary obedience degenerate promptly into something as weak and despicable as the Diet of the Holy Roman Empire in the eighteenth century? Coercion would be out of the question, partly because of the distance between the strong powers who would necessarily furnish the major part of any army which the confederation might form, but chiefly because the confederation could not possibly keep under arms an army large enough to coerce one of the four large states. It would be as hopeless to attack Brazil as to coerce the United States. There has been some dispute among political scientists as to how far force is necessary for the existence of a strong government, but the general opinion seems to be that adequate force must be at least latent and potential, and the will of the community to use it thoroughly well understood. In the United States the existence of that force is now admitted, but it is not so generally conceded in Latin America. Certainly, any confederation supposedly created for the common interests of twenty-one sovereign states, four of which could virtually nullify any of its decisions, could never have had any really strong corporate existence.

The experience of confederations of sovereign states in the past proves only too conclusively that

ADMINISTRATIVE AND LEGAL PROBLEMS

a union between numerous small communities and two or three large states, with one state as large as all the rest, invariably results either in the domination of the confederation by that single state or in the administrative weakness and practical nullity of the confederation as a result of the union of the majority against the one. Either eventuality would be fatal to Pan-Americanism; the actual superiority of the United States would lead either to its domination of the confederation or to its disruption. A political deputation once waited upon Lincoln with some request which he deemed unreasonable, and was asked by the President how many legs a sheep would have if you called its tail a leg. They promptly replied, as was expected, "Five." "No," said Lincoln, "calling its tail a leg would not make it one." Calling the United States, therefore, the equal of each of the twenty Latin-American republics would not change the fact that the United States is more populous, wealthy, and powerful than the twenty added together. We who live in the United States are apt to forget this. It is rarely, if ever, forgotten south of the Rio Grande.

We shall have made as students little progress toward the comprehension of currents of thought in Latin America if we have failed to appreciate the strength of the democratic movement. They are glad to have the United States protect them from European aggression, they are anxious to call in England or Germany to protect them from the United States; but they have not the slightest intention of forming an alliance of any sort with any power which will give the latter any influence or control, or which will involve any sort of organic union with it. They wish to achieve for Latin America an actual independence of the rest of the world. They consider that they have as much right to political independence as any nation, and as little reason to accept dictation, guidance, instruction, or assistance as the United States itself or any nation in Europe. They look upon themselves as our peers. We shall be lacking in candor if we decline to admit that the impulse behind this movement is identical with the motive of our own Revolution. We denied the right of England to advise us, guide us, help us; we declined to recognize any need for advice or help. Pan-Americanism means in Latin America a united movement by the Latin-American republics against the pretentions of the United States. There is a good deal more active agitation going on south of the Rio Grande for this purpose than for any other purpose the republics have in common.

ADMINISTRATIVE AND LEGAL PROBLEMS

But they are no less determined to preserve their political independence of one another and have not the slightest intention of sacrificing one jot or tittle of sovereignty to a Latin-American confederation, any more than they have of yielding to the domination of the United States or of Europe. By democracy they understand self-government, the government of a political entity by its own people, and the recognition by the rest of the world of any government they see fit to organize, whether or not it is in harmony with the definition of government in other countries. They themselves have the right, and the exclusive right, to decide what is good government for them; any attempt to interfere with their right to reach a conclusion is domination and conquest, whatever ethical and commercial precepts acceptable to other nations may be quoted in its defense. It is condemned as undemocratic, and unwarranted by the mere fact that it is made, either by arms, by proclamation, or by diplomatic correspondence. The methods and the reasons are not to the point; the thing itself is offensive and wrong, and they will have none of it. They see no more reason for the United States to undertake the alteration of Mexican government than to attempt the reformation of the government of Russia. The present current of South American thought tends strongly toward national independence for the republics individually, not only of the United States and of Europe, but of one another.

CHAPTER VI

SOCIAL OBSTACLES

INTIMATE intercourse between the peoples of the various American states, and in particular between Latin Americans as a whole and the citizens of the United States, will be an essential and fundamental factor in any close or successful bond between them. Upon it alone will depend the mutual faith and confidence which each ought to have for the other; to the extent that it is intimate and real will be the depth and verity of the common confidence. Without some such intercourse, the establishment of any kind of bond between the American republics must be problematical and temporary. Without it any administrative connection will be weak and meaningless. Without an actual acquaintanceship of citizens, all diplomatic arrangements between the republics as sovereign states will be empty and artificial forms. Democracy is a very real thing, and a democratic government over the twenty-one republics presumes the coöperation and therefore the acquaintanceship of the individual citizens.

A necessary postulate of Pan-Americanism is the legal equality of the citizens of all of the republics with one another; its unavoidable corollary is social equality. The South Americans frankly and freely discuss the mixed racial character of the various countries, and make no secret of the intermingling of the blood of the red man and of the black man with that of the white man. Mixed marriages are common with full-blooded Indians or negroes, and do not receive social reprobation of any sort. Full-blooded Indians or negroes have risen to positions of great prominence, have, indeed, been presidents of some of the states, and have occupied in the political and social life of Latin America truly significant positions. Their democracy knows nothing of race, color, or previous condition of servitude.

There can be no doubt that South America contains many people as broadly intellectual, as widely read, as highly cultivated, with as high moral standards and noble character as the average men and women in the United States. Let us not argue the question whether the ablest South Americans are the equals of the ablest men and

SOCIAL OBSTACLES

women in the United States. There can certainly be no doubt that there are many in South America who are easily the equals in every respect of those who consider themselves in the United States people of education and culture. Abroad, especially in Paris, the South Americans have no more difficulty in securing social recognition than the citizens of the United States have. Indeed, any North American who has spent any length of time in Paris has very likely had the experience of saying that he is an American, and of hearing the query, "A South American?" Unquestionably the South Americans would demand and expect the fullest possible recognition of social equality in all parts of the United States. There is no reason to-day why they should not expect it as a result of the present diplomatic relations. In particular they would expect freedom of access to hotels, theaters, trains, and public places of all sorts without so much as a whisper or a fleeting suspicion in anyone's mind that they did not belong there. Intermarriage would inevitably follow, and this, too, without thought or expectation of any loss of cast or status by either one of the contracting parties. Any other basis of intimate association than this with the South Americans is unthinkable and would be rejected by them with the scorn it would deserve.

Nevertheless, the obstacles in the way of the establishment of such social equality are undeniably great; and the obstacles in the way of its acceptance by large bodies of men and women in certain sections of the United States are indubitably greater. "Half-breeds and their descendants," says Calderon, "govern the Ibero-American democracy." "The native race, the Spanish race, and the Negro race are everywhere mingled in similar proportions." "The people of the United States hate the half-breed. . . . No manifestation of Pan-Americanism could suffice to destroy the racial prejudice as it exists north of Mexico." These temperate but determined sentences represent a feeling of almost passionate strength which usually finds expression among South Americans in anything but a restrained and judicial manner.

The color problem is indeed the most serious question open to consideration in connection with the future of that great continent; but it is not, indeed, the social equality of the various peoples which is under consideration. The real problem of South America lies in the fact that the present inhabitants are the result of the mixture of the Spanish conquerors with a native people whose cultural development had reached the period of middle barbarism only in the most advanced tribes, who were at the time of the conquest perhaps hundreds of thousands of years in development behind the oldest peoples of whom we have any record in Europe. To this mixture of the civilized white and the barbarian was added before it had fairly became a mixture a third element still more incongruous. The negroes, brought as slaves during the seventeenth and eighteenth centuries to Latin America were literally savages, and were further behind the Indian in ethnical development than the Indian was behind the white man. Of the three elements the whites were numerically the weakest, and in the natural growth of the population the whites and their descendants have not grown as rapidly as the full-blooded types. In the course of time, however the three have become intermingled beyond recognition, and there are few to-day who can prove themselves possessed of pure blood in the ordinarily accepted sense of the word. These three elements thus combined were located by the accident of history upon a tropical soil where industry was difficult, and where agriculture and surface mining were, for many, many decades, the only possible occupations. Generous nature poured before them a profusion of products suited to their needs for sustenance and deprived them of the incentive of work for the purpose of preserving life. According to American and European ideas they have not been industrious as a race, and the problem of labor is a very vital one.

The real issue, causing at present grave concern in the minds of the extremely intelligent leaders is the future of this mixed people. Have they the qualities necessary to enable them to continue indefinitely to own their own land? Are they sufficiently industrious, intelligent, and susceptible of instruction, to perform in South America, with capital borrowed from Europe, and with the aid of European or American engineers and scientists, a feat similar to that achieved by the Japanese? Unquestionably, a considerable proportion of the population has already demonstrated its possession of these qualities, but we must not forget that there are millions of people in South America who are not yet so advanced, and whose capacity and industry still remain open to question. This section of the population is poor, densely ignorant, superstitious, and apparently lacks any disposition of its own toward the accumulation of information, wealth, or cultivation. They are satisfied with what they have; the natural produce of the country suffices for their simple wants and they are unconscious of their own deficiencies judged by other standards. They do not conceive any useful purpose in hard labor and unremitting toil for the acquisition of wealth which they would not know how to spend and whose mere possession would not give them satisfaction. A large proportion of this section of the population are full-blooded Indians, and a considerable number are full-blooded negroes. In the interior regions, still almost unexplored, are a good many hundred thousand savages whose number and condition is a matter of conjecture. Although the one may not be large, the other is in all probability such that it will increase the difficulty of existing problems.

Can this apparently inert population be roused to actual efficiency? Are the more developed really capable of grappling with this stupendous problem of the less developed? Have they the necessary qualifications of leadership as well as the indispensable information and powers of analysis? Have they the practical organizing capacity, the disillusionizing common sense that solves great practical issues and reaches the bottom of vital problems? If South America is to continue in the hands of South Americans for the next century, the people now living in South America and their descendants must show some of these qualities. The leaders already realize that political independence will be only nominal until economic and intellectual development has reached a point which makes the South American states equals in every respect to the great communities in Europe. Equality must be a reality, or independence, real independence, and the actual control of the future and destiny of those peoples will always be in question.

Thus the social problem underlies all others and looms portentous upon the political and economic horizon. They see the fate of the Indian in the United States: the continued dispossession, the lack of social equality of Indians as Indians (except for the few individuals), the lack of legal status, the certainty that the Indian people as a race is about to disappear as the individuals now composing it are slowly absorbed into the community of the whites. The Indian himself has never shown at any time in the United States a capacity of organization sufficient to make effective resistance. Communities like the Creeks and Cherokees, who were certainly as highly trained in agriculture and industry, as capable in organization and administration as the vast majority in many South American states, were unable to resist the steady pressure of the white man's superior development and capacity, and lost little by little their identity and national existence as well as their national independence. As Indians, they are gone. The Cherokee Nation is no more. When the Latin Americans see the great waves of European and Asiatic immigration rolling toward their shores, when they view the communities already founded, their scorn for the half-breed's methods, their readiness to dispossess him and take his land, their belief that they will one day rule him in the person of their descendants, they are apprehensive lest it portend the beginning in Latin America of that same process now almost complete in the United States. They are considering restrictions on immigration, the possibility of erecting a political barrier that will exclude the white man, or at any rate retard this process. Whether or not Latin America can attain this reality of racial independence and perpetuate its present political independence will depend upon the extent to which as a whole they possess the racial qualities essential to the formation and maintenance of strong, efficient governments, capable of peaceful administration, and also to the development of their economic resources by their own labor and intelligence. In particular the future demands leadership from those South

Americans who have already attained individually to European standards of efficiency and culture. If they can solve these problems, if, in particular, they can energize the great bulk of the population, they will be able in time to make real this vision of South American independence, this hope of South American democracy, this dream of a South America for South Americans; states which will be powerful, wealthy, cultured, and respected in the Congress of Nations.

They see in the refusal of the United States to recognize their racial capacity and social equality the evidence of a disposition on the part of the United States to interfere with this process before it is well begun. The claims for intervention to preserve stable government, the insistence upon a need for outside help in administration and finance, is to them the denial of the capacity of the more intelligent and educated to grapple successfully with this problem. They fear the intention of the United States to take the problem from their hands and repeat in Central and South America in due time that dread process, slow as the limping foot of time, sure as the coming of death, which spells the racial and national annihilation of these halfbreeds. They resent passionately the very notion that they are incapable of solving their own problems. They are furious that the United States should be unwilling to allow them to try to solve their own problems and should not have faith and confidence that time and experience might teach them to deal successfully with them. Mr. Wilson's attitude toward Mexico they understand and admire. It means for the first time the handing over of the problem to the natives of the country for them to settle, even although they regard as regrettable Mr. Wilson's statement that the settlement must eventually accord with American concepts of business, order, and efficiency.

All of these things then, the social problem connotes to the Latin American of intelligence. The racial prejudice against half-breeds in the United States connotes the same fears. Nor is it certain that this social line in the United States is not a most tangible obstacle in the way of convincing the Latin American that we do not intend aggression and conquest.

It is, therefore, thoroughly unfortunate that any attempt to create a closer bond of Pan-Americanism should lead at once to claims of social equality which it would be fatal for us to deny, and which it would be almost equally ruinous to grant. How could we logically continue to maintain the present social barrier in the United States against the negro and the Indian? There have been numerous instances where individuals of both races have received under certain circumstances public and distinguished consideration; there are even parts of the country where something approaching social equality for all exists; but there can be no doubt that there is a feeling as wide-spread as the country that it would not be advisable to invite a negro or an Indian to dine in a conventional way, nor desirable to marry him to one's daughter. These are the vital things. To tolerate negroes and Indians in hotels, theaters, and sleeping-cars is a very slight concession, although one which is yet to be obtained in broad areas of the United States; but actual social intercourse on precisely the same plane with white people, and, chiefest of all, intermarriage; these are not seriously contemplated anywhere in the United States, while the mere suggestion arouses in the South and West passionate aversion. The social position of negroes and Indians of culture and intelligence is already difficult; it would become unendurable the moment Pan-Americanism became a reality. Its flagrant inconsistency with our own democratic and social premises would become so patent that it could not be maintained in decency after actual equality had been conceded to the Latin Americans. It is highly probable that an actual majority of the people of the United States would reject any closer union with Latin America, if they once clearly understood that it involved beyond doubt or question the granting of social as well as legal equality to Indians and negroes in the United States. It is only too clear that any closer union would be unanimously rejected south of the Rio Grande which did not provide the most explicit pledges of social equality. Indeed, before any sort of organic connection becomes possible, real demonstrations of social equality for Latin Americans, proving that they are actually accepted as equals in the United States, would be expected and sought by the leaders. If we have the slightest impartiality or candor as students, we shall recognize that they would be foolish even to contemplate anything less.

How far we are from actual union with Latin America, from coöperation based upon mutual trust, confidence, acquaintanceship should be patent to the least informed. Those to whom these considerations are new can scarcely conceive how hollow and vain the talk of close association sounds to those who have long known these facts. While such a social barrier exists, faith, confidence, respect, mutual credit in each other's protestations seem difficult to predicate. The Latin Americans see it, however, as a corollary of the great premise that the world is made for the white man, and that only white men are truly civilized or able to help the darker races toward civilization, or capable of assuming their guardianship through the long generations while they are being transformed into the white man's image. That the red man and the black man do not desire transformation seems never to have occurred to the white man, nor do their protestations and resistance usually avail. The time is at hand when those races in the world which are not white are about to challenge these claims of the white man and question their justice and ethics from the vantage ground of the white man's own premises of democracy. They see in the white man's country multitudes of unsolved problems, combining sorrow, cruelty, want, and ignorance. If the premises of democracy and of the white man's logic confer upon him the right to solve those problems in his own country and to exclude the interference of others, simply because the country is his and because he ought for that reason to solve problems,—they fail to understand how

SOCIAL OBSTACLES

that same logic can vest in the white man not only a right but a bounden duty to interfere in their country for a solution of those same problems. Why should the white man deny a social equality to the red man, and the yellow man, and the black man, while he refuses them the right to deny him equality in their country? It is the premises and not the conclusions upon which we differ from the Latin Americans; upon things that are as indelible and impossible to change or conceal as race, color, and previous condition of servitude.

CHAPTER VII

DEFENSIVE WEAKNESS

WHAT now of Pan-Americanism as a solution of the problems which the republics in the Western Hemisphere will have to meet when Europe's victor appears? Would a Pan-American union bar his progress and foil his designs? Would a simple defensive alliance between the United States and the Latin republics accomplish the same end? It will surely be important for us to cast aside at this stage of our inquiry hypotheses and expectations, to consider only what seem to be veritable facts, and to estimate the probable success of such a joint attempt to defend the Western Hemisphere from European aggression. If we can show that the United States and Latin America may by their joint efforts conceivably shield each other from the conqueror, and achieve in concert what neither could have hoped to accomplish alone, we shall demonstrate something of the very first importance.

DEFENSIVE WEAKNESS

We shall prove something of equal significance, if it becomes probable or even possible that the joint efforts of the republics would not be likely to resist the victor with success.

Edward Everett Hale struck the keynote of the Pan-American situation in a phrase intended for a very different purpose: "No one ever heard of a man shouldering his musket to defend his boarding-house." To arouse individuals to self-sacrifice and lead them forth coolly to face death, there must be some object to defend precious beyond the need of explanation or exhortation. Even if we assume the possession of entirely adequate force by the nations in the Western Hemisphere to resist the victor, united action would still be exceedingly problematical, because the United States and the Latin republics lack a mutual interest to defend. The weakness of Pan-Americanism as a supposed solution of future difficulties lies in the almost certain impossibility of securing the coöperation for any such object.

It is a fallacy of the first importance to suppose that Latin America needs our protection: its political independence is not threatened by Europe because the motive for conquest is almost entirely lacking. If generations in England have deemed it inadvisable to make any attempt to secure dominion by a conquest requiring the use in a distant continent of a large European army, Germany has even more vital objections to such a policy for her position between France and Russia makes dangerous in the extreme the dispatching of any considerable force from the Fatherland. Nor would the conquest of South America be possible without the use of a truly huge army. Its defensive strength is great, not only because of its size, but because the lack of communication at all suitable for military needs between its various entities and between the coast and the interior would make a series of campaigns, rather than a single campaign, an absolute necessity. To subdue one state would be eminently possible; to subdue a group of states would require military operations of the most serious description; the continent would have to be conquered piecemeal. Even if we estimate the military ability of Latin America at the minimum and take little account of its fierce determination to preserve its independence, we shall be compelled to admit that conquest is so difficult as to be almost beyond the resources of even a first-class European power.

Latin America, however, is already lost! It has been in England's hands for nearly a century, and, far from regretting the circumstance, has

DEFENSIVE WEAKNESS

found the connection profitable and one desirable to continue. All the republics know thoroughly well that England cherishes no designs against their political independence; they believe Germany to be also without intention to conquer them or even to invade them; they fear colonization but have no other reason to dread a closer economic connection with England or Germany. Their interests are the same as those of the Europeans and so long as neither conquest nor colonization is involved, the advantages are mutual beyond dispute.

It would not be wise at this great crisis for us to deny or indeed to fail to recognize frankly the Latin-American belief that the real enemy against whom they need protection and of whose political domination they are certainly afraid is the United States. They would consider the weakening of the position of the United States in the Western Hemisphere at the hands of Europe's victor far from detrimental to them, because the present arrangement between the United States and England, by which the United States has actual control of the Gulf of Mexico, has been almost their only reason for grave apprehension. If the result of the present war should be the expulsion of the United States from their waters, there would be few serious thinkers south of the Rio Grande who would not regard the change as *prima facie* beneficial.

The second danger of which they are vividly conscious lies in the possibility of the creation by the United States of some artificial situation which would either exclude Europeans from the Latin-American trade in favor of Americans, or which would in some way make intercourse with Europe more difficult. The Monroe Doctrine they are well aware was aimed originally at England rather than at Spain and is still supposed to portend the continued supremacy of the United States in the Western Hemisphere and the right actually to exclude Europeans. If such be its meaning, its maintenance or enforcement would not be to the best interests of Latin America. Inasmuch as the present supremacy of the United States and its claim of paramount interest over European nations in the Western Hemisphere will be the factor really threatened by the victor, the interests of South America are identical with those of European nations and are therefore not threatened. Indeed an alliance with the United States against Europe's victor would be an alliance intended to maintain and preserve the very situation which the Latin Americans consider least desirable and

DEFENSIVE WEAKNESS

whose continued existence is their chief source of anxiety.

Not less deadly to coöperation between Latin America and the United States than this divergence of interests is the lack of mutual confidence. The fear in the southern countries of aggression from North America would vitally hamper any defensive armament or any concerted action. They would surely fear that the defeat of the victor by combined effort would so strengthen the United States as to put the whole Western Hemisphere permanently in her hands and make possible the schemes of aggression which they believe have been thwarted hitherto by the protection of England. Our pacific intentions proclaimed by certain presidents and diplomats arouse interest but not credulity. They see too clearly what we could do to be willing to credit the supposition that if circumstances should ever permit, we would not embrace the opportunity. This lack of mutual confidence would make doubtful the formation even of a defensive alliance, while the difficulties in the way of legal and administrative efficiency would make any closer bond too weak to be of value for defense. When it is so highly improbable that a Pan-American Confederation would be able to hold itself together and govern its own largest members, where shall we suppose it would find the necessary strength and efficiency to protect itself and its members from European invasion? If a confederation should be formed between the United States and the Latin republics, it would be an artificial unit with so slender a basis that it could hardly survive a clash of interests or the shock of attack.

These formidable obstacles make the defense of the Western Hemisphere by joint effort against the European victor improbable. It remains for us to ask whether such a defense is possible from a military and naval point of view. The control of the sea would undoubtedly be indispensable. Until the combined navies were prepared to maintain intercourse by water between the members of the Confederation, or between the various members of a defensive alliance, defense would be out of the question. The strategic weakness of the position is apparent and alarming. Thousands of miles of coast must be patrolled, the great commercial centers, whose defense would be imperative against action by hostile fleets, are separated from each other by distances so great that they could not be protected by a single fleet. New York is farther in point of time from the Amazon and the Amazon in turn from the Rio de la Plata than the

United States is from Europe. It is hardly credible even that a single fleet could defend Galveston, Panama, and the Amazon. It certainly could not do so while England held the Bahamas, the Bermudas, the Windward Islands, Jamaica, Trinidad, and Barbados. These points alone control all the water routes, and a very strong fleet would be needed to take them or to check the operations of a comparatively few commerce destroyers from such bases.

We should have to maintain three fleets, each large enough to dispose successfully of any forces likely to be dispatched from Europe: one off the United States plying between New York and the Chesapeake; one in the Gulf of Mexico; and one in the South Atlantic. Another enormous fleet, large enough to control the whole Atlantic in actual fact and patrol it effectively from one end to the other, would be needed in addition. Coöperation between them in case of attack would be literally impossible; the victor could reach any of them from Europe in practically the same time that assistance could reach them from the other fleets.

At present there is no such fleet in existence and scarcely more than a basis for one of such size, since our navy, even if we assume its defenders' statements to be true, is barely sufficient to protect the United States. Nor are the facilities on either continent adequate for building so large a fleet in time to be of any avail. Even if it could be done, only the United States could build it, and by whatever name it was called it would be none the less in reality the United States fleet and would have to be manned in all probability by Americans. The Latin Americans would be more afraid of it than of the combined English and German navies, because they believe we have a motive to use a fleet against them which they do not believe either the Germans or the English possess. Indeed they very much prefer that the supremacy on the sea should remain where it is, and, if lost by England, should pass to any other nation than the United States. To allay such suspicions by the creation of a unit to be owned by the various republics and stationed at times of peace in their harbors, would create a fleet of no use in time of war because the distance between the various points is so great as to preclude prompt coöperation. Even should the United States and certain groups of the Latin republics create separate fleets, the suspicions of the intentions of the United States would still remain and the superior naval ability of the Americans would still arouse apprehension

DEFENSIVE WEAKNESS

and in time lead to quarrels and war. No candid student can fail to conclude that the United States is not now in a position to protect South America against European fleets and possesses at present no facilities adequate for creating a navy large enough to perform the task.

Could the United States army protect South America from invasion by European armies? We are supposing, of course, that the fleet has failed to keep the Europeans at a distance. The difficulty of the military defense of South America against invasion is similar to the defense of the Atlantic Ocean. A strategic position controlling the whole continent is entirely lacking; the districts needing defense are widely separated; and the overland communications are so inadequate for military needs that armies located at certain centers would be incapable of movement to other points, in time to prevent a successful invasion by European contingents landed by the fleet controlling the sea. The facility with which the aggressor could shift his attack would seem to make the defence of Latin America by an American army out of the question, even if we assume that there was such an army and that it could be sent to South America in time. In addition, we should have to face a problem of maintaining an army in the southern continent quite as difficult as that before the invader, because the distance by sea to the principal South American centers from our own chief ports is practically the same as from the great European ports. The distance by land through Central America is much greater and the difficulty of maintaining an army overland would be enormous even if there were all-rail communications between the two continents. Without such communications, our lack of control on the sea would spell our inability to place an army in South America, or to maintain or re-enforce it, if by good fortune we should land it there. Nor must we forget that we are not a military nation, and not being prepared to manufacture munitions of war at the rate which modern warfare demands, we should not be able to maintain an army, because we should not be able to make the needed supplies fast enough.

Needless to say, no adequate army at present exists for the defense of Pan-Americanism. The United States army is small; the South American armies are not much larger; the quality of all is much in dispute. While the United States army technically numbers about eighty thousand men, its most ardent advocates are able to demonstrate the existence of only about forty thousand—a

DEFENSIVE WEAKNESS

single army corps—which would be available for defense against invasion in the United States or for dispatch to South America. There is grave doubt expressed even by the defenders of the army's efficiency, of the adequacy of its equipment, of its artillery, and of its supplies of ammunition. Sincere and honest men who have at least no obvious prejudice make no secret of their opinion that it is not at all what it should be, while the more radical are apt to deny it any efficiency at all. These disputes however have little relation to the real issue we are discussing. Adequacy is determined, not by the quality of the force, but by the requirements of the operation. A hundred thousand excellent troops are of no avail at all where a million are necessary. The lowest figures cited by military students for an army to defend the United States is half a million. If there is any question at all as to our ability to equip and maintain indefinitely one hundred thousand men, it will be entirely obvious that we are not in the least prepared to equip and maintain half a million men. Nor should we forget that the defense of Pan-Americanism against invasion will mean the maintenance at a number of points of a force of men amply large enough to meet any forces which an invader might attempt to land,

and that no invader would probably consider coming with a force as small as one hundred thousand men. When we cannot protect ourselves, how shall we also defend Latin America?

Conquest by a European aggressor, it seems more than probable, none of the American republics need fear, though South America is much more nearly immune than is the United States. Invasion is beyond doubt a physical possibility for a first-class European power as there are at present neither naval nor military forces in North or South America adequate in size to prevent it. There are many reasons to suppose that European aggression against the United States may be undertaken to put an end for a generation at least to any chance of American expansion in Latin America. Far from its being true that Pan-Americanism is in danger from Europe, the probabilities seem to indicate that it is the United States which is about to be assailed by Europe in the interests of Latin America. Such are the ideas which convince the Latin Americans that our claim to defend them from European aggression is *prima facie* an excuse for aggression on our own part.

CHAPTER VIII

THE FUTURE OF PAN-AMERICANISM

IT is difficult for an impartial student, who studies honestly the facts of the situation without purposes of his own to subserve, to see that Pan-Americanism has a future. Beyond all question it has had no past existence and is not a present reality. If we now conclude that it has no future, we must declare it a dream or a nightmare, a vision of peaceful associations or of crude barbarian conquest according as our fundamental premises direct. The postulates which were laid down in a previous chapter would seem to be reasonable, conservative, and inevitable. Pan-Americanism assumes at least the geographical proximity of the two American continents and their apparent isolation from Europe, with mutual interests between them and a divergence of interests with Europe. Only from such broad geographic and economic features can a closer bond of any sort derive strength. For America thus to declare and insist upon its independence from Europe predicates as well the self-sufficiency of the Western Hemisphere and its political and economic independence of Europe. It does not necessarily connote absolute isolation or the refusal to trade with Europe, but an ability to dispense with the European connection should it become advisable or expedient in time of war. Not less important would be mutual trust and confidence between the various American states, with its roots deep in mutual intercourse and association. The purpose of a closer union would be the need for mutual aid and protection against Europe (for against Europe Pan-Americanism is directed), and the probability that the American states would be able to furnish each other from their own resources the military or naval strength to make good their independence of Europe, should it be questioned in arms.

Unless we are grievously misled by Latin Americans themselves, as well as by foreign observers, none of these prerequisites exist, and without them, he will be indeed a bold man who will suppose that any sort of a connection worthy of the name can be established. The weakest conceivable relation —a defensive military and naval understanding between the sovereign republics as sovereign

THE FUTURE OF PAN-AMERICANISM

states without administrative relations of any sort —predicates mutual confidence and a mutual need for protection. Neither exists. The weakest economic and financial bond—a customs or fiscal union of some sort providing for freedom of trade and a uniformity of currency, weights, and measures—would rest upon the belief that the commercial relations between the American states were more important to them than their relations with Europe. The contrary seems to be the truth. A Pan-American Court for business disputes, requiring a compromise between the legal precepts of the southern continent and those of the United States, would be a possibility, but could hardly be efficient, strong, or popular without a greater degree of mutual understanding and acquaintanceship than seems to exist. A Pan-American confederation and administrative bond between sovereign states, with something approaching a federal executive and possibly a legislature, can be real, only as the expression in institutional life of a mutuality of economic interests and an identity of political ideas, of a mutual confidence and an identity of policy. None of these exist. In short, not one of these conceptions from the slightest to the more elaborate seems based upon realities. On the contrary, Pan-Americanism is likely to impress an impartial mind as an absolutely artificial and sentimental concept, diametrically opposed to the racial, economic, political, legal, and social interests of the American republics. A concept so contrary to all the fundamental factors in the situation on whose existence all observers quite agree, an ideal which so clearly lacks an adequate motive in its own fundamental assumptions, demonstrates to the South Americans very convincingly that the advocacy of Pan-Americanism is intended to further the aggressive schemes of the United States by clothing them in so gracious and idealistic a form.

The day is at hand when the Latin American republics will challenge Pan-Americanism, the Monroe Doctrine, and the assumption by the United States of the supremacy of the Western Hemisphere. As soon as a convenient occasion offers, some public manifestation of this intention will appear. The movement is sweeping and inclusive. It will deny that there is any such thing as the rightful supremacy of the Western Hemisphere; it will deny the United States any greater interests, any more significant position, any broader rights, or any more extended privilege than the smallest Central American republic. Equality for all independent nations in the West-

THE FUTURE OF PAN-AMERICANISM

ern Hemisphere, the economic and political equality of European powers and of all American powers will be proclaimed as the true doctrine of Pan-Americanism. It will place the assumption of supremacy or of paramount interests in the Western Hemisphere by any one of the resident powers on the same basis and subject to the same obloquy and scorn as the advancement of a similar claim by one of the European powers. It will demand recognition of the salient features of the situation as they really are and insist upon the acceptance of political and economic postulates based upon them, instead of upon economic and political phenomena of the past which have been obsolete for generations. There seems to be at present no essential reason why the same sort of relationship should not prevail between the republics in the Western Hemisphere as obtain between those same states and European nations. There are no fundamental obstacles in the way of the creation and acceptance of an identity of relations which do not exist between European nations; there are present all the fundamental factors of international association upon which rest the diplomatic intercourse of the great powers themselves. In Latin America, Pan-Americanism stands for equality in the Western Hemisphere, not for supremacy; it stands for the inter-relationship of the American states with each other and with European states on the same basis; it predicates no supremacy for one but the independence of all, not the paramount interests of one, but complementary interests in all. So far as the other is concerned, each should become foreign territory and stand upon the same political, diplomatic, and economic footing as the great powers in their relations with one another.

Future alliances in Latin America are not likely to include all the republics within one administrative or fiscal bond and still less within a single military alliance. Several confederations are more probable than one and the continuance of the present political independence of all is more probable than either contingency. If any closer relationship should be established between the Latin American republics and some other power, it will not be inter-continental but international; its basis will not be a geographical assumption or the accident of historical discovery and colonization, but the strong racial, temperamental, and administrative ties binding South and Central America to the Latin races in Europe—Spain, Portugal, Italy, and France. With them an economic bond would be also far more mutual than any alliance with the United States could conceivably be, although at

THE FUTURE OF PAN-AMERICANISM

present the closest economic ties are those with England and Germany. Political conquest by European nations of South America is as remote as the conquest of the United States. Immigration from Europe is as probable and will very likely be as potent in its effect upon the southern continent as has been European immigration in the United States. The real conquest indeed which South and Central America have to fear is the steady influx of alien blood, institutions, language, and interests, which slowly but surely may dominate the existing peoples, their ideals and governmental methods by reason of their greater virility, and create a new South America in which the descendants of the present population might conceivably be robbed of all direction, so that their imprint upon the country and its habits of thought would be erased.

BOOK IV
THE FUTURE

The Future

CHAPTER I

CONCRETE ISSUES

AT present four concrete problems or groups of problems face the American people.[1] First and foremost, we must take into consideration the entire control of the ocean highways to the United States by a European power and the complete dependence of the foreign trade of the United States upon foreign merchant marines. This is the natural effect, the inevitable

[1] The author wishes to remind his readers that he is dealing in the Fourth Book, "The Future," with possibilities and probabilities, and is attempting to balance against each other the more plausible and important solutions suggested. He is not to be understood as in any sense advocating one rather than another. In particular, he disclaims any attempt to represent his own views. In these as in other chapters, many statements, if isolated and compared with similarly isolated fragments from earlier chapters, will appear contradictory unless the student carefully remembers that they are intended to represent the contradictory views held by different sections of the community.

legacy of the supremacy of the sea. It is now necessary for us to ask whether this is desirable. Should we view its continuance with favor and regard with complacency our dependence, for our contact with the rest of the world and with the rest of the Western Hemisphere, upon the good will of some European nation? Should we calculate literally that its forbearance or its own peculiar interests and the complications of international politics together with the strength of the strategic position of the United States would counsel it to extend our privileges to the point of freedom of trade? Will a change in the mistress of the seas, a shifting of the balance of power in Europe, and the rise of new and powerful economic entities in Europe change the policy of the nation controlling the sea to our detriment? If we decide that our dependence and existence by the sufferance and good will of some foreign nation is either undesirable or inexpedient, the prerequisites of substantial independence of all nations will be a subject of the utmost moment. The type of preparedness which it would involve, the extent of armament required should war become inevitable,—these will be more than merely interesting subjects.

If on the other hand it seems for any reason whatever desirable to depend upon the present connection or relationship, will it be expedient for us to raise, with insistence, questions that may imperil our cordial relations with the sea-power, and shall we continue to espouse policies in direct contravention to its well-known precepts and interests? The consequences, if we act in this manner, we must carefully appreciate. Nor must we forget that the supremacy of the Pacific affects us as well as the supremacy of the Atlantic and of the Gulf of Mexico. Should a German victory throw the one into the hands of Germany, the other will unquestionably fall into the hands of Japan, and the tensity of our present relations with that nation will then force us to ask whether we are now in a position to maintain our present contentions with Japan the moment she becomes mistress of the Pacific. Will not a new policy in the far East become imperative, at the sacrifice of consistency and even of existing interests?

We have long claimed the supremacy of the Western Hemisphere and have predicated our paramount interests in it as against any European power, but our claim has not yet been admitted in Europe and in South America and is more than likely to be challenged in the near future by both. If either or both raise the question of the validity of such an interpretation of the Monroe Doctrine, can we maintain it? Is it desirable or expedient that we should do so? Assuming that we might attain the actual supremacy of the Western Hemisphere, does a paramount interest exist which makes such action essential or desirable?

The third issue which we have to face is that of imperialism, of expansion in the Western Hemisphere, of the maintenance of the Monroe Doctrine in the sense of policing the Gulf of Mexico and the smaller Latin-American countries. If we assume this is just, can we also prove that it is expedient? If we believe that it is consonant with their interests, can we also show that it accords with our own? Indeed, it will be imperative for us to ask ourselves whether we have national ambitions for the acquisition of territory outside the present continental limitations of the United States and to reach some conclusion as to the object of acquiring such territory, of the likelihood of opposition, and of our ability to meet it successfully.

In the imperialist problem of the far East lies the fourth question for decision. Are the Philippines the key to the open door of the Eastern trade? Shall we defend them if they are assailed, not out of any love for the Filipinos, not with any notion that they are commercially profitable

CONCRETE ISSUES

to the Government or to us as individuals, but because their strategic position makes us a far Eastern power and gives us a position, if not a right, from which to defend and promote our economic interests in China? If we decide to exclude the Japanese from the United States, will it not affect our relations in the far East? Shall we ask full privileges in Japan for Americans and deny the Japanese similar privileges in the United States? Will not our ambitions in Asia, provided we have them, dictate our treatment of Asiatics in the United States?

These problems—an independent position on the sea, the supremacy of the Western Hemisphere, imperialism in Asia—are neither complementary nor entirely consistent unless we maintain a strong affirmative, and therefore an aggressive, position upon all of them. We cannot expect to maintain our supremacy in the Western Hemisphere and continue to depend upon some European power for the use of its merchant marine; we cannot hope to play an important part in Asia unless we are within measurable distance of controlling the Pacific; we can scarcely expect to acquire territory in the Gulf of Mexico without meeting opposition and without sacrificing the ideals of Pan-Americanism.

PAN-AMERICANISM

Inevitably, one and all reduce themselves to the question of armament. If certain policies are desirable, if certain objects are to be attained, if we cherish certain ambitions, extensive armament will be a prerequisite of their consummation. The non-military character of our organization, our traditional policy of peace, and our dislike of aggression must be carefully considered in relation to these four problems. If we shall decide against extensive armament, it will be, so far as these problems are concerned, equivalent to a decision for disarmament. Inadequate force will be the same as no force at all; the expenditure of a thousand dollars is sheer waste when a million is necessary.

CHAPTER II

THE PREREQUISITES OF INDEPENDENCE

THAT American goods should be carried in American ships and protected by a strong United States navy is a proposition unlikely to be disputed but nevertheless one which we must examine rather closely before answering categorically. If patriotism seems to counsel an affirmative reply, discretion and expediency, with economic advantages in mind, may argue in the negative. Nor will a decision that must be advanced at all costs prove by any means that the prerequisites of its attainment are within our power.

The ethics of independence are literally those of self-defense: the unassailable right of every nation to control the factors essential to its territorial integrity, its economic prosperity, and its international status. As against other communities the interests of the United States must be supreme and of this principle we can admit no contraven-

PAN-AMERICANISM

tion. Our national interests and in particular our national honor can never make anything less than independence a fact to be regarded by the American people with complacency and satisfaction.

The economic desirability of independence is by no means to-day a matter of assumption. Since the United States became an integral part of the interdependent international economic fabric, its access to the markets of the world is not merely desirable, nor in the least something permissive, but an economic necessity imperative for our welfare. On the assumption of the continuance of intercourse our whole economic fabric is built. We definitely depend upon the sale of our products and manufactured goods to other nations and are as thoroughly dependent for our physical existence upon the prompt return of their commodities. This fact has changed in all its more important aspects the relations of the power in control of the sea to other nations. In the past, England found a great navy the bulwark of her existence because it protected the imports of food and raw materials upon which her national existence depended. Other nations were able to acquiesce in her supremacy because their importations were by no means as essential to

THE PREREQUISITES OF INDEPENDENCE

their own welfare. While it is still true that England draws from foreign sources a larger proportion of her maintenance than other nations, it is no longer true that her prosperity is more dependent than that of others upon freedom of access to the world's markets. The difference is now one in degree rather than in kind and is apparent rather than substantive. The Germans have built a large merchant marine and have created a great fleet for the express purpose of holding in their own hands factors able to establish that continued contact with the markets of the world which is to-day the paramount interest of Germany. Advisedly, she has decided that independence of the sea-power is indispensable. This change in the situation may prevent other nations from conceding longer England's paramount interest in the sea and lead them to insist that all nations now possess the same interest in freedom of intercourse, even though it may differ in degree. Freedom of access to the world's markets beyond the possibility of interference by any nation may become an international premise.

The economic results to the United States of independence of the sea-power are therefore clear. It would provide for the continuance of our contact with the international market upon which depends our prosperity. The profits of freight, brokerage, and insurance, which now are paid to England, would come to us. It would free American trade from all the influence of alterations in European alliances and from the effects of political and military events in Europe, placing us beyond that inevitable influence, which all such events exert to-day upon international markets and the world's trade. From arbitrary interference of any kind it would deliver us. We would be able to compel others to accord our interests the same attention they would expect all nations of equal wealth and international standing to accord their own. It would assure beyond cavil our international economic status and privileges.

Nor are the economic gains of independence by any means those of greatest interest to us in this inquiry. Independence of the sea-power is in itself a prerequisite of independent action by the United States in foreign affairs, a prerequisite of territorial expansion, of imperialism, of Pan-Americanism, and indeed of any clash with Europe's victor into which we entered with reasonable expectation of a successful issue. Until we are free from the English merchant fleet and from the control of all the approaches to the Western Hemisphere by the English navy, we shall not be able to act in foreign affairs contrary to the policies and interests of the sea-power without immediately entailing upon ourselves an economic crisis of the first magnitude. To attempt independent action in diplomacy before we take control of the sea in earnest will actually compel the sea-power, whether in the hands of England or Germany, to destroy our commerce with the rest of the world, and ruin our economic fabric. Independence is not a commercial problem alone but a question of international status. Yet in the last analysis the desirability of our complete independence of the sea-power involves the probable cost not only of winning it but of retaining it, as well as the desirability of independent action in foreign affairs and the probability of our desire to prosecute policies contrary to the interests of the power likely to control the seas. If policies contrary to the past or present interests of the sea-power are essential to our future prosperity, independence will become a fundamental prerequisite of our policy. If the ends we must subserve are practically identical with those of the sea-power, an alliance with it will secure them.

The first prerequisite of independence is not at all a merchant marine, but an adequate merchant marine,—one large enough to render us independent in fact of the world itself, one considerable enough to carry the whole of our exports and imports in time of war, when the belligerent status of part of the world's fleets might otherwise deprive us of our necessary contact. In other words we must gauge the essentials of independence not by the requirements necessary to cope with normal conditions but with those imperative in handling any abnormal situation which might arise. When we speak of independence therefore we are talking less of existing facts than of possibilities.

The second essential is a system of exchange in the hands of American bankers, providing not only adequate exchange facilities with Europe but the establishment in all parts of the world of such branch banks as are needed to deal without question with the entire volume of American trade. At present, like most countries, we are largely dependent upon London exchange, and through London our business with all the less developed parts of the world is done. No independence can be real until we are freed absolutely from this situation. Nor is this demand to be satisfied by the creation of agencies which merely make direct exchange with all parts of the world possible. The facilities provided must be such as to make

THE PREREQUISITES OF INDEPENDENCE

direct exchange profitable and desirable, not only for American merchants but for their foreign customers.

The third indispensable prerequisite is the control of the ocean highways by the United States fleet, so that our contact with Europe and the Mediterranean, our control of the Panama Canal, our trade in South America, and our commerce with the far East and the Islands of the East, is assured beyond peradventure. Here however we are not able to measure the means and methods necessary to secure independence by calculations based upon the probable exigencies of our own polity. While the European situation retains its present characteristics, the power controlling the sea will consider its authority a domestic necessity of primary importance and will never maintain it purely for the sake of controlling the approaches to the United States or of dictating to us our relationship with other nations. It will be necessary for us to realize that when we challenge it in our own interests we raise the much larger issue of the national integrity of the sea-power and its domestic defenses against European aggression. For Germany this is no more a purely international issue than it is for England; both regard it as a domestic issue of the very first consequence. We must prepare to assail the means England has taken to protect her international status and her actual existence, not merely her dispositions for patrolling the Atlantic or her fleet in American waters; to challenge her control of our approaches will at once raise the issue of her supremacy anywhere, even in the English Channel. To build a fleet large enough to conquer the European power in control of the sea may not be necessary, but we must have a fleet at least large enough to threaten its existence by making a battle too dangerous to be accepted. Undoubtedly this will mean a very large fleet of high efficiency.

England will object almost as vitally to a great American merchant marine. Her notion of an adequate merchant marine for herself is based upon the number of ships needed in time of war to carry the supplies on which she depends. In other words, her merchant marine must be placed in time of peace on a war footing and requires for its support in time of peace a very great volume of freight for transport. So large a merchant marine cannot be maintained by subsidies and the nation can afford to own it only as long as it sustains itself. Inasmuch as the amount of trade in the world at any one time is more or less

THE PREREQUISITES OF INDEPENDENCE

limited, the English must secure an abnormal amount of ocean commerce to keep their merchant marine on this war footing in time of peace. The prosperity of her fleet and therefore its existence is immediately threatened by the creation of other great fleets which rob her own of its livelihood by taking from it a part of the world's carrying trade. As the English fleet already conveys the bulk of the world's trade, the creation of any other merchant marine is certain to affect its profits, and if to the German fleet is added a great American merchant fleet, a serious crisis will result for English shipping of a nature which the sea-power can solve only by aggressive action.

An army is absolutely essential to prevent the existing sea-power from putting undue pressure upon us while our own fleets are building. If England or Germany invades us with an army they can of course take possession of that which the sea-power is intended to protect, the country itself. Unless we are ready to defend ourselves on land, we can be periodically compelled to sacrifice everything gained on the sea in order to rid ourselves of the invading army. Independence cannot therefore be attempted without the creation at home of an army large enough to render a successful invasion of the country so problematical

PAN-AMERICANISM

that no European power will attempt it. We do not wish to fight, but under the circumstances we can avoid fighting only by making it more dangerous to the aggressor than a victory will be worth. An army of less than half a million men will be entirely inadequate, and only circumstances can show whether a half-million men, thoroughly trained and elaborately equipped, will be sufficient to make us immune.

Let us not evade the real issue by needless quibbling. Under present circumstances an attempt by the United States to ensure its independence of the sea-power involves an attack upon England and an extensive alteration in England's present position in the world; nor will the situation be strikingly different should Germany take England's place. Whatever our purpose, whatever its justification, we shall still be adopting a policy whose results for other nations cannot fail to be interpreted as aggression. From them we shall be attempting to take something which they now have—a circumstance which will go far to close their ears to any arguments tending to prove that they never should have had it and that they possess at the present day no right to it. The fact will still remain—they are losing something and we are getting it. To them it will be aggression and

THE PREREQUISITES OF INDEPENDENCE

with it they will deal accordingly. However just therefore or expedient independence may be for us, we must not forget that it will practically involve us in military and naval measures essentially identical with a lively aggressive attack upon the power in control of the sea. If we hesitate before adopting a policy which is aggression even in appearance, or to maintain it with the utmost determination by extensive military and naval measures, we shall do well to refrain from talking of the desirability of independence. It is to be secured and maintained in no other way, once we have won it.

The difference between security and independence is almost as great as the distance between the antipodes. For security we ask merely a probable safety from actual violence, and it does not make a great deal of difference to us whether our security rests upon arms or upon strategic factors in our own or the European situation. That we are not in actual present danger of violent conquest suffices. For independence on the other hand, it is scarcely enough to be certain beyond any reasonable doubt that we can resist any possible assault which can be delivered. All eventualities and possibilities become of importance and we must prepare for all as if they were actually upon us. In providing for security we may eliminate everything beyond the clearest probabilities; in preparing for independence we must make ready to meet even the remotest possibilities. In the one, we shall be satisfied if we can avoid the worst; in the other, we consciously set our aim upon the attainment of the best possible and make up our minds to be satisfied with nothing less.

The character of modern warfare makes opposition to the victor by the United States futile unless we undertake truly elaborate preparations in the very near future. Those who expect him to be too exhausted at the end of the war for aggression in pursuit of his ambition are reckoning without their host. Whatever the economic exhaustion in Europe may be, the army and navy which control the land and sea will undoubtedly be the largest and best equipped that the world has ever known, while their training and equipment will have been carried by the war itself to a point of perfection of which men scarcely dream to-day. To meet such a victor must we prepare, and unless we make adequate preparations for the conflict it were better that we made none at all. Security we may attain at a relatively small cost; but for independence we shall have to pay

THE PREREQUISITES OF INDEPENDENCE

the price which the victor sets upon it and not a price which we ourselves predetermine.

Can we afford independence? Will not the cost of adequate armament be prohibitive? No impartial student will hesitate to reply in the negative. We can easily afford with our vast resources to do what the European states have done with half as much, if only we consider the object worthy. Indeed we already have the expense of armament without its protection. While the United States army is hardly as bad as the most radical of its critics claim, there can be no doubt whatever that in comparison with European armies it is by far the most expensive and the least efficient in the world. Our army annually costs (according to figures recently compiled by one of the Peace Foundations) $1314 a man while the German army costs $306, the French army $291, and the English $378. Our average expense is more than four times that of any European nation for the men actually in the field, and, while we pay our men higher wages than any other nation, the real difference in expense is not in that item.

If we put the issue thus, the result is little short of staggering. We have paid recently over one hundred millions of dollars a year for our army while Germany has expended on hers two hundred millions. She has produced the largest and best-equipped standing army the world has known, one seven times as numerous as ours and, at a moderate computation, more than ten times as efficient, at just about double the cost. The total expenditure of France in 1912 was two hundred and fifty-nine millions of dollars for which she had to show, a navy fourth in size and at least third in efficiency in the world, an active army of over six hundred thousand men and a reserve army of about four millions, which were put into the field at a few days' notice. The French artillery corps was supposedly the largest and finest in the world. The United States spent in that same year on its army and navy combined *only fifteen millions of dollars less* and had to show a navy of considerable size but not of commensurable efficiency and an army of barely eighty thousand men, with no reserves, no artillery to speak of, and no supplies of ammunition. Belgium put three hundred thousand well-equipped men into the field at a very few days' notice and her annual military budget is listed at thirteen millions of dollars—four times as many men well equipped at a cost of about one-eighth of what we pay for one quarter as many men, the adequacy of whose equipment is open to the gravest doubt. This army of

THE PREREQUISITES OF INDEPENDENCE

course was largely composed of reserves, but the Italian standing army, counting over three hundred thousand men, is maintained at a cost of a little more than half our military budget. The size of our army has increased little in the last four decades *but its expense has quadrupled*.

The figures in regard to the navy are also thoroughly instructive. The Germans are supposed to have been spending prodigious amounts in recent years and have certainly built up a fleet enormous in size and of undoubted efficiency. They spent in 1912 and 1913 one hundred and eleven millions of dollars; *the United States spent twenty-five millions of dollars more;* England, with the largest navy in the world and supposedly the greatest bill of expenditure, spent two hundred and sixteen millions of dollars; and France with the fourth largest navy spent eighty-one millions of dollars. The English navy has cost something over a third more than the United States navy and its efficiency is perhaps three times as great. Our present army and navy are in fact the result of good money misspent, the bulk of which seems unrepresented by anything military or naval. These figures have been published so often that the truth ought to have been thoroughly well-known long before this. We can easily afford armament because we are already paying for adequate armament, if the sums spent by European nations are any criterion of what armament costs.

If further expenditure becomes necessary there are two very simple methods by which vast sums can easily be saved. The first is by economy in national administration. Lack of business methods and incompetent clerks cost us annually many millions. A resolute application to the departments in Washington, and particularly to the Post Office and Customs Service, of advanced business methods will save more millions a year than an American likes to contemplate. Every European post office is an asset in the annual budget of a good many millions, whereas the United States post office can produce a small credit balance only by a process which is called in private business "juggling the accounts," and by compelling the railroads to perform much of the service of carrying the mails, including the whole of the parcels post, without recompense. If the so-called "Pork Barrel" alone can be stopped, a good many battleships can annually be built from that great sum of money which is now apportioned out in contracts for the constituents of congressmen. We have built a good many har-

THE PREREQUISITES OF INDEPENDENCE

bors which ships never enter and deepened a good many rivers which have no water in them at certain seasons of the year. There is some truth in the parody of the famous remark: "Millions for graft, but not one cent for safety."

War and armament are both expensive, but we can easily afford independence, if we decide it is desirable, by foregoing a variety of luxuries and extravagancies which are quite as void of permanent importance as armament. Any one who will take the trouble to turn to the census and see the millions and millions spent annually upon tobacco, beer, fine clothes, theaters, automobiles, will see that a small fraction of the total sum, which is as decidedly wasted each year so far as the future is concerned as if it had been burned up, would provide us with an armament sufficiently large to achieve every conceivable purpose the American people might ever have. We can afford armament without really burdening ourselves at all, if we can spend honestly the sums already appropriated, and we can place the matter beyond all doubt by a little economy in national administration plus a very slight sacrifice in our own luxuries.

Realizing then that independence of the seapower is a prerequisite of aggressive action by

PAN-AMERICANISM

the United States, let us assume that independence attainable and consider the desirability of the territorial expansion which it will make possible.

CHAPTER III

THE ECONOMICS OF EXPANSION

MANY European statesmen have advisedly reached the conclusion that the truly significant factor in the national warfare is its rate of economic progress, the continuance of which must be assured at all costs and the consequences of whose diminution is to be dreaded as a calamity fatal to the national prosperity. Do the economic premises of European expansion apply at all to the United States? Shall we need in the future new territory to develop and new markets to exploit? Are we wrong in supposing that our interests are different in character from those of European nations and that the logic which they find convincing does not apply to our needs or interests? What are the prospects for the continuance of the recent rapid economic development in this country and what will be the probable consequence of its retardation?

First and foremost, the rate of American growth

has been the result of immigration. A young country with plenty of land, and an abundance of natural resources needed merely the application of labor to produce commodities and profit. Roughly speaking, the capital was in existence and the amount of it that could be utilized, its rate of development, depended entirely upon the number of hands which could be put to work. The normal rate of progress would be the normal annual increase in the number of hands that were put to work, which, if dependent upon the ordinary growth of the population, would not in any one year be large. Rapid immigration, by furnishing us with an abnormal increase of hands every year, caused an utterly unprecedented and abnormal rate of development. In the next place, we put these hands to work upon virgin resources—upon lands which had never been cropped, in forests untouched by the ax, or upon deposits of free mineral which could be dug with a spade. Our resources were as extraordinary in quality as the increase in the number of hands was abnormal; even the crudest and most wasteful of methods yielded astonishing profits. The first impulse of machinery and the new facilities of transportation, communication, and intercourse, gave an added stimulus to the rate of progress.

THE ECONOMICS OF EXPANSION

Never before in history had it been so easy to move men from one place to another, to locate the resources awaiting development, and to put hands promptly at work. From the first use of machinery came an astounding increase in the output, and from the new transportation an unexpected ease of distribution.

We are already beginning to feel a slackening of this rate of growth, for all three of the factors which created it are far less potent than before. Immigration has fallen off not only in actual numbers, not only in proportion to population, but in quality. The hands which now come are not directed by as good heads as formerly. Then our exuberance has exhausted practically all of our virgin resources: the best land is already tilled; the free minerals are nearly exhausted; our great forests have been so denuded as to cause the utmost concern. The pace of development is no longer accelerated by the advent of new inventions of former potency, and the future will scarcely see the introduction of as epoch-making devices. The rate of growth is already retarded and may slacken to a degree that we would not now consider progress.

From these changes, as well as from the benefits of the previous development, has resulted a striking transportation. The market in America in the past for crude, rough labor was phenomenal and entirely abnormal because we were compelled to perform a multitude of operations badly rather than not at all; to-day we are seeking skilled labor rather than unskilled. Such a demand proceeds from the necessity of careful, intensive work upon resources which no longer yield the same rate of return. The days of extensive farming are numbered and the days of intensive cultivation are here.

In the past our rate of growth was fostered almost entirely by forces in America, because we did actually stand somewhat apart from the European fabric, and because the world as a whole was by no means closely related in business. The creation of an interdependent international economic fabric has made prosperity in one country dependent upon the existence of healthy, normal conditions elsewhere. When we write of identity of interests and of interdependence, we mean simply that one nation is as dependent upon another's buying what it produces, as the second is upon selling to the first what it has produced itself. Neither produces all it needs; neither makes the slightest attempt to produce everything; each counts definitely upon obtaining

THE ECONOMICS OF EXPANSION

from others what it does not make and of supplying to them in turn the surplus of commodities which it does not consume at home. This is to-day the premise of international trade. Its concrete result is to make domestic prosperity for any nation largely dependent upon the continuance of its foreign trade, to make our prosperity in America depend not so much upon what we produce as upon what other nations buy from us. Obviously, a situation which prevents our customers in foreign countries from purchasing leaves our own commodities unsold and unsalable, while the failure of foreign nations to produce prevents us from obtaining commodities which we vitally need. If the war has destroyed the market for American copper abroad, it has badly crippled manufacturers here who use aniline dyes or potash. Kid skins we have imported from France; dyes and potash from Germany; the war, which we did not create, immediately interfered with the normality of American business because the United States is an integral part of the interdependent economic structure of the world. There could scarcely be a fact more significant than this: that American prosperity is as dependent upon conditions in foreign countries and upon their domestic well-being as it is upon forces and factors primarily

American. In the future, we shall need to take carefully into account probabilities and developments in Europe, South America, Africa, and the far East, if we are to envisage those factors vital to the future prosperity of American citizens.

Undoubtedly the reaction upon economic conditions of the facility of communication and intercourse between nations tends to diminish the rate of progress in all nations and to equalize it. To the least developed sections and districts, where the imperative need for capital and labor results in high rates of interest and high wages, capital and labor usually hasten, until the demand has been filled and the supply more nearly assumes the normal ratio to the demand in other sections of this interdependent fabric. Each year progress is made because the increase in population provides new mouths to feed, new bodies to house and clothe, and more individuals with economic cravings to satisfy. To this increased demand each nation normally contributes; of the larger supply needed to meet it each produces its part, which will naturally bear some rough proportion to its own previous economic efficiency. An abnormal share of this new demand will be necessary for the nation which is eager to develop at an abnormal rate, and the actual amount of goods to be annually sold will be greater because the same proportion of the new demand is annually larger by that year's increase in the population of the world. The continuance of this abnormal degree of growth Germany has decided she must ensure by forcible methods; all other European nations are not less determined to obtain it if they can, and are driven to seek new markets in which they can develop new trade more easily than they can secure a larger share of the increased demand in each other's markets.

There is no nation in Europe, not even Germany, where economic growth has moved at as unprecedented a speed as it has in the United States. A century ago the pioneers of settlement had scarcely crossed the Mississippi and now the surging tide of industrialism has transferred the center of population and industry from the Atlantic coast to the Mississippi valley. No state in Europe was as dependent upon another as we were a century ago upon Europe; none was as backward in manufactures, as deficient in the finer arts of civilization, as unfamiliar with the greatest traditions of the race. To-day the disparity no longer exists, for we are the peers of any European state in economic development. Where Germany has risen from poverty to affluence, we have conquered a continent with our own bare hands and dragged from the earth by unremitting toil an aggregate wealth comparable to that of nations whose accumulations of capital are as old as Europe. Such an achievement is without parallel in the annals of the race.

We are apt to forget that the United States has been in the past a seeker for labor and capital, the possessor of an insatiable demand rather than of a surplus supply. We ourselves have furnished Europe with that vast and ever expanding market which enabled European industry to advance by leaps and bounds during the last century. Here England and France found the outlet for their surplus; here the profitable location for their investments of capital; here has been sold the swelling volume of the new Germany's produce; here has been in the past Europe's greatest field for development, the world's most extended market, the one demand which was increasing faster than the rate of production in Europe could keep pace with. And the benefit was mutual! We needed their capital and labor and their market for our raw products and their supplies of manufactured goods while we were developing our own industry.

But this market is now a thing of the past; the

THE ECONOMICS OF EXPANSION

demand no longer exists; and in its place stands a new supply seeking a market. It is not too much to say that the cause of the present struggle for markets in Europe is the attempt to replace the market which the United States once afforded their produce but which it provides no longer. Here is the root of Pan-Germanism, the secret of the interest in Morocco, in China, in South America. Europe has always depended upon selling to a rapidly developing market and has adjusted her economic fabric to an ever increasing demand. For at least two centuries the United States furnished that market and, now that it does so no longer, it must be replaced. There is this great and significant difference in the situation: the company of nations seeking markets numbers one more. The United States itself is now an independent and integral part of the world's interdependent and interlocking economic fabric; its interests with Europe are still mutual but no longer different; complementary to those of European nations rather than their counterpart; identical in character, purposes, and needs. We no longer furnish them a market whose demands it is as much our interest as theirs for them to supply, but we produce a portion of the world's supply as necessary to them as theirs to us, and are seeking ourselves markets for the annual increase in our output.

Already the problem is in existence and a solution desirable; soon the need will be imperative. Inevitably, from the retardation of the rate of progress will come a change in the aspect of business for the ordinary man, because two hands and two legs are every year capable of rendering less valuable service to the community and the unskilled work will be increasingly hard to find. The old superabundance of food which has become almost a tradition in America is already a thing of the past. There has been too much food; the tendency will steadily be to provide just enough. Scientific farming and production makes it easy to avoid overproduction and the growth of more diversified interests will rapidly reduce the proportion of the population which devotes its time to agriculture. Inevitably will come a rise in the price of necessities, and, as unskilled labor will steadily command a smaller price, the degree of comfort to be had for the same quality and quantity of work will diminish. From the exhaustion of virgin resources and of the first impulse from machinery will result in a gradual cessation of immigration, the rate at which the home market has increased in the past will diminish steadily, and we shall tend to produce in the future only to meet the normal increase of demand due to our own normal increase in population, and to meet our share of the same normal increase in foreign countries. We shall face therefore in a not distant future the same issues England has already faced and which Germany is now attempting to meet; we shall experience the same difficulties in meeting them and may conceivably find the only available expedients to solve them those which England has already used and which Pan-Germanism is attempting to provide—new markets.

We can easily house in the United States three hundred millions of people and provide them with work, but we cannot continue for many more decades to provide work for our own people at present wages and supply them with the same amount of commodities at present prices. If we continue to retain our increasing population within our own borders, if we continue to add to it artificially by immigration, inevitably there will be proportionately less work and therefore less wages, because there will be proportionately more laborers; inevitably there will be less food and more mouths and therefore higher prices and less to eat per individual. We can grow indefinitely in the United States but not at the present rate of growth nor with the present degree of individual comfort. If precedent affords us the slightest glimpse of the future, we shall soon be seeking new markets, new fields to which capital and labor may emigrate.

From such new economic demands will follow, unless precedent is again misleading, new demands upon national policy and statecraft. The capital and labor who wish to emigrate will desire, as they have in the past, assurances from the national government of protection in their new residence, or will demand as in the case of the cotton culture the creation of new economic opportunities by political agencies. In the path of our economic expansion we shall find as other nations have a great number of obstacles placed there partly by chance, partly by past history, and partly by the designs of other nations to secure for themselves unusual privileges. Already it is almost an axiom of European politics that a chief duty of the modern government lies in the removal of artificial obstacles standing in the way of the economic interests of the nation and in the prevention of arbitrary interference with its interests by other nations, whether by tariffs, fleets, or armies. They see clearly in Europe that the most vital interest of the state is economic, because economic prosperity is the foundation of political independence, of national unity, and of international status; they see that prosperity depends upon the continuance of the rate of growth, and that political and military action ought to protect and further these economic interests. The present European conflicts are based primarily upon these economic contentions. This then is an economic war—a war for markets, for colonies or dependencies in which markets may be developed, for access and perhaps preferential rights in those of Asiatic communities. Precisely these factors are already present in the United States, and, if precedent be any criterion, will before long lead our statesmen and citizens to a conviction that the supreme duty of the state is to provide for the economic welfare of its citizens, whence it is but a step to territorial expansion, to an insistence upon new markets, secured by political, diplomatic, and it may be by military and naval agencies.

The interests of the United States therefore are identical with those which have led the present nations into this war so far as our interest in their prosperity extends. American business is affected by all events in Europe—political alliances between different nations, changes in their internal conditions, their domestic or governmental efficiency as reflected in their economic structure, and in the part they play in the international fabric of which we are an integral part, in the welfare of which we are as much concerned as they. We have no choice, the world is interdependent and we are a part of it, whether we like it or not; whether we know it or not.

International friendships and antipathies are based upon contact, upon constant intercourse and acquaintanceship between the nations concerned, though in the past close alliances and vigorous hatreds were pretty generally confined to nations physically contiguous. Before the days of railroads and steamships, a nation's interests were not likely to extend much beyond its own borders or to be vitally affected by events which did not happen in its immediate vicinity. But to-day the interests of the United States, like those of all great nations, are bounded, not by the territorial limits of North America, but by the activities of American citizens.

The extension of the economic fabric promptly spread our interests to the confines of the globe and made us potentially the allies or enemies of any country upon it. The old traditions taught that no European alliance could subserve the true

THE ECONOMICS OF EXPANSION

interests of the United States; that the Atlantic isolated us from Europe, freed us from its tangle of political alliances, and left us without mutual interests with any European state beyond those which could be advanced by diplomacy. There was indeed a feeling of antipathy towards Europe, a belief almost that their existence was hostile to our welfare, and that we were by no means as interested in their welfare as they were in ours. To the Revolutionists the colonies were being exploited for the profit of English merchants; to the eager advocates of protective tariffs, American labor was being exploited by foreign countries and undersold by the products of underpaid foreign labor. All this is past. Vital interests of the United States exist to-day in every country in the world. The railroad, steamship, and telegraph have put all nations in all parts of the globe into immediate contact, have created interests where none existed, and have made possible international alliances and wars based upon interests that seem widely sundered. To-day we have interests which can be furthered by foreign alliances, and which may actually dictate the nature of our own alliances. The variety and extent of the interests which make our entrance inevitable into international politics render the

United States an ally of consequence for any nation, and a power to be feared and courted. Our past traditions, our present intentions, our nobler ideals will not alter the work of economic force whose potency has transformed the face of Nature and habits of mankind. With their work we must reckon and realize speedily that our unwillingness to recognize and failure to accept these fundamental changes will simply plunge us into crises whose origin and character we shall not comprehend and therefore shall not be able to solve, or will leave us at the mercy of foreign nations who have seen their comprehension worth unlimited time and infinite trouble. We too must understand that we may not be taken by surprise; we must prepare to meet the attempts of other nations to utilize these forces, and to mold the international future in their own image for the promotion of their own special interests.

CHAPTER IV

THE ETHICS OF EXPANSION

IF we are able to demonstrate convincingly the desirability and expediency of territorial expansion or of imperialism, shall we also be able to prove their consonance with ethical standards? If the Monroe Doctrine is expedient, is it also just? If the supremacy of the Western Hemisphere is profitable to maintain, is it also praiseworthy? We shall need to justify Pan-Americanism and show that it accords with motives deserving the regard of the American people. Assuming that the Japanese in California and in Latin America are inimical to our economic interests, have we the ethical right to protest? We are challenging England's treatment of neutral shipping and protesting in one way or another against her control of the sea; there is a movement on foot to increase the American merchant marine and to establish as nearly as possible our actual independence of the sea-power; the justification of both is by no means an issue of indifference to the American people. Are any of these legitimate ambitions? Do all or any of them fulfill the ideal which the American people seem to cherish of noble and disinterested action at this present crisis?

The ethics of expansion and the justification of any policy pursued by the United States in the past or adopted in the future, depend entirely upon our definition of the word ethics. For a good many generations there has been a more or less active debate over the existence or non-existence of a permanent standard by which ethical values at different periods and in different countries could be compared and measured. Obviously, if such a standard exists we must test our behavior by it and accept the verdict; but, fortunately or unfortunately, there are almost as many ethical standards as there are notions of right conduct. The most we can do is to apply the better known successively to the facts and note the result. Many are inclined to contend that the lack of agreement upon an ethical standard robs any conclusion of practical value as a guide to statesmen or individuals. To maintain such a position is plainly to make expediency the only test of rightness and to treat any further inquiry as academic and therefore inconsequential.

THE ETHICS OF EXPANSION

At least two of the notions of ethical conduct, at present widely supported, declare any and all policies of expansion or imperialism *prima facie* unethical and *ipso facto* wrong. The pacifist assumes that anything gained by compulsion or armed force is wrong: war is abnormal, unnatural, and criminal, proceeding from the worst of motives involving the most despicable conceivable behavior, and resulting in brutality, inhuman cruelty, and unnecessary destruction. From this there is no escape if once we grant the premise. More subtly the principles of individualist ethics, to be found in the bulk of ethical treatises and espoused by nearly all teachers and thinkers who look upon themselves as ethicists, militate against these conceptions of expansion which we are considering. If the analysis of a layman in such controverted matters is not entirely at fault, the object of individualist ethics is really the contentment of the individual in this present life and the welfare of his soul after death. The layman has in mind that sort of right conduct which will lead to his happiness here and to his spiritual salvation hereafter, and naturally demands the furtherance of such ends by the development of spiritual and mental qualities, minimizing as a matter of course the importance and even questioning the value of the acquisition of wealth and the struggle for economic advantage. Indeed the temporalities of life sink into the background and become almost non-ethical because of their comparative powerlessness, long demonstrated by experience, to advance the contentment of the inner man in this present existence beyond a relatively elemental point, or to satisfy him of their ability to save his soul in the next world. The quasi-religious tinge, so marked in present ethical teaching, has its effective origin in the blending of certain features of Christianity with certain aspects of Greek and Roman philosophic teaching.

Economic forces are essentially non-ethical because unadapted to the advancement of the highest ethical ends; economic prosperity is non-ethical because it is also almost powerless to advance the aims cherished by ethicists. While thinkers have not denied the rightness of a desire nor a certain moderate degree of physical comfort and have even laid stress upon the importance, for the development of the loftier motives, of an entire freedom from anxiety concerning actual subsistence, they have strongly doubted the expediency of recognizing among ethical motives the desire for worldly position or for economic advantage. Those who have admitted such impulses

THE ETHICS OF EXPANSION

to a place, have usually accorded them a very secondary and subordinate position and have plainly regarded the decision as a concession grudgingly made to the fallibility of human nature, rather than the recognition of a tenet desirable or necessary. The result is most strikingly seen in the divergence between the teachings of ethicists and the notions of right conduct ordinarily followed in the business community. The economic world has not unnaturally regarded as inadmissible a series of principles which virtually accorded the business world the position of an excrescence on the community, and recognized its continued existence as scarcely likely to further the highest aims of individual or state and only too apt to foster notions destructive of the truest good of both. According to such ethical premises, there are no ethics in business.

If we test by these same tenets the territorial expansion of nations and imperialist policies, the premise will infallibly demonstrate the non-ethical character of both and their lack of consonance with the true ends and desires of the community. If not actually base and despicable they will hardly appear noble or praiseworthy.

The premise of expansion and imperialism is in fact the necessity and desirability of economic gain and of material well-being, continued beyond the needs of national subsistence to the acquisition of as great a degree of prosperity and wealth as can be attained. Any rate of progress less than the maximum involves sacrifice and (constructively) suffering. With freedom from actual penury and starvation and even with the attainment of comparative comfort, imperialists are dissatisfied; they demand wealth, the possession of as much more than just enough as can be had. The ethics of expansion, if we may fairly claim that it exists, has sought to define and delimit the economic selfishness of individuals and nations in order to determine how far and why certain particular notions for obtaining wealth are expedient. It has tried to list means and methods permissible in furthering designs for the increase of bodily comfort and material prosperity here on earth. It is builded upon the tenets of political economy rather than upon those of ethics, and it naturally reproduces faithfully the non-ethical and non-moral character of economic postulates which the founders of political economy readily admitted were true if they were tested by such notions of ethics or morals. Indeed, if ethics apparently excludes from consideration the science of accumulating wealth, political economy no less firmly insists

THE ETHICS OF EXPANSION

that the admission of "ethical" or "moral" impulses will at once vitiate its logic. If ethics assumes that the chief end of life is spiritual contentment and salvation, political economy predicates the increase of individual wealth as the sole purpose of life. Each admits the other's existence; both practically declare that the logic of one destroys that of the other.

Shall we not be wise to recognize here a conflict of standards, or a lack of consonance between standards, rather than a lack of ethical qualities in what we are judging? In other words ethical values seem to be comparative and temporary rather than positive or permanent, resulting not from the character of the thing judged but from its consonance with certain preconceived premises. Conduct or policy will be ethical or not according to its relation to certain postulates which we must always include as the most essential element of our decision. Ethical values are not only comparative but relative.

From the slightest investigation of the deeds and policies of nations and individuals in the past, we shall learn that these ideas of ethics have never been applied by a community to the problems of its existence or of its economic welfare. While adhesion to the general desirability of these concepts has been readily accorded, the conduct of individuals and of nations has been regulated by a very different set of precepts. No great amount of thought will be needed to discover also that nations have never recognized as applicable to them the rules of individual ethics. The reason is only too obvious: the conduct of nations for the increase of their economic welfare or the preservation of their territorial integrity cannot very well be judged by rules intended to promote the peace of mind and the spiritual salvation of individuals.

The premise of international ethics seems to be an application of the notion of individual self-defense to the larger entity. From the very earliest times the individual has been accorded the right to take another's life in defense of his own; he has demanded and ordinarily received, subject of course to examination and verification, the right to judge of the imminence of danger to his own safety and the consequent necessity for taking the other's life. In this principle statesmen have seen a direct analogy to the threatening of national existence by invasion, and from it they have drawn justification for such measures as they deemed imperative for defense. In crises they have justified severe measures with individuals and other nations by the plea that they were indispensable to the preservation of the national independence. The discretionary right to judge of the existence of the necessity and to pass upon the means requisite to meet it, they have always arrogated and they have invariably denied—though not with invariable success—any right to censure the use of this discretion after the event had proved their judgment bad. Of the desirability of such right of self-defense there has never been much question, but such circumstances are not those recently challenged by ethicists.

We have to deal to-day with a very subtle type of self-defense, which does not assume direct aggression in arms nor yet any injury of the sort hitherto recognized as a justification. Does a desire to ensure the future economic welfare of the nation stand upon the same footing as its right to repel armed invasion of its own territory? Has a nation a right to regard as hostile a series of economic developments, which no individual or nation created or originated, which are entirely impersonal, and which affect nearly all nations in some degree, because they seem likely to interfere in the future with that nation's degree of economic prosperity? The danger is of course contingent; it is in the next place impersonal; and in the third place, it is not an intentional injury even although it may conceivably involve great peril to national integrity. This is the danger which the demand for expanding markets, territorial expansion, and imperialism pleads. That it would not be in accordance with international ethics for one nation to assail another's domain, simply for the sake of increasing its own territory or to add forcibly to its own movable property, is pretty generally agreed. Is the ethical aspect of the situation altered when it is possible to allege a plausible future economic difficulty? Can economic "threats" justify reprisal in arms? May one nation draw into its hands the trade and consequent profit which another has at present, so long as the trade itself is not the actual object or the direct result of an armed invasion? Above all, does even a great and impending economic catastrophe justify a nation in defending itself *by the conquest of those individuals or nations who are not themselves in any conceivable way responsible for the economic forces likely to produce this calamity?* Such a defense Germany has alleged for her invasion of Belgium; such a defense must France give for her rights in Morocco; such must be the defense of the United States in the maintenance of its supremacy on the Western Hemisphere, of the Monroe Doctrine, or of any degree of intervention in Latin America.

The issue is exceedingly subtle and entirely without precedent in previous international disputes. The danger exists only in the future and its character is purely economic. No nation can be proved the aggressor, and in addition the solution is to be obtained at the expense of those people least involved in the production of the crisis itself. If it is wicked to kill a man with a gun, and considered murder to poison him; if it is unethical to make war by means of many men armed with guns, and wrong to poison the water supply of great cities; is it ethical to deprive these same people of their means of livelihood and reduce them to penury because some one else believes his welfare depends upon it? We agree that we must not rob individuals and nations with arms. May we rob them by economic methods? We are not allowed to steal territory from each other or from third parties simply that we may possess it. Are we justified in taking that property or rights in it by armed invasion on the plea that it is essential to our future economic welfare?

In reality, our ethical inquiry involves not so much an investigation of methods as an inquiry into ends and purposes. The old international ethics concerned itself pretty exclusively with methods and permitted the use of arms for the purpose of defense, upon the assumption that defense would normally be limited to actual invasion of the national territory. Few nations then possessed interests at any distance from their own frontier and still fewer were able to pursue an aggressive policy. From the moment however that modern transportation and communication extended the interests of nations to the confines of the globe and made possible the pursuance of aggression by any nation in any part of the globe it might select, aggression and therefore defense promptly assumed a new complexion, which the old definition of international ethics by no means contemplated. The same economic forces which spread the national interests placed new weapons in the national hands—economic weapons of the utmost potency, whose use did not in the least involve warfare in the old sense, but whose results were not essentially different from those of conquest, lacking only the destruction of life and property. Was this kind of aggression justifiable? The old international ethics would have pronounced in the affirmative because it involved no actual armed invasion of the other's territory. If therefore we limit ourselves to methods employed rather

THE ETHICS OF EXPANSION

than the thing done and adopt the position of most pacifists that the really objectionable thing is armed warfare, we shall justify and permit a great variety of practices by which nations may impoverish and conquer each other without the firing of guns, much more effectively and permanently than they could have in the past by means of actual armed conquest. This logic also deprives the nations thus assailed by economic weapons of all right to defend themselves. By declaring the use of arms unjustifiable in resistance to anything except armed aggression against the national territory, the nation appealing to arms against the new economic weapons becomes the aggressor, and is promptly called upon to shoulder the blame for the war.

Some sort of an agreement as to the meaning of the words "expansion" and "imperialism" is therefore essential to any conclusion as to the ethics of either. It should be obvious that between the actual assumption of political control as the result of armed invasion, and no interference at all, there are a great variety of possible stages. The whereabouts of the line between justifiable intercourse will promptly establish the ethics of any particular event. Shall we consider it just for the United States to preserve the peace in

Central American republics when the process may involve interference with their elections or ministries? May we rightly insist upon economic privileges for American citizens in Latin America? Both of these involve no control over that nation by our own Government. It is then possible to take a further step and take control of the revenue of these states on the ground that debts are due American citizens which cannot be paid because of the financial methods in vogue among the natives. This involves practically an economic control over the native government exerted by the Government of the United States. It results as effectively in depriving it of the perception of its own taxes as if we had conquered that country and had appointed tax collectors to represent us, instead of claiming that the ones we do appoint represent the natives. It will be obvious to the least informed that they are appointed in the interests of American capitalists and that their only reason for existence is the inability or unwillingness of the natives to conform to what we believe to be American interests. This we assume to be ethical. It is then possible for the United States to assume military control of a country to restore order and create conditions which we deem advisable, but of which very clearly the natives do

THE ETHICS OF EXPANSION

not approve, for if they did approve our intervention would not be necessary. This, it is claimed, does not involve economic control nor does it interfere in the least with the political independence of the natives.

Ordinarily, Europeans and Americans have declared that any variety or degree of interference or control over undeveloped peoples was beneficial to them, lenient, and entirely ethical, so long as it did not actually involve the assumption of technical sovereignty. To deprive the natives of political independence, to annex their territory and actually call it a part of the territory of some European nation has generally been deemed unethical, whether done by armies or by influence. Everything except the fiction of political independence has been continually taken from the natives of undeveloped countries by all European nations and by the United States and has generally been deemed in accordance with international ethics, even though obtained by the actual use of force. The ethical line therefore between conquest and the actual economic or military possession of the country has been tenuous and dubious. The important fact to establish is therefore the purpose or aim of the action taken rather than the method employed.

PAN-AMERICANISM

In any proper sense of the word, expansion is an attempt to procure rights and privileges which we should not normally have and which the inhabitants of the country concerned would not voluntarily give us. It employs abnormal political influence to establish an abnormal economic relationship between the countries and obtain an abnormal economic profit. Any conception at all worthy of the name of ethics will place in the same category every variety of control which tends to this end, whether it is economic, military, or political; whether it is called intervention, protection, assistance, assimilation, penetration, the Monroe Doctrine, or conquest. If it aims at obtaining something we should not normally get, it will be on a par with the assumption of control. If it is wrong to obtain certain things, it will make no difference by what method we acquire them. If the method used be the criterion of blame, nothing acquired in any other way can be wrong.

Any application at all of what are ordinarily called ethical precepts will show that the threat to use force by the United States is as much aggressive action against some small Latin-American state as the actual dispatch of a military expedition or of a squadron. An ultimatum to Mexico

THE ETHICS OF EXPANSION

employs as a political club the potential force which the greater size and wealth of the United States would allow us to exert. If armed aggression is wrong, threats really supported by potential armed aggression also are wrong. If we are asking for something for which it might be necessary to use armed force, and we deny the rightness of violence, then it will be equally wrong for us to obtain in any other way. The United States has established its economic preponderance in certain of the West Indian islands and in certain of the Central American republics by methods known to the Europeans as peaceful penetration, and the natives of those countries consider that they have lost all rights save the shadow of political independence. If so much was ethical, the assumption of actual political control will not deprive the natives of anything really valuable, since everything of importance is already lost. If this last step is not justifiable, it is difficult to see how any part of the process can be called ethical. Let us however once more remind ourselves that ethics is a question of definition and not a positive quality and that right conduct depends more upon our premise than upon what we do. We ought simply to realize that an ethical line cannot be drawn between certain types of behavior which are distinguished by the technical and artificial rather than by substantive differences.

In what way can we demonstrate the ethics or justice of the claim of the United States to supremacy in the Western Hemisphere? By what right shall we rule the Latin Americans? This issue involves the very difficult ethical question of the treatment of red men, black men, and heathens by white Christians. Are all entitled to precisely the same rights? If we are in duty bound to recognize the rights of red men and black men as equal to our own, we shall not be able to make good our claim to supremacy. Admittedly we should resist any claim advanced by England or Germany to supremacy over us; admittedly they would resent our claim of superiority over them; but we are able calmly to discuss and assert our supremacy in the Western Hemisphere as something almost too axiomatic to debate, just as the Germans and English assert with equal nonchalance their superiority and supremacy in Africa and Asia. Are any of them based upon ethical or moral contentions? If we regard the tenets of Christianity we shall admit that all men stand upon an equal footing without regard to race or color, and ethicists and pacifists as a body accord-

THE ETHICS OF EXPANSION

ingly deny the rightfulness of any assertion of supremacy by the white race.

No such contention has ever been admitted in actual practice. The white race has arrogated the right to rule all other races and has thus far made good its title to supremacy and superiority. Nor has the United States taken an attitude upon this issue different from that of other white nations. The Indians and negroes have only very recently been accorded legal status and we have yet as a nation to act upon the assumption that the Indians possess rights paramount in the land to those of the white man. Such land as the white man did not wish to use, the Indians have been allowed to occupy, but the moment the white man desired it, reasons in plenty have been discovered for handing possession over to him. The basis of the opinion seems to be the distinction between the Christian and the heathen, and the general assumption, true for many centuries, that the white race alone would be Christian. There could be of course no question but that the Christians were to rule and that they must so deal with the heathen as to save their souls. Inevitably this meant that the white race took under its guidance and tutelage all other races and was to provide as best it could for their salvation, by the institution of churches and by good government and education. According to the ethics of the Crusaders and of the Inquisition, the Spaniards and the English who occupied the Western Hemisphere assumed the right to coerce the bodies of Indians and of negroes for the purpose of saving their souls. It was early recognized that political control and the direction of the labor of the natives by the white man was a necessary consequence of conversion and was indispensable to the maintenance of the tutelage of the whites.

The Protestant Reformation in the sixteenth century had a peculiar influence upon this tenet, tending on the whole greatly to strengthen it. Whereas Catholics had taught that the act of baptism was sufficient to save the heathen's soul, even if the individual could not comprehend the doctrine, the Protestants insisted upon the actual comprehension of the teaching, and, while the Catholics in practice placed the heathen upon a par with infants and assumed that the offices of the church must procure their salvation because they were not capable of assisting, the Protestants were of the opinion that Christians would not perform their whole duty unless they made the heathen capable of saving his own soul. That anyone else could save it for him they denied. To

THE ETHICS OF EXPANSION

educate him to the point of comprehension meant however the continuance of the tutelage and supervision until such time as the less developed races should become Christians in something more than name and educated in something more than the outward signs of Christian character. Hence came the assumption that the Christian nations must watch over the lesser developed peoples in the Western Hemisphere in order to make real their Christianity and their ultimate salvation. It became a religious duty which could not be shirked or avoided; some white nation must be responsible for these peoples who so recently were heathen. If therefore Spain lost the supremacy, England must take it up, and, if it did not pass to England, the United States must assume it. It was a part of the white man's burden, a trust to be discharged as a part of his own duty toward God.

International ethics therefore is a subtle and most peculiar mixture of the law of individual self-defense, the ethics of business, and the ethics of the Crusaders. So far as we are concerned, we can hardly claim to-day a real necessity for self-defense against actual aggression from South America, such as would in any sense justify us in taking military and naval control of the Western

Hemisphere. In order to base our supremacy upon the necessity of the continuance of guardianship by a Christian nation, we must assume that the intellectual attainments of Latin Americans are as yet too rudimentary to permit their real comprehension of the tenets of Christianity, to say nothing of the imputation that the offices of the Catholic Church are entirely unable to ensure their salvation. To state such a proposition is to show its present absurdity as a basis of American policy. Unless we can justify our expansion by the ethics of business, the ethics of peaceful penetration, the ethics of future markets, or of territory to develop, we shall not be able to justify it at all.

In the end we return to the issue with which we started: what is ethics; what are the criteria of justice? Our premise will determine our conclusion; there is no escaping this fact; but what ethical premise will justify peaceful penetration? There is only one such standard: the actual conduct of nations in the past. If then we consider ethics right conduct and take as its standard the present conduct of nations, as well as our own past actions and those of the greater European nations, employing actual cases as against hypothetical assumptions, we shall have little difficulty in

THE ETHICS OF EXPANSION

concluding that the expansion of the United States into Central and South America for the purpose of assuring its economic welfare in the future would be entirely in accordance with international ethics, as *applied* by white men in their relations with the lesser developed countries during the last three centuries. The practices of the past justify such ambitions. We can demonstrate the consonance of any sort of conduct with ethics if only we assume the right premise. Is it not possible after all that a search for the principles by which certain conduct could be proved ethical, would not only bear a close resemblance to the ancient logical fallacy of arguing in a circle but would also be scarcely recognizable as an ethical inquiry?

CHAPTER V

THE EXPEDIENCY OF THE MONROE DOCTRINE

THE history of international diplomacy contains nothing more elusive and difficult of definition than the Monroe Doctrine.[1] It has been quoted in the past in justification of a great variety of conflicting purposes and has shown an apparent flexibility and fluidity which approach contradiction. At times it has been limited to defensive measures; at others extended to justify forcible aggression; from a mere right to preserve our own independence has been developed a right to annex Latin-American territory, to build a canal, and to intervene in other nations' affairs. Where some presidents have seen in it a permissive relationship, others have found it mandatory. The historians have not been less confused than the diplomats have been contra-

[1] The author wishes to remind the reader that he is attempting in this chapter to state the pros and cons and not to prove that expansion and imperialism are expedient or desirable.

dictory; yet the American people are clearly agreed that the Monroe Doctrine contains something fundamental which they are not at all inclined to sacrifice and to which they attach a prodigious importance.

A possible explanation of this peculiar situation may be suggested. The Monroe Doctrine seems to be couched, in true Anglo-Saxon fashion, rather in the specific application of the principle involved than in a statement of the principle itself.

Continually we have been given the effect rather than the cause; the actual decision rather than the generalization from which it proceeded. The Monroe Doctrine has stood in reality for two definitive and fundamental conceptions of American polity, and the American people have rightly gaged its essential quality. First, it stands for our incontrovertible right of self-defense, expressed originally in a practical application of that principle to the situation of 1823. At that moment our political independence seemed absolutely safe from European powers in Europe, but by no means as secure from European states located in America. To ensure our independence therefore we had to prevent European states from projecting themselves into the Western Hemisphere. In the second place, the Monroe Doctrine has stood for the equally undoubted right of the United States to champion and protect its primary economic interests against Europe or America; we asserted our fundamental duty of defending and guaranteeing by all means in our power our economic independence. Monroe applied the principle to the situation of 1823 at a moment when our paramount interests had been for a century and still were freedom of trade with the West India Islands, and when the economic bond between the colonists in the Western Hemisphere was mutual in the strictest sense. America for Americans, the exclusion of Europeans, was not only a possibility but a desirability. Subsequent presidents and diplomats, as the particular issues changed, reasserted constantly not the general principle but its application to the situation. They made the Monroe Doctrine therefore a complex of all the varied ideas and notions which our statesmen have had in the past with regard to the maintenance of our political independence of Europe and the desirability of our economic independence. To protect the one and provide for the other has been the nearest approach to a primary interest which the United States has ever had.

Each particular expedient for advancing these

EXPEDIENCY OF THE MONROE DOCTRINE

fundamental interests has rarely held the foreground for more than a brief period. While freedom of access to the West Indies was really essential to American trade, the bulk of our diplomatic policies was directed against the English control of the Gulf of Mexico. While there were still great areas of unoccupied land in North America, American statesmen were apprehensive of colonization by European states and proceeded to purchase the land in question, to annex it or conquer it. During the French Revolution and the Napoleonic wars, neutral trade with France in foodstuffs was a prominent interest and led promptly to the War of 1812. The Peace of Vienna brought into the foreground this whole complex of motives, so that they appeared simultaneously in the various phases of the diplomatic negotiations of Monroe's period and included in its utterances precedent for most contingencies, rendering it the most important single period in our diplomatic history.

No sooner had the Doctrine been enunciated than the interest which it had primarily been intended to further disappeared by the operation of economic and political forces over which we had no control. Other forces for whose growth we were as little responsible appeared in the

PAN-AMERICANISM

United States and in Europe and entirely changed the aspect of the two fundamental problems of political independence and our economic dependence upon Europe. The growth of the cotton culture had now made the annexation of land suitable for cotton our primary interest, and had promptly taken the place in American policy of an insistence upon freedom of trade in the Gulf of Mexico. The fundamental problems were the same; the particular expedient by which we were attempting to provide an adequate medium of exchange with Europe was entirely different, and led therefore to the assertion of a practical solution, unrelated to the earlier suggested solution. It was still called the Monroe Doctrine, partly no doubt to claim for it the antiquity and correspondence with past precedent it deserved and partly because no better descriptive term suggested itself. The Civil War, the freeing of the slaves, the new economic development again changed the situation and therefore changed the practical expedient suggested for advancing our two most important interests. The moment the United States had become an integral part of the interdependent international fabric and had assumed, because of the rise of the German navy, actual supremacy in the Western Hemisphere, every

EXPEDIENCY OF THE MONROE DOCTRINE

practical consideration relating to these problems was again revolutionized and hence their practical expression was apparently entirely at odds with the earlier statements of the Monroe Doctrine. It could not have been otherwise, for the fundamental problems themselves were transformed beyond recognition.

The inconsistencies of the Monroe Doctrine, its fluidity and flexibility, are therefore apparent rather than real. The fundamental principles are to-day what they always have been: our undoubted right to political independence, our incontrovertible duty to ensure our economic welfare and prevent arbitrary interference with it by European nations in their own interests. Such principles we cannot abandon without sacrificing all that is vital to our national integrity and national honor. Less than this we could not assert; more than this we cannot yield. It is not however international law and it has never been accepted by other nations, though its basic meaning they are not inclined to dispute because the same principles are implicit in their own polity. They recognize our right to maintain them as they expect us to grant their own necessity of acting in accordance with the same postulates.

It will be essential for us to recognize to-day,

as has been so frequently admitted in the past, that a change of circumstances renders obsolete certain particular applications of the Doctrine. We are not obligated now and never have considered ourselves obligated in the past to reaffirm any particular solution, or to require from other nations a recognition of any of its past applications. To question the expediency of any particular application has never been and is not now to question the validity of the Doctrine itself, but involves simply a consideration of the ways and means, of the ends and methods expedient under existing circumstances. We are therefore entirely free to apply the Doctrine at any time to any new set of circumstances without considering ourselves bound by past problems or precedents. Consistency of action and statement with the past the circumstances of the new situation may render inexpedient, and compel us either to sacrifice the fundamental principle itself or our own previous attempts to further it. What has been already changed so often may be modified in the future as the exigencies of the case suggest.

Hence it is expedient for us to recognize in the first place that the specific applications of the Doctrine in the past have been rendered entirely obsolete by the disappearance of the situations

EXPEDIENCY OF THE MONROE DOCTRINE

to which they applied. Monroe and Adams saw in 1823 a natural geographical separation between the Old World and the New, a natural affinity of interests between republican peoples in the New World, and their common antipathy to monarchical governments in the Old, besides the mutual economic interests between the peoples in the Western Hemisphere in the West India trade. All these have since disappeared. To-day a geographical relationship between the Americas closer than that between the Western Hemisphere and Europe is a fiction. The development of the nineteenth century has produced a greater similarity between our Government and that of England or France, than between the United States and the Latin-American republics, while the latter's methods of administration and general premises of political thought are so utterly different from ours that the United States Government hesitates to recognize them as truly republican. The mutual interest in the West India trade disappeared ten years after Monroe's message was read and has never existed since. As for a threat to our political independence involved in the location of a European state in North America or the Gulf of Mexico, such as terrified Jefferson, Monroe, and Calhoun, there is not now and for fifty years has not been the slightest danger to our political independence from any such source; the growth of the United States in population and in wealth has effectually exorcised such perils. Nor are the interests which seemed so vital to American statesmen in the decades preceding the Civil War more significant. The territorial expansion of America in order to increase the area of cotton land has been rendered of consequence by the new machinery for ginning cotton, by the new fertilizers which have made the upland cotton available, and which have solved the cotton problem by making profitable the cultivation of other land besides virgin soil. The crop has grown by leaps and bounds and nothing but a slackening demand can prevent its continued growth.

Adams doubted in 1823 whether any pronunciamento by the United States could protect South America from Europe; certainly it could not exclude England who already controlled Latin America, and he saw no reason to doubt her ability to defend South America single-handed. Circumstances proved the correctness of his ideas. Before Monroe's message was enunciated an agreement between England and France to protect the republics solved the difficulty. If both were opposed to reconquest the restoration of Spanish

EXPEDIENCY OF THE MONROE DOCTRINE

authority was impossible. Nor has there appeared to this day good reason to doubt the correctness of the claim advanced by England and the South Americans that their defense from aggression has depended upon the English control of the sea and upon the lack of sufficient motive to challenge it. We are therefore at present under no obligation to continue a protection of South America which never was real, and if we decline to reaffirm a particular application of the Monroe Doctrine, primarily applied to the West Indies, we shall not rob the South Americans of anything on which they depend. The political independence of South America seems as well assured as that of the United States and in as little danger from Europe. The South Americans do not dread any such eventuality; our aid against Europe they do not desire, nor do they ask us to defend them. They do not believe us better prepared to fight for them than they are to protect themselves.

If by the Monroe Doctrine we mean Pan-Americanism, America for the Americans, the exclusion of Europeans and of European influence as a matter of principle, we must recognize that we are advocating a scheme which the South Americans believe inimical to their interests. Any closer connection between the United

States and the Latin-American republics they consider so abnormal and artificial, so lacking in mutuality, and so entirely devoid of popular confidence that we must recognize frankly the full meaning of its adoption as an American policy. It spells imperialism and territorial expansion. Of this the South Americans have no doubt. "The Republicans think only of imperialism," says Calderon, "Will a generous élite succeed in withstanding this racial tendency? Perhaps, but nothing can check the onward march of the United States. Their imperialism is an unavoidable phenomena." It is from the very lack of mutuality in Pan-Americanism that he draws this conclusion. The ostensible objects of that movement are so clearly artificial, so entirely in favor of the United States, so clearly hostile to the best interests of Latin America, that Latin Americans feel driven to the conclusion that it is merely a cloak for the ambition of the United States and of its intention to conquer South America in the interests of its own economic future. The defeat of Europe's victor would be the necessary preliminary to the extension of American supremacy, and for the United States to claim its bounden duty to exclude Europe's victor from the Western Hemisphere would, in face of the facts, merely prove its intention to play the part of conqueror itself. Even if we decline to accept this logic as true, we shall still be conscious that it is not a phase of the situation which we can neglect.

If we invoke the Monroe Doctrine in its primal meaning of our bounden duty and right to ensure our present and future economic welfare by any means in our power, we shall find ready at hand the ethics of economic expansion recently developed in Europe and there considered valid and significant. That we may need in the near future new markets and new territory to develop is by no means improbable, and there is no district so thoroughly well fitted for our economic needs as Latin America. If we decide to utilize the Monroe Doctrine to justify territorial expansion, we must recognize fully and frankly that the defense we are seeking is in the future and is not at present existent, and that it is a far cry from the type of defense which the framers of this Doctrine originally had in mind. It will still be conquest, aggression against those innocent of any intention to harm us, who are not themselves the perpetrators of the evil we are trying to remedy.

Unquestionably, territorial expansion, imperialism, by whatever name we call it,—and if we follow past precedent we shall once more term it the Monroe Doctrine,—means only one thing: war with Europe's victor in the first place and with South America in the second place. We should also apparently put ourselves in the very peculiar diplomatic position of fighting the Latin Americans to compel them to allow us to protect them from European aggression. We should also be quarreling with our own best friends in Europe, who cherish no designs against South America, in order to render assistance to those who fear us, even when we come bearing gifts which they do not require and which they would not need even should they be attacked. This is at present the only proposed application of the Monroe Doctrine. Our medium of foreign exchange is assured beyond the possibility of doubt; our political independence is not likely to be threatened. Our dangers lie in the future and are contingent rather than actual, while the steps to promote them are desirable rather than imperative, but they all involve aggression or expansion, interference with the control of the sea, and with Latin America. They cannot be described as defensive measures of the older type and we must look for their justification to the ethics of modern expansion as seen in Pan-Germanism and in recent international developments.

EXPEDIENCY OF THE MONROE DOCTRINE

Assuming however that expansion is desirable and ethical, is it attainable? Should we have a reasonable chance of success, if we attempted it? This is the true meaning of the phrase, "the expediency of the Monroe Doctrine." In a word, it means militarism; nothing else can justify it, nothing less can protect it. Its prerequisites include the establishment of our independence of the sea-power, both in the Atlantic and in the Pacific, by the development of a great navy and of a great merchant marine, one large enough to terrorize England, Germany, and Japan, the other sufficient in size to transport the whole volume of our foreign trade. We shall then need to provide an exchange system adequate for the transaction of the whole volume of our international trade, for if we challenge the sea-power we shall immediately deprive ourselves of her services as distributor and exchanger. A further indispensable military measure would be the occupation of Mexico and Central America in order to assure ourselves of the land approaches to the Panama Canal. So much would be needed to cope with Europe's victor. Until we have dealt with him and have made ourselves in the truest sense supreme over all the powers in the New World, aggression and expansion are not to be thought of. He too will have claims upon South America, and if we attempt to challenge them we must be prepared to do so in sufficient force to make good our protest.

There would then remain the Latin Americans to deal with. Our control of the Western Hemisphere would of course permit us to stop their trade with Europe, but the task of invasion would be stupendous. The area of Latin America is three times that of the United States. Not having been arranged by Nature for the purpose of facilitating military campaigns it is strewn with mountains, intersected by numerous rivers, fringed by a broad band of territory along the coast where the climate, swamps, and insects provide conditions of maximum difficulty for armies. The population is by no means negligible in numbers and is of proved courage. Even the peoples of the smaller states in Central America have merely to retire to the interior, and leave us to struggle with the enormous difficulty of crossing the hot coast district to achieve the privilege of chasing them around through the mountains and plateaus. To transport an army and provision it in Central America would require a merchant marine of great size and would certainly interfere considerably with the adequacy of our merchant marine for foreign commerce. Between the various states of Latin America there seems to be no legitimate strategic relationship. Each would have to be subdued separately if it were subdued at all and a series of campaigns, which would require years for completion, would be necessary unless the movement were undertaken by an army of truly phenomenal size and efficiency. In any case, an army of occupation would have to be left to retain control, unless an entirely unlikely result should eventuate, and gain us the willing submission of the inhabitants and their coöperation in the future. The conquest of even the smallest Central American state is beyond the power of the present United States army. The protection of its communications would not be possible with the present United States fleet. A navy at least as efficient as the present German navy and an army of a million men would be very likely adequate, but we could not definitely assume their adequacy until circumstances proved it. The expediency of the Monroe Doctrine in the sense of territorial expansion or imperialism involves this question: is the end itself sufficiently important to justify any such portentous efforts as would clearly be necessary to accomplish it?

To answer this question will require wisdom, discretion, and insight. Though we need not suggest a solution, we must not forget that our economic interests are primarily with Europe and not with South America. Adams and Monroe were entirely mistaken in expecting that the development of the future would accentuate the mutuality of interests between the United States and Latin America. Subsequent development has proved that the connection between the two is abnormal and that the true economic interests of both were with Europe. This much is certainly clear: it is not expedient for us to quarrel with Europe to extend our relations with Latin America. Indeed, it is an open question whether it would be to our economic advantage to close the markets of Europe temporarily by a conflict with the sea-power in order to monopolize eventually the markets of Latin America. The temporary loss in the European trade might conceivably exceed the total profits for many years in the trade with the new market. Whether we can extend our ægis over Latin America and exclude the European, without causing a general war with Europe, only the situation at the close of the present European war can decide. If we are not armed and ready when peace is signed, we may be foreclosed even before the attempt is made.

CHAPTER VI

THE ARGUMENT FOR DISARMAMENT

THE finest and in many ways the most attractive argument advanced in favor of total disarmament by the United States is the pacifist declaration of the duty of the United States to take advantage of its peculiar strategic position and set Europe an example.[1] Our position makes such a step more possible for us without endangering our national independence than for any European or Asiatic power. It is therefore for us to lead and not to wait in the expectation that some nation less favored than we will take the initiative. Such a step would be entirely in accordance with the general non-military character of our institutions and organization; and to conjure with such a precedent is ordinarily effective. If such an act is to accomplish its object, however, it will be

[1] This chapter is an attempt to state forcibly the arguments for disarmament as the succeeding is intended to state those against it.

highly necessary that the step should be taken as the result of a determination reached by the vast majority of the American people after due deliberation and discussion,—perhaps only after some great presidential campaign upon this specific issue of disarmament,—so that all the world might know that the chief ground and reason for the action was ethical and pacifist and not merely a motive of economy or a mixture of selfish and base influences. Expediency, economy, selfishness must be rigorously exorcised or the very purpose of the act will be frustrated.

Our disinterested conduct and our attempt at generous action must also be made crystal-clear to European nations by our behavior in things of lesser moment. To disarm from the most splendid of ethical motives and then to insist upon exacting from England a degree of consideration in matters of neutral trade which England felt greater than she could grant consistently with her safety; to act from motives of good will toward men and then to insist that the Japanese could not own property in the United States, or to decline to recognize that sort of government in Central American countries which they themselves deemed expedient, these would be so inconsistent with our general premises as to throw suspicion and doubt upon the purity of our original motive. Nobility in great things will compel us to act with generosity in small things, even though by it we should sacrifice much. Shall we make the greater sacrifice and balk at the less? Shall we yield the essential and hesitate before the unimportant?

Truly glorious would be the renunciation by the people of the United States of all ambition outside continental United States, the explicit surrender of all our outlying possessions, the abandoning of the Monroe Doctrine in any and every form, either as intervention, interference, or conquest. Economic advantages we would resolutely put behind us which the sword or threats might secure. The use of our wealth and potential strength as a club we would also explicitly forego, and declare openly to all men our intention in future to depend upon fair and honorable dealing and the great natural advantages of our position to promote our economic prosperity and secure for us all things truly necessary, declaring aught else wrong and unethical.

Another argument for disarmament is to be found in humanitarian motives—the horrors of war, the loss of life, suffering entailed upon the helpless and innocent, needless destruction of property resulting in no advantage to the belligerents, and in poverty and suffering to non-combatants. To many, such motives make a powerful appeal.

There are many reasons for believing that disarmament might be effected without involving real danger to our integrity. We are defended at present by our strategic position, the principal factors of which are the subtlety and delicate balance of European alliances and relationships rather than our actual geographical location, factors not easily supplemented by armies and navies and for which armament is a poor substitute. Were it more probable that a radical change would take place as a result of this war in the European balance of power, armament would be more justifiable. It seems likely that the vanquished will be beaten and humiliated but not crushed and that the balance of power will not be more changed than in 1815 or in 1870—and neither of these events produced a situation dangerous to the United States. That armament will be indispensable to our national integrity seems unlikely and disarmament in the near future for that reason appears to be comparatively safe. To this consideration we should add the fact that political control of the present territory of the United States is not as yet advantageous to any European nation or coalition in the settlement of its disputes in Europe and would be hardly essential to the extension of its authority elsewhere.

Our danger of invasion is really slight and disarmament comparatively safe, because the victor would lack the motive for invasion rather than the power. He will be seeking markets in undeveloped territory which will furnish him an opportunity for the investment of capital and for an increase of the productive and consumptive capacity of that community at an entirely abnormal rate. Such a field the United States will not present. It is already too highly developed and already too independent and elaborate an economic structure to furnish him anything beyond the normal market which he will expect to find in the greater states. We cannot in the nature of things be his prey.

Nor should we probably sacrifice our access to foreign markets by abandoning any attempt to dispute the control of the sea with Europe's victor. The mere fact that our trade is carried in foreign ships, our exchange performed by foreign banking houses, and our intercourse dependent upon the good will and sufferance of foreign nations, is not necessarily dangerous and undesirable, even though it might conceivably be both. The really significant fact is that of interdependence, for the continuance of trade is as important and essential to all other nations as it is to us, and could not be stopped by the victor on the sea without causing an international crisis of such magnitude that the whole world must rise and crush the sea-power in order to rid itself of the incubus. No nation controlling the sea can so act and subserve its own immediate ends, nor interfere with the freedom of passage of neutral nations without endangering its control and existence. Our interest in the sea is one that we share with the world at large and therefore one in which the world at large is as much interested as we are; hence it is one which the victor will be driven to recognize.

It is idle for us to seek independence on the sea from England or Germany. Reasons of domestic policy entirely unaffected by us or our policies impel both of them to assert rights in the ocean which neither could allow us to challenge. Our protestations they could not recognize as against their own paramount interests in the sea-power for defense. While intercourse is essential for our commercial prosperity, the control of the ocean highways is the prerequisite of England's existence or of Germany's international status. So long as England controls the sea, we need only remember the generosity and forbearance of her conduct in the past to assure ourselves of its continuance in the future. She understands thoroughly well the limitations and obligations of her position and is not in the least inclined to make intolerable to others what she deems necessary for herself. It is her peculiar geographical position, her peculiar economic condition, which makes real encroachment upon the rights of others difficult and dangerous for her. There can be in the nature of things no power in the world so well fitted to possess the sea-power as England, if we concede that any nation should have it. There can certainly be no power in the world whose possession of the sea-power would be so much to our own advantage; indeed, it is an open question whether we should be in a stronger and more advantageous position if we were more independent on the sea than we are at present. Not only her position but her experience in the past fits England to rule: she has learned her lesson and has demonstrated her ability to rule with efficiency and due regard for justice. The United States also possesses a heavy pledge of her generous interpretation of our requirements in the advantage she derives from our economic support in times of crises. Unless she can rely upon the complementary economic structure of the United States, England's position has a special weakness because in times of great stress her fleets cannot open the way to the markets in the Baltic and Black Seas whence come her necessities of life. So essential are our supplies to her that she must sacrifice even the reality of her overlordship on the sea to obtain our ungrudging support. The importance of this fact, many allege it is impossible to overestimate when we are considering the expediency of disarmament. With a change in the supremacy of the sea which would so revolutionize conditions as to make it essential for us to dispute its control with the victor we need not deal; for the English regard it so essential to their own existence that they will not allow another nation to possess it so long as England survives. Such a contingency as her literal destruction by the victor is so improbable as to be beyond the realm of hypothetics. Should Germany take her place, there are few advocates of disarmament who seem to believe that she would not fall heir to England's caution and generosity.

If we believe armament unnecessary for defense of our independence or of our economic welfare, is it not imperative for aggression? Do we not after all need to prepare to obtain by arms things

THE ARGUMENT FOR DISARMAMENT

merely desirable? Those who argue for disarmament deny specifically and generally that any adequate motives exist for aggression. With its ethics they disagree, and pronounce them as insufficient as the ethical notions behind Pan-Germanism which the vast majority of the American people have already condemned. Is this not sufficient, we are asked? Have not the people spoken? In addition, aggression is contrary to the non-military character of past precedent and to the tenets so often enunciated by our leaders of letting Europe alone. Turning from general principles to specific facts, we are told that aggression is not a possible policy for us because our strategic position is physically so weak that only a huge army can accomplish our object. Where the effort is so great, the stake must indeed be large to justify the undertaking, and the United States has not and never can have, it is claimed, interests which such aggression would be needed to subserve. And even if it had, we are now so late in commencing the elaborate preparations indispensable to the conduct of modern warfare that ten years of effort would scarcely put us in a condition to meet the victor of this present war. If he is exhausted by the struggle, he will not be capable of aggression and we shall need no defense;

PAN-AMERICANISM

while the great force to ensure the accomplishment of any legitimate ambitions which the United States may cherish will be unnecessary because he will be in no position to oppose. If, on the other hand, as it seems more probable, his army and navy are not only extraordinary in size but unusual in efficiency, any attempt at aggression would be futile for the United States because the war will probably not last long enough to permit us to complete adequate preparations. Nor should we forget, they tell us, that until we have secured independence on the sea we are forbidden aggression and the assurance of ambitions which development alone cannot obtain. The creation of a merchant marine and a great navy is too serious a task to be completed in a shorter period than a number of years, and before it could be finished the opportunity for an aggressive move of which it was the prerequisite would have entirely disappeared. Would we not also be foolish if we supposed that England and Germany would fail to fathom the scheme and wait until we had completed our preparations before attacking us?

To many the economic inexpediency of disarmament is convincing.[1] To attempt by aggression

[1] The student should read carefully Mr. Norman Angell's books.

THE ARGUMENT FOR DISARMAMENT

to protect economic factors and provide for our future prosperity seems to a growing constituency one of the worst of fallacies. Economic purposes are neither aided or created by fighting; economic factors are the results of economic causes; economic benefits are obtained by the operation of economic forces which legislation and good will are as powerless as guns and battleships to create. Money cannot be made by war; profit is not a matter of force but the result of the application of labor to capital. So far as the United States possesses a strong economic position, it is beyond the reach of others; to the extent the United States is weak, force is incapable to remedy its economic deficiency. If we have any true interest in South American trade, we shall have no difficulty in obtaining our profit, because they will be as anxious to sell or buy from us as we shall be to buy or sell to them. If we have capital to loan on terms they consider favorable, they will be more anxious to borrow than we are to loan. When they buy goods from us, they must pay us in goods; when they borrow capital, they must pay the interest and principal by exports whose amount will therefore be regulated by the true interests of the countries concerned. In the long run—and it must be remembered that all economic calculations are based upon the normal operation of economic forces during long years—nothing can interfere with this process and nothing can take its place. Whatever the economic facts are, war is powerless to alter them.

In addition, it is claimed that the United States itself presents possibilities of development so vast and resources so extraordinary that American capital and labor may easily find adequate employment here for decades. If we add to the capital and labor available for our own development the amount which we would otherwise spend upon armament, we shall have in the process of time an enormous accumulation of commodities, of capital, of economic satisfactions and comforts for the community itself, far greater in volume than anything aggression could have provided, and we shall have avoided all possibility of loss. To add to our own capital by the work of our own hands is a process whose profits are absolutely certain; to attempt aggression for the development of resources located at a distance, means experiencing risk out of all proportion to the degree of profit expected and without certainty of any profit at all. At the price of armament we do not need expansion.

To these weighty factors is added commonly

THE ARGUMENT FOR DISARMAMENT

the assertion that the expense of armament is enormous and continuous, and, worse than either, an economic waste. With our labor and capital we create certain commodities which possess no utility, except for a species of exertion which is in itself not only useless but destructive. To spend great sums of money and years of time in the creation of things which are useless is not the sort of a proposition supposed to commend itself to men and women of sanity, but when this time and effort are used to create things whose only purpose is the destruction of human life and of the necessities and comforts of existence, such expenditure becomes not only foolish but criminal. It is not so much the amount to which the pacifists object as the expenditure of labor and capital for things which are useless save for the promotion of destruction. While conceivably such actions may be in accordance with the passions of man, they can hardly be supposed to accord with his interests and cannot by any stretch of the imagination be termed expedient in an economic sense. The science of economics is a science of wealth, of production, of the creation of what was not before. War is the science of destruction and cannot by any conceivable possibility be economic; its very premise excludes it from consideration.

PAN-AMERICANISM

What policy then shall the United States, once disarmed, espouse? What position will she occupy? How can she possibly maintain the respect of other nations and procure consideration for her institutions from those powers at whose mercy she will place herself?

The nobility of her action should in itself secure for her an international status and leadership otherwise impossible of attainment. If the general economic premises above listed are valid, the United States could not lose anything of value. One thing and only one would be desirable. The true policy of the United States would then without question lie in a firm alliance with the sea power, which would *in its own interest* fight our defensive battles for us and in exchange for our economic assistance further our legitimate ambitions in South America and in the far East. Such an understanding the United States already possesses with England and by virtue of it we are supreme to-day in the Western Hemisphere, the owners of the Panama Canal, the possessors of the Philippines, and exert great influence in Latin American affairs. To all intents and purposes we are at present disarmed and there would be no obstacle in the way of the continuance of this understanding with England

THE ARGUMENT FOR DISARMAMENT

and no great probability she would desire to exclude us from the position which we at present occupy. By such an alliance we have already achieved more than we could have possibly obtained by a truly enormous armament: the sea power was in a position to give us what we wished without having to fight for it ourselves and without requiring us to fight either to obtain it or maintain it. So long as we ally to all intents and purposes with the sea power, whether that alliance is written in documents or exists merely as a tacit understanding capable of change at any moment, we may expect all that consideration which we could reasonably hope to obtain from armament. Should the sea-power change hands, it would be necessary for us to consummate as soon as possible a similar understanding with its new possessor. It would not be essential for us to arm. In this argument there is much that is plausible, while it certainly accords with the facts of the recent situation. Should the result of the war leave the international situation in the Western Hemisphere in all essentials what it is now, such reasoning would be valid, though not necessarily conclusive.

CHAPTER VII

THE PRICE OF DISARMAMENT

IF armament will cost money, so will disarmament. The most futile of all suppositions is that either will be without expense or without gain: from both will come gain, but a different sort of gain; both will cost money, commodities, and it may be human life, though perhaps in different degree and for a different purpose. A little cool thought will show that neither can be clear gain and that the true difficulty in the American problem lies in the balancing of the gains of one against its losses, of weighing the gains of one against those of the other, and the losses of one against those of the other. The law of compensation is inexorable: we get nothing without paying for it. If certain ends are to be achieved, disarmament may be our best method; if we have set our hearts upon accomplishing certain other ends, disarmament may compel us to sacrifice them. Neither armament or dis-

THE PRICE OF DISARMAMENT

armament is in itself an end; both are simply the means to ends. Only a lack of perspective can lead a statesman or student to regard armament or disarmament as desirable in themselves. Both are relative to losses that are to be avoided and to gains to be achieved.

What is the difference between disarmament and our present military and naval condition? A difference of name rather than of substance, for a force inadequate for the purpose in hand is as valuable as no force at all. At present our army is a police force intended chiefly to cope with the Indian problem which, because of the peculiar constitutional status of the Indian, could not be handed over to an ordinary constabulary. The army in the Philippines performs a similar duty. Our navy is a coast patrol because it is not adequate in the least to control the ocean approaches, our Island possessions, and the Panama Canal against the power supreme upon the sea. We shall be indeed lacking in a perception of the realities of the situation if we attempt to measure the adequacy of our navy by comparison with the strength of navies as insufficient as our own; it cannot be adequate until large enough to compel something more than respect from England. So long as a fleet can blockade our harbors without entering them, our coast defenses are of no particular importance for the control of the sea or for our intercourse with foreign nations. There is little purpose in keeping open a harbor which shipping cannot reach. If our navy were really capable of undertaking an aggressive campaign against the sea-power, harbor fortifications would relieve it of the necessity of detaching squadrons to keep open our harbors and so add to its offensive strength. Coast defenses can add to existing naval strength but can never supply its deficiencies; they defend the land and not the sea, and require in reality the coöperation of a large army rather than of a large fleet. They will not be really defensive until the American army is large enough to protect them from military assault from the rear. So long as the victor with the control of the sea in his hands can land military forces at will, he will find the problem simple of capturing our coast defenses. The latter are indeed vital to an adequate army in conflict with the sea-power but are of no real utility to a country whose only strength lies in a navy too small to cope with the sea-power. Let us not fall into the error of supposing that, because our army and navy are not adequate for such a task, they are therefore of no value at all. They perform well enough the tasks for which they are calculated, but the army is obviously not measured by the needs of the country for defense against invasion, nor is the navy built to take control of the sea from England, or to protect in transit a merchant marine. So far as defense or offense are concerned, the securing of our independence of the sea-power and the ensuring of our economic intercourse with foreign nations, we are already disarmed, because we possess no force in the least adequate to provide for any of these ends.

The real debate lies therefore between a more logical continuance of our present policy. We must resolutely reduce our navy to the same status as the army, making it a police patrol rather than a weapon of defense or offense, or prepare for clear and well-considered reasons for an armament adequate to win our independence of the sea-power and to promote such national ambitions and interests as the people may decide are imperative or significant. The chief cost of disarmament (one might almost say its first price) lies in the inability of easily reversing the decision and of afterwards meeting such contingencies as present themselves. So elaborate and vast are the preparations for modern warfare that adequate measures for defense or offense cannot be taken when the need is pressing.

To disarm therefore means to renounce beforehand, without knowing whether it may some day be imperative, expedient, advisable, or desirable for us to exert our potential strength, any possibility of using it for any purpose however reasonable. To say that there could be no such purpose is to speak without real comprehension of the unexpected and unforeseen events of the last two decades. The present war is the result of factors not as old as the men who are fighting in it, and whose significance has been realized by scarcely two generations of statesmen. Such radical and rapid shifts of the situation have occurred in time of peace and as a result of non-military factors. Shall we forget that armies and navies are busily at work transforming the international situation, perhaps revolutionizing every element in it of consequence to us? We shall not need to wait for a generation to witness cataclysmic upheavals in conditions. Invaders and conquerors have by no means limited their assaults against foes who gave them adequate reason. The history of our own country affords conspicuous examples of a need for armament to accomplish an object whose desirability no one now questions. If we decide to disarm, the present conditions of warfare will make it practically impossible for us afterward

THE PRICE OF DISARMAMENT

to alter the decision. If we are to modify our policy we must do so now in order that we may be able in the near future to meet imperative exigencies or further desirable ends.

It may be well for us to remember that we are annually paying enough money to provide an army and navy able to cope with any probability if only it can be efficiently spent instead of wasted. Indeed from some points of view the issue of disarmament might be phrased as the abandonment of our present pretense of armament, for which we pay so vast a sum without return or the attempt to make adequate the army and navy which we already support. What will it cost us to stop spending money beyond the needs of the police work which both now perform? What will that saving of a hundred and fifty million dollars a year cost us?

Will it cost us our security? Not necessarily, but quite possibly. We must remember that the props have been withdrawn from under our strategic structure which at one time made us practically invulnerable. We can be invaded to-day and might be assailed with conspicuous success; there will certainly be at the close of this war one if not two armies in existence large enough to conquer the United States. That any European country will have a motive for such a step is unlikely but by no means impossible. Our own defenses at present are the subtleties of the European situation itself, the delicate balance which makes it dangerous for a European nation to dispatch across the sea a large enough army to do us any damage or a large enough navy to attempt to assail our coast. But over these factors we exercise no control, and to disarm is to allow the exigencies of European politics and the interests of European nations to decide our destinies beyond a peradventure, without allowing us in any way to participate in molding the situation upon which our future depends or to protest against a result inimical to our interests and integrity. The tradition of American life is definitely non-military but if we are to decide advisedly that it is the most important American ideal to be continued at any cost, we should realize the price. Armies and navies are no longer permissive or abnormal elements in our strategic situation, though it is by no means certain that our security or integrity depends upon either.

Will disarmament cost us that access to the markets of the world upon which our economic existence depends? In all probability no, because it would not be expedient for the sea-power to try to prevent it. So long as the business of the world is as closely interlocked as at present, the prosperity of all nations depends upon continued access to each other. We are an integral part of the fabric and as long as their access to us is precisely as important as ours to them, they will be as anxious as we could possibly be to provide for the complete freedom of intercourse we desire. For the nation in control of the sea to threaten in any fashion the interests of all other nations would produce at once that very protest against its position which the sea-power must avoid at all costs. This aspect of the situation must influence German policy as definitely as it does English. Disarmament can hardly injure our commercial position so far as the continuance of intercourse is concerned.

Disarmament will surely cost us all our national ambitions, present and future. While it may not rob us of anything imperative for our existence, it will be likely to deprive us of nearly everything desirable or advisable which the interests of other nations do not impel them to yield to us. First we shall be compelled to renounce finally all notions of controlling the sea, and shall therefore be forced to throw ourselves upon the mercy of England or Germany in the Atlantic and of Japan in the Pacific, and depend upon their forbearance, generosity, and keen sense of their own interests to allow us such rights as are indispensable. Controversies with the sea-power growing out of its supremacy or out of other aspects of its international position, we shall be forbidden. Representations we may make, and we shall gain our point if they are willing to grant it, but we must realize at the outset that we shall never be able to force the issue upon them by presenting them with an ultimatum. Our privileges will necessarily be measured by their interests rather than by ours, while their policies rather than our needs will dictate the lineaments of our international position. An adequate merchant marine we shall be compelled to renounce and perforce rest satisfied with such facilities of ocean transport as the sea-power provides us, or which it allows others to furnish us, in addition to such a merchant fleet as it is willing to have us build. A merchant marine, capable of carrying all our commerce and of maintaining our independence, we can never have, for its very existence will at once arouse the apprehensions of the European power whose control of the sea rests fundamentally upon its own defensive needs and which will therefore scent aggression and

THE PRICE OF DISARMAMENT

danger and decline to permit us to develop such a merchant fleet.

South America we must recognize as foreign territory, occupied by foreign nations, in which we have neither rights nor interests. The Monroe Doctrine will promptly become impertinent and impossible. America for the Americans will be no longer a conceivable policy for us to maintain beyond the point which they are willing to accept. Although we may still assert our right of political independence and our right to ensure our economic independence, the two fundamental postulates of the Monroe Doctrine, they will both be expressions of opinion rather than policies, because we shall have definitely decided never to use force to support either. Without the possibility of its use we shall be totally unable to preserve political or economic independence, and will be compelled to accept as much of either as other nations find it in accordance with their interests to allow us to retain. That this will be considerable, our geographical position makes certain, but it will by no means guarantee as full a recognition of those principles as the American people may deem essential.

Our possessions outside the borders of the United States we shall retain, if we disarm, at the sufferance of the sea-power and of such nations as are able to reach them by land. In all probability we shall not keep them long. The control of the Gulf of Mexico and the supremacy of the Western Hemisphere to such an extent as we have possessed it, we must surrender forever, unless it becomes the interest of other nations literally to place their possessions in our hands for temporary safe-keeping. Everything outside the boundaries of continental United States including the Panama Canal will be sacrificed by disarmament and lost irretrievably. With them will disappear all possibility of aggression, control, overlordship, interference of any sort or kind in other countries, and any rights or privileges which aggressive action may be needed to obtain or maintain. Latin America, the Chinese trade, preferential rights in undeveloped countries we shall not have, and tariff laws and navigation acts militating against our trade we may be compelled to endure in silence. We shall possess outside the United States only what the good will and the interests of other nations voluntarily concede and we shall be compelled to accept patiently such action as they may take where they conceive that their interests run counter to ours.

The practical effect of our position when we

are once disarmed may thus be illustrated. We shall find it necessary to accept England's interpretation of the rights of neutrals and regard as final her list of contraband the moment she insists upon it. Intervention and watchful waiting in Mexico will become impossible, for the whole weight of our action depends upon Mexico's fear that we may use our strength against her. Once they know we have pledged ourselves not to employ it, they will not pay the slightest attention to our representations beyond that dictated by international courtesy. In our various quarrels with Japan, we shall immediately be driven to accept their view of the situation and accord them such privileges as they demand in the United States, or insist upon our own contention at the expense of sacrificing all privileges in Japan and in the Japanese trade which they would take away from us in retaliation. If Germany or England seize the Panama Canal, take Cuba, appropriate the property of American citizens in Central America, a dignified diplomatic protest will be the extent of our power. Our position and the rights of American citizens will be measured by the lack of motives in other nations to do us harm, because the moment a reason arises urging them to deprive American citizens of rights there will be nothing to prevent their doing it.

Will disarmament cost us economic prosperity? Not at present, but in the future the degree of our prosperity, due to the operation of economic forces, will in all probability seriously reduce our margin of profit. To suppose as many do that our lack of strategic relation to the European field of war gives us no interest in their difficulties and makes their problems and affairs matters of indifference to us, is to cherish a fallacy of the most dangerous description. Our economic interests are complementary to theirs and absolutely identical in character. The economic phenomena in Europe which are at the roots of the present war exist in America and will be operative here in the very near future to a degree not greatly different from that in Europe. True, we do not have their precise difficulties to cope with, but we have the other end of the same situation, and if it does not manifest itself here in the same specific instances, we shall still be foolish to conclude that it will not affect our interests and our prosperity.

Disarmament will prevent us from obtaining access to the markets of the world except on terms favorable to other nations and consequently on

THE PRICE OF DISARMAMENT

terms less advantageous to us than to them. There is at any one moment only so much trade. If all remain satisfied with the share which the normal workings of economic forces allots to them, we shall have nothing of which to complain, but the most striking feature of the present situation is the insistence of some nations that they ought to get more than their normal share. To obtain it some have gone to war with others, whom they claim already have more than their share, and the latter are trying to retain it. So far as the United States is concerned, it will not make a great deal of difference which of the European nations obtains or retains an abnormal share of the world's trade. Obviously the strongest will get it, and the others will share what is left in some rough proportion to their strength, while the nation least fitted to compel others to consider its needs, will get only as much as the victors do not feel it worth their trouble to take. This interference by military and political forces with the working of economic factors must not be exaggerated: the economic factors themselves prevent its going beyond a certain point. It cannot entirely ruin our prosperity, if we actually have goods to sell which other nations wish to buy. But it can interfere in the future as it has in the past with the rate of our development and with our degree of profit. It will first reduce our trade with the lesser developed nations where the proportionate profits are large, and will compel us to deal with the highly developed nations where the normal profits are small and the competition great. Access to markets where competition has been minimized by political forces and the profits consequently enhanced will not be for us.

To meet the situation we will be driven to develop intensively our own resources and work hard to produce things which the world must have and for which it is ready to pay. It will mean of course economic pressure, an increase in the number of hands beyond the demand for work, and the creation of a more or less permanent body of individuals not able to find employment. We have hitherto had in the United States practically no poverty in the European sense and no margin of existence. These phenomena are just appearing and their development will be accelerated by any slackening in our rate of progress. At the same time the surplus population can emigrate without danger to our political independence because the size of our population will be of no military consequence once we have disarmed. Our geographical location will in all probability continue to make political conquest inexpedient for nations strong enough to undertake it. As the intensified development of our own resources proceeds, the supplies of minerals will decrease at a faster rate than at present, the land will yield constantly diminishing returns to a greater degree, and we shall be steadily looting the capital which Nature has furnished us. In each decade more labor will be required to secure the same degree of profit and as men continue to increase and the resources to decrease it will not be many decades before the pressure of existence will become apparent. We are already deeply in debt to Europe for the capital which we have borrowed in the past and some day we must pay the principal. It can be discharged only from profits, and the moment we reduce the present rate of development and therefore the present profit, the annual payment on our debt will become a larger and larger share of our net income, not because the sum is greater but because the income is diminishing. Above all we must remember that the pressure of these problems will steadily increase, bringing lower wages, higher prices, less to eat, less to wear, while a larger and more permanent part of the population is unemployed and lives on the margin of existence. The present standard of comfort in the United States can be maintained only by maintaining our present rate of progress.

Disarmament therefore will ask the present generation to sacrifice something of its present comfort, a good deal of its future well-being, and the possibilities of enhancing its economic prosperity and that of subsequent generations. It will prevent us from attempting to remove by force, arbitrary and artificial interference by other nations with the workings of the economic processes upon which our present prosperity depends. No European statesman supposes to-day that economic forces can be created by war or by legislative fiat, but they do believe that their operation can at times be consciously assisted and that political factors can always prevent interference by the political or military strength of other nations in their own interests. This protection disarmament will compel us entirely to forgo. We shall trust ourselves to the sufferance and good will of the other nations of the world, not expecting them to aggrandize themselves at our expense, but ready to accept the worst if they decide to act selfishly rather than with generosity. Is it not perhaps wise for us to ask whether they are at present ready to treat us in the spirit in which we purpose to deal with them? Do they show at present a conspicuous willingness to advance each other's interests? Have they forborne to promote their own where they knew them to be inimical to others? Have they hesitated to employ the force at their command to further their interests against peoples unprotected and utterly innocent of offense? Can we wisely accept their interpretation of their interests as the measure of our privileges?

We may also ask whether the sacrifice of the United States in the interests of universal peace will accomplish its object. The utility of disarmament as an argument for peace will depend entirely upon the extent to which other nations accept our decision as actuated by noble motives rather than by a mixture of vanity and selfishness. Europeans claim to-day that the condition of our army and navy is due to the fact that we do not believe ourselves threatened rather than to our belief in the wickedness of war; that we would act as they have if the situation were similar. Disarmament is cheaper for us and not dangerous, they insist. There are indeed so many economic and quasi-economic motives cited in support of disarmament which do appeal to certain selfish instincts in every population that the purity of our motive in reaching that decision will be only too open to question by those who seek to impugn our sincerity. Unfortunately, too, the true distinction between war and peace seems hardly to be that of armament or disarmament. The line is difficult to draw to-day on account of the interrelated aspect of the economic world which spreads the interests of any nation to the confines of the globe. Where mine begins and thine leaves off is very difficult to state when we deal with the complex affairs of nations. Until we shall include in war every and any method of interfering unduly with the ordinary operations of life, we shall not make a distinction of any importance between war and peace. It is only too evident that the crux of the difficulty in international politics is the desire to secure an abnormal share of the world's trade, a valuable dependency, the right to exploit a certain people or a tract of land. Until the attempt to take another's property shall be deemed equally bad whether or not it results in actual warfare, no lasting result can be obtained. Indeed, a true comprehension of the present situation seems to show that warfare is really directed against the furtherance of economic ends by economic aggression and unfair dealing in other ways than war. Shall we therefore say to those who see their property being

THE PRICE OF DISARMAMENT

filched from them by "peaceful" methods, that they must not resist, because war is wrong? They see and feel a very real wrong and they perceive very clearly that nothing except force can save them; to it therefore they appeal with promptitude and dispatch. The true aggressor is the man they assail, for they regard themselves as pushed already into the last ditch and driven to defend their firesides by means which they would otherwise have preferred not to employ. The horrors of war, its dangers and risks they fully appreciate, but they feel that they cannot yield all they hold dear without a struggle.

Peace in fact is not a temporal condition, nor merely abstinence from war: it is a state of mind which will become universal when men no longer desire to take another's property by methods whose fairness the other will deny. Such a state of morality is not something which can be created in a brief time by agitation, example, precedent, or oratory. It is a condition and is no more something into which the community can be dragged or argued, than men can be coerced into it by shooting off cannon. The fact that it does not exist is the clearest possible evidence that the prerequisites are not yet true and are beyond the reach of argument or logic. Force is not the difficulty; the trouble lies in selfishness, wickedness, ignorance, and a lack of morality and Christianity in mankind. Nothing short of the slow process of education and growth, by which the bad will be made good and the covetous and greedy will be reformed seems capable of creating universal peace. Some difficulties, argument may avoid, some troubles may be explained, needless misunderstandings adjusted and the toll of suffering and destruction somewhat reduced.

If this is in a measure true, are we wise to entrust our national integrity and our future prosperity to the present moral and ethical impulses of European nations in the expectation of thus promoting the cause of peace? Will it be expedient to advertise beforehand our intention not to defend ourselves from robbery of any sort and our reliance upon the goodness of other nations? Will the victor look upon our interests as his own, and forbear to take from us more than we will gladly give him? Will he listen in the future to our representations of economic distress and trade difficulties and sacrifice something of his own welfare to advance ours?

Bibliography

WHILE the diplomatic history of the nineteenth century in Europe remains a sealed book, the evidence available in contemporary history must differ widely from the line and precept which investigators in other fields than diplomatic history are accustomed to demand. For this reason the evidential precepts for sifting, evaluating, and comparing evidence at other periods, "result when applied strictly to the history of the last quarter of a century, in a series of negations and colorless affirmations which neither describe nor explain events." We must either deny the movements of our own time historicity, until we ourselves have passed from the scene, or recognize frankly and fully that we shall have to be satisfied with a good deal less than certainty and be content when we have produced an approximation of the truth which an investigator of the Stuart period would stigmatize as mere guesswork. Never should the student of contemporary affairs forget this probability of error in conclusions which seem undoubtedly sound; nor allow his reader to forget that some of his boldest statements would be regarded in treating almost any period of the past as conjectures scarcely worth hazarding. He must do the best he can with the bricks he has, and leave the production of a final and accurate account for his children and grand-children.

The question of evidence reduces itself to two propositions: the relative importance of data whose correctness is certain and the relative credibility of testimony which would be important if it were true. Indeed, in most cases, we have to deal as students less with evidence than with testimony, itself explicit, clear, and from authoritative sources. The real difficulty lies in the amount of this testimony, its conflicting statements, and the apparently unimpeachable character of all the witnesses. It may often be clear that a witness might know the whole truth about the facts we are investigating; but this will not prove that he has chosen to tell us any of it.[1]

Minute details, forests of dates, economic statistics by the thousand, innumerable biographical data, we have; to provide them for the period of Julius Cæsar is difficult and exhausting and takes much of our time; we need not look for

[1] Usher, *Pan-Germanism*, revised edition, 1915, p. 346.

BIBLIOGRAPHY

them in contemporary history; they fairly throng upon us; but are the least valuable and essential part of the story. In the second category, testimony, belongs nearly everything of an interpretative nature or which tends in any degree to elucidate these teeming facts and piece them into something resembling a picture. Beyond doubt these are the vital things. These, the secrets of senates and presidents, we know in the past centuries; these we lack almost entirely to-day. Letters by the hundred, memoirs, interviews we have, but they are all testimony, important only if true. And those who hold the key are distressingly discreet. Apparently, these difficulties are less serious in American than in European history, but the difference is more seeming than real; for where we can be quite sure we see the American side of the picture clearly and accurately, the clouds and mist which shroud the European background prevent us from apprehending beyond mistake the meaning of the whole.

In deciding what was credible and whom to believe I have tried to apply a few relatively simple tests. Of most importance seems to me the logic of events, the reading which best explains the really potent happenings, like the building of the Panama Canal, the annexation of the Philippines

—*les faits accomplis*. It must too always be a reading in accord with the logic of events in modern Europe, for if one thing is more conspicuously true than another it is the world aspect of international politics. No country is isolated; no country unaffected by the sea-power of England or the ambitions of the Pan-Germanists.

To rely upon this logic of events, as I have called it is merely to accept, *faute de mieux*, the guidance of indirect testimony which could not have been manufactured for a purpose, in preference to a choice between several equally plausible explanations provided for us by those whose interests are obvious in guiding our opinions. We simply insist "upon a reasonably complete chain of indirect or circumstantial evidence, composed of actual events, however minute, as superior evidentially to any amount of direct testimony which is open to the suspicion of manufacture for the purpose of forming opinion, if not with the intention actually to mislead it." A comparison of this logic of events with direct testimony, American and foreign, with the ideas of competent foreign observers, with what we believe to be true of the European situation itself, and with the actions of our own and foreign governments seems to me to provide eventually the only approach to certainty we are likely to achieve during our own lifetime. To detail this process of reasoning to the reader would be tedious and not informative, for usually a brief inspection of the situation in the light of the general premises will show him the trend of reasoning. I have contented myself with stating results and not processes. Until testimony will stand the test of indirect evidence, I regard it as too uncertain for me.

These postulates at once exclude from the student's consideration all propaganda of any sort, except as evidence of what such partizans advocate; all newspaper and magazine material, except as providing testimony or as the factual background. In the former category belong the literature of peace societies and political associations—rhetoric in Congress, in the press, and between covers. Testimony is testimony and not evidence, whenever and wherever found. So, too, natives or returned travelers from South America, Mexico, or Japan are not necessarily equipped with more accurate information about the sentiments of the population or governmental policies, even after a residence of years, than we are about the secrets of the United States after a residence of a lifetime. We must demonstrate first that our witness really ought to know what we are seeking and then prove that he has some adequate motive to tell us.

The excellent bibliographies of American history —J. N. Larned's *Literature of American History*, Channing, Hart, and Turner's *Guide to American History*, and the bibliographies of Hart's *American Nation*—render a work of supererogation the listing of even that part of the voluminous literature which any student must perforce utilize. The Library of Congress publishes careful lists of all government publications, and has also compiled elaborate bibliographies on Cuba, Hawaii, the far East, and the like, thoroughly covering American interests. On a less elaborate scale and less accurately the Pan-American Union has done something of the sort for the literature in English about Latin America. For the less expert student the following titles and brief comments may prove useful as indications of books likely to be helpful.

I

THE UNITED STATES

a. Strategic Position.

MAHAN, A. T. *The Influence of the Sea Power upon History, 1660–1783.* Boston, 1890.

An epoch-making book of the first caliber, which even the casual reader will do well to

BIBLIOGRAPHY

ponder carefully. It has revolutionized the conceptions of men who guide empires.

—— *Sea Power in its Relations to the War of 1812.* Boston, 1905.

—— *The Interest of America in Sea Power, Present and Future.* Boston, 1898.

—— *Naval Administration and Warfare.* Boston, 1908.

Undoubtedly, Admiral Mahan's books form the most important single contribution to an understanding of the polity of the United States.

SEELEY, J. R. *Expansion of England.* London, 1883.

An extraordinary book, also epoch-making, in its analysis of England as colonizer and empire builder.

SEMPLE, E. C. *American History and its Geographic Conditions.* 1903.

BRIGHAM, A. P. *Geographic Influences in American History.* 1903.

Slighter and less valuable than Miss Semple's fine contribution.

b. *American Development.*

USHER, R. G. *The Rise of the American People.* New York, 1914.

BIBLIOGRAPHY

The present author has here set forth at greater length the fundamental notions of American history which underlie the present volume. There his defense can be found.

ADAMS, BROOKS. *America's Economic Development*. 1900.

On the West India trade, the best work is Edward Channing's *History of the United States*, ii., iii.

c. Foreign Relations.

MOORE, J. B. *American Diplomacy*. New York, 1905.

A relatively brief but thoroughly excellent sketch by probably the best equipped American authority.

LATANÉ, J. H. *Diplomatic Relations of the United States and Spanish America*. Baltimore, 1900.

COOLIDGE, A. C. *The United States as a World Power*. New York, 1908.

DUNNING, H. A. *The British Empire and the United States*. New York, 1914.

A semi-official history, written for the Centennial of the Peace of Ghent. Careful, astute, as valuable for what it avoids as for what it says.

BIBLIOGRAPHY

TRAVIS, IRA DUDLEY. *The History of the Clayton-Bulwer Treaty.* Ann Arbor, 1900.

JOHNSON, W. F. *Four Centuries of the Panama Canal.* 1906.

MOORE, J. B. *Digest of International Law.* 8 vols. 1906.

> For reference only.

d. *The Monroe Doctrine.*

HAMILTON, S. M. *The Writings of James Monroe,* vi. New York and London, 1898–1903.

> Contains the correspondence and the messages up to 1823. A useful selection of subsequent statements has been printed in American History Leaflet, No. 4. A bibliography of the literature is in D. C. Gilman's *Monroe.*

HENDERSON, J. B., JR. *American Diplomatic Questions.* 1901.

> The discussion of the Monroe Doctrine is particularly full and satisfactory.

LAWRENCE, T. J. *Essays on Some Disputed Questions in Modern International Law.* 2d ed., Cambridge, England, 1885.

> The views of a distinguished English international lawyer.

REDDAWAY, W. F. *The Monroe Doctrine.* Cambridge, England, 1898.

BIBLIOGRAPHY

An English discussion, temperate and excellent. See also J. A. Cook in the *Fortnightly Review*, Sept., 1898, pp. 357–368.

PÉTIN, HECTOR. *Les États Unis et la Doctrine de Monroe*. Paris, 1901.

A French point of view.

ONCKEN, HERMANN. *Historisch-politische Aufsätze und Reden*, i., 37–95. München, 1914.

The interesting views of a leading German historian and publicist.

BINGHAM, HIRAM. *The Monroe Doctrine, an Obsolete Shibboleth*. New Haven, 1913.

e. The Influence of International Politics on the United States.

USHER, R. G. *Pan-Germanism*. Boston, 1913. Revised edition, enlarged, 1915.

In this volume the present author has stated his general conception of the European situation. The bibliography in the revised edition contains numerous authorities.

MAHAN, A. T. *The Interest of America in International Conditions*. Boston, 1910.

The least valuable of his writings.

—— *The Problem of Asia and its Effect on International Politics*. Boston, 1900.

BIBLIOGRAPHY

ARNOLD, W. T. *German Ambitions as they Affect the United States.*

REINSCH, P. S. *World Politics at the End of the Nineteenth Century as Influenced by the Oriental Situation.* New York, 1900.

GRIFFIS, H. E. *America in the East: A Glance at our History, Prospects, Problems, and Duties in the Pacific Ocean.* New York, 1914.

MASAOKA, N. *Japan to America.* New York, 1914.

> A series of papers by Japanese leaders on relations with the United States. It is testimony, not evidence, except of what they wish us to believe.

LEA, HOMER. *The Valor of Ignorance.*

> Written by an American soldier of fortune, who knew the far East well.

f. Imperialism: Expansion.

WILLOUGHBY, W. F. *Territories and Dependencies of the United States.* New York, 1905.

RANDOLPH, C. F. *Law and Policy of Annexation.* New York, 1901.

> The constitutional aspects of imperialism. The bibliographies give titles of many less pretentious but more important articles and reviews.

BIBLIOGRAPHY

g. *Peace and Disarmament.*

The publications of the Association for International Conciliation, of the World's Peace Foundation, and of the American Peace Society.

ANGELL, NORMAN. *The Great Illusion.* New York and London, 1910.

—— *Arms and Industry.* New York and London, 1914.

MAHAN, A. T. *Armaments and Arbitration, the Place of Force in the International Relations of States.* New York, 1912.

—— *Some Neglected Aspects of War.* Boston, 1907.

II

LATIN AMERICA

CALDERON, F. GARCIA. *Latin America; Its Rise and Progress.* New York, 1913.

The best book in English by a Latin American.

MEROU, M. G. *Historia de la Diplomacia Americana.* Buenos Ayres, 1904.

BRYCE, JAMES. *South America, Observations and Impressions.* New York, 1913. Revised edition, 1914.

BIBLIOGRAPHY

The work of a scholar of international repute, of a statesman, and diplomatist, written almost from a cosmopolitan point of view, and by a man with deep insight into the American people and the way in which things must be put to reach them.

CLEMENCEAU, GEORGES. *South America To-day: A Study of Conditions, Social, Political, and Commercial.* New York, 1911.

A study by an eminent French statesman and publicist, whose natural sympathies are with the Latin Americans.

DOMVILLE-FIFE, C. W. *The Great States of South America.* London, 1910.

An honest, readable English account from the English point of view.

"Latin Americans and the United States," by various authors. *Annals of the American Academy of Political and Social Science,* July, 1903.

CRICHFIELD, G. W. *American Supremacy: The Rise and Progress of the Latin American Republics and their Relations to the United States under the Monroe Doctrine.* New York, 1908.

Perhaps the best of the veritable deluge of literature issued by enterprising publishers.

BIBLIOGRAPHY

CRICHFIELD, G. W. *The South American Year Book*. London. Louis Cassier Co., Ltd.

> Invaluable for statistical information.

PALMER, F. *Central America and Its Problems*. New York, 1910.

> A frank story of what the noted correspondent saw.

—— *The South American Series*. Scribners, New York.

> This series of descriptive books seems to be the best at present available.

The reader's attention is called to the admirable articles in the last edition of the *Encyclopedia Britannica;* they contain perhaps the latest information from authoritative sources. The periodical literature on Latin America is more than usually important because of the paucity of good books and because of the contemporary character of the subject. While the *North American Review*, the *Political Science Quarterly*, the *American Journal of International Law* contain valuable articles from time to time, the English, French, and German reviews are ordinarily better informed and more apt to print extended surveys because their audiences have long been interested in Latin America from something more than academic reasons. *Archives Diplomatiques, Questions Diplo-*

BIBLIOGRAPHY

matiques et Coloniales, *Revue Générale de Droit International Public*, the *Fortnightly*, *Contemporary*, *Nineteenth Century and After*, and the South American Supplement of the London *Times* are to be strongly recommended. The interest in Germany is more recent and the articles less numerous. *France-Amérique*, published at Paris, and *Union Ibero-Americano*, published at Madrid, make a specialty of Latin American news. There is also a *Pan-American Magazine*, published at New Orleans.

III

PAN-AMERICANISM

BARRETT, JOHN. *The Pan-American Union: Peace, Friendship, Commerce.* Washington, 1911, pp. 251.

    An official account by the Director-General of the Union.

CHANDLER, C. L. "The Beginnings of Pan-Americanism." *Bulletin of the Pan-American Union*, Sept., 1911.

FORTESCUE, G. "The Pan-American Ideal." *Bulletin of the Pan-American Union*, Jan., 1912.

GARRIGO, ROQUE F. *America para los Americanos.* New York, 1910.

BIBLIOGRAPHY

LIMA, OLIVEIRA MANOEL. *Pan-Americanismo* (Monroe, Bolivar, Roosevelt). Rio de Janeiro, 1907. pp. 342.

LOBO, H. *De Monroe á Rio Branco*. Rio de Janeiro, 1912. pp. 155.

ORLANDO, ARTHUR. *Pan-Americanismo*. Rio de Janeiro, 1906. pp. 220.

ROOT, ELIHU. "The Pan-American Spirit." *Outlook*, Oct. 20, 1906.

SHERRILL, C. H. *The Pan-Americanism of Henry Clay, Sarmiento, and Root*. Buenos Ayres, 1909. pp. 11.

—— "The South American Point of View." *American Association of International Conciliation, Bulletin* No. 52, 1913.

TORRES-CAICEDO, J. M. *Union Latino-Americano; pensamiento de Bolivar para formar una Liga Americana, su Origen y sus Desarroelos y Estudio sobre la Cuestion ó un Gobièrno legitimo es responsable par los Claños y Perguicios occasionados a los Extrangeros par las Facciones*. Paris, 1865.

URRUTIA, F. G. *El idèal international de Bolivar*. Quito, 1911. pp. 105.

To this meager literature may be added a few scattered magazine articles of lesser moment: South American Supplement to the London *Times* for July 30, 1912; W. C. Fox in the *Forum*, vol. xxx., 294; the New York *Nation*, vol. xxii., 505; xxiii., 332. The correspondence and state papers of Clay and Blaine contain some illustrative material. The publications of the Pan-American Union are devoted almost entirely to trade statistics and descriptive material of an elementary character intended for those entirely ignorant of Latin America. The material in Spanish intended for circulation in Latin America is also largely descriptive. Excerpts and translations from the novelists and agitators anent the United States appear from time to time in the *Review of Reviews*, the *Literary Digest*, and similar periodicals.

INDEX

Acquaintanceship, lack of, between United States and Latin America, 228-31

Adams, John Quincy, Secretary of State, 76, 77, 78, 80, 88

Administrative problems of Pan-Americanism, 267-78

Aggression, United States not created by, 7-8, 257; independence of the sea-power the prerequisite of, 336-7; nature of, to-day, 371-9, 401-2

Alaska, 155

America, use of the word, 21, note, 28, note. *See* United States

—— Central. *See* Central America

—— Latin. *See* Latin America

—— South. *See* South America

American people, resolved to play disinterested part in crisis, 8-9; non-military character of, 17; must decide future policy, 18; effect of English sea-power on, 39-40; attitude toward England after Revolution, 50-1; attitude toward Latin America, 203, 226-33, 250-3, 261, 286-8, 291, 299-301; present issues before, 3-18, 327-32

Argentine Republic, 273

Armament, the prerequisite of aggression, expansion, or independence of sea-power, 332, 401-2; what its lack would compel us to sacrifice, 422-42; distinction from disarmament, 422-3, 438-9

Army, place of, in strategic fabric of United States, 13, 14, 23-5, 27, 45-50, 52, 101-8

—— United States, 29, 57, 196, 341-2; present condition of, 314-5, 422-3; present cost of, 345-6, 427

Atlantic Ocean, influence of, upon United States, 21-5, 30, 33-5, 98-100

Balance of power in Europe, effect on United States of, 25-7, 107-8

Belgium, 4

Brazil, 273

California, Japanese in, 197-8

Canada, 32, 52-3, 122, 156-7

Canning, English Foreign Secretary, 74, 77, 81, 83, 88

Capital, in Latin America, 81, 95, 131-4, 146-7, 163-5, 244-9; in United States, 358; future condition of, 362-6

Central America, 96; influence of United States in, 154-5, 234, 254-6

Clayton-Bulwer Treaty, 88

Coast defenses of United States, 423-4

Communication, condition of, in past, 21-5; improvements of nineteenth century in, 98-101, 356-7; influence of, on South America, 127-34, 218-25

Confederation, Pan-American, prerequisites of, 207-11; administrative and legal problems of, 267-84; weakness of, 309-10, 320-1

Conquest of United States, prerequisites of, 27-30, 35-6, 136

Contraband, 168-174

Cotton culture, provides me-

461

INDEX

Cotton culture—*Continued*
  dium of exchange with Europe, 84–7

Customs union, Pan-American, 232, 267, 319

Democracy, in United States, 24; in Pan-Americanism, 267–84; in Latin America, 285–303

Democratic party, influence of, on issue of neutral trade, 178–9, 183

Disarmament, argument for, 407–21; price of, 422–42; distinction from armament, 422–3, 438–9

Economic aspects of Pan-Americanism, 232–49

Economic factors in American development, 21, 31–3, 59–65, 80–8, 93–5, 98–108, 351–66

Economic factors in modern Europe, 31–3, 111–23, 137–8, 157–65, 362–6; in Japan, 189–91; in United States, 351–66, 434–7

Economic inexpediency of armament or war, 416–19

Economics of expansion, 351–66

Emigration, modern problem of, 116–23, 161, 360–2

England, American independence of, 21–5, 32–7; influence of, on United States, 39–40; nature of sea-power of, 41–4; limitations of sea-power of, 44–52; moderation in use of sea-power of, 55–6; influence of sea-power on United States, 56–8; economic interests of, 42–3, 160–3, 334–5; in War of 1812, 51–2; merchant marine of, 55–6, 340–1; double rôle played by, in our colonial history, 68; control of West Indies and South America by, 71–4, 80–3; Monroe Doctrine aimed at, 79; objects to territorial expansion of United States, 87; supremacy of, in Western Hemisphere lost by building of German navy, 91; arranges to hand supremacy to the United States, 92–4; economic motives of, to-day, 111–23; past solution of present economic problems of, 120–1; Latin America easiest concession for, to a victorious Germany, 146–7; possibilities of clash of, with United States, 151–83; attitude toward neutral trade, 51, 68–9, 166–83; holds strategic points of, Western Hemisphere, 152–3; loss of supremacy of Pacific to Japan, 188–9, 192–5. *See also* Sea Power *and* Supremacy of Western Hemisphere

Equality, legal, between citizens of United States and Latin America, 268–9, 278–81

—— social, between citizens of United States and Latin America, 289–303

Ethics of expansion, 367–89

Ethics of white conquerors, 257–66, 384–7

Exchange facilities for United States with Latin America, 234–7; with rest of the world, 180, 276

Exchange, medium of, difficulty of securing, in colonial days, 60–4; after the Revolution, 50–3, 60–7, 70, 78; provided by cotton, 84–7

Expansion, territorial, of the United States, caused by demand for cotton, 85–7, 254; resulting from our

INDEX

Expansion—*Continued*
supremacy in the Western Hemisphere, 92–7, 254–5; problem of to-day, 330, 336–7, 371–2, 375–81; the economics of, 351–66; ethics of, 367–89; present expediency of, 396–406; made impossible by disarmament, 429–33

Europe, strategic relations of North America with, 24–8 30–1, 98–108; economic interests of, in Western Hemisphere, 31–3; economic motives of, 111–23; geographic relationship with North and South America compared, 218–24; dependence of Western Hemisphere intellectually upon, 225–6; interdependence of United States with, 364–6

Far East, 94–7, 184–200, 330–1
Foreign policy of United States, 10–11, 252–3. *See* Monroe Doctrine
France, 5, 51, 73, 97, 345–6; influence of, on Latin America, 225–6, 239, 265

Germany, influence upon United States of development of, 90–2; economic motives of, 111–23, 137–8; probabilities of clash with United States, 135–50; use of English sea-power against, 166–71

Hawaii, 195–6
Holy Alliance, 73–4

Immigration, influence of, upon United States, 351–3; upon South America, 297
Imperialism, 252, 330, 399–406; premise of, 371–2
Independence of United States of sea-power, 327–9; ethics of, 333; prerequisites of, 337–43; cost of, 343–50
Independence of United States, foundation of political, 21–38
India, 143, 194
Indians, treatment of, in United States, 86, 258–9, 264, 281, 296–7; problem of, in Latin America, 257–66, 281, 290–303
International economics, 237–49, 351–66
International ethics, 375–89
Invasion of United States, prerequisites of, 27–31, 35–6
Inventions of nineteenth century, influence on United States and its position, 98–108; on Europe, 114–6; on South America, 221–2
Isolation, of United States from Europe, 21–5; disappearance of, 100–1; of South America from Europe, 218–24

Japan, character of people, 184–5; strategic position of, 186–7; building of fleet secures supremacy of Pacific, 187–8; object of Japanese ambition, 189; relations with England, 190–95; with United States, 195–200

Latin America, basis of notion of mutual interest with United States, 59–60, 65–7, 70, 78–9; early relations of England with, 71–3, 80–3; winning independence for, 72; economic basis of English monopoly of trade with, 80–1, 89; economic interest of United States with, 80–1, 94–5; conditions in, 138–43, 272–6, 278; strategic position of, 146, 305–7, 310–13; future relations of England

INDEX

Latin America—*Continued*
to, 157-65; extension of American trade with, 158-9; isolation in time from North America, 221-3; dependence of, on Europe, 223-4; lack of economic mutuality of, with United States, 232-49; race problem in, 229, 257-66, 281, 289-303; independence of United States about to be declared, 320-3; bibliography of, 454-7

Latin Americans, character and attainments of, 140-1, 220-2, 226-8, 239, 290-303; attitude toward England, 71-4, 81-3, 306-7; attitude toward Germany, 148-50, 307; attitude toward United States, 226-33, 250-1, 253-7, 261, 285-8, 291, 296-9, 301-3, 307-10, 312, 320-3, 399-400

Legal equality between citizens of United States and Latin America, 268-9, 278-81

Legal problems of Pan-Americanism, 278-84

Markets, expanding, necessity for, in American colonies, 61-79; necessity for, in modern Europe, 111-23, 371-6; for Germany, 137-8; for England, 157-65; for Japan, 189-91; for United States, 351-66, 401-6; disarmament will exclude United States from, 434-6

Merchant marine, American, 69, 166, 337-8, 340-1; English, 55-6, 340-1; German, 335

Mexico, 32, 86-7, 214, 256, 403

Monroe, James, President, 75, 79, 83, 88

Monroe Doctrine, clash of victor with, 5; origin of, 70-9; change in, as result of cotton, 83-7; supposed abrogation by Clayton-Bulwer Treaty, 88; attitude of Germany toward, 149-50; of England, 75-9, 154; of Japan, 196-9; of Latin America, 203, 215-7, 225, 232-3, 261, 308, 320, 399-400; importance of, at this time, 330; true principle of, 390-2; past expedients to advance, 392-95; present expediency of, 395-406; bibliography of, 451-2

Navy, English, protects American colonies, 34-44; used against United States, 50-3, 66-9; protects Latin American independence, 72-4, 77, 81-2, 255. *See also* Seapower

—— German, robs England of supremacy of Western Hemisphere, 90-1; and hands it to United States, 91-7; robs England of supremacy of Pacific, 192

—— Japanese, 187-9, 192-6

—— United States, 52, 67, 177; basis of, 57-8, 94-5, 196; present cost of, 347-8, 427; condition of, 339-41, 423-5

Negro, treatment of, by white men, 259-60, 264, 281

Negro problem in Latin America, 260-4, 281, 290-303

Neutral trade, rights of, 51, 67-8, 166-83

Pacific Ocean, 184-6
Pacifist ethics and ideals, 368, 407-21
Panama Canal, 94, 96, 148-9, 153, 195, 219, 254, 432-3
Pan-American courts, 268, 278-83, 319
Pan-American Union, 213-4

INDEX

Pan-Americanism, relation to present crisis, 17–18; economic motives behind, 111–23, 232–49; meaning of term, 203, 215; not now a reality, 203, 212, 216–7, 310; importance of, 204, 216–7; past history of, 212–4; present status of, 214–6; premises of, 205–7; as an hypothesis for the future, 204–5; prerequisites of, 207–11, 267–8, 290, 300, 317–8; probable results of its establishment, 212; fundamental fallacies of, 218–31, 250–66; lack of economic mutuality in, 232–49; South American view of, 203, 232–3, 251–6, 285–8, 291, 296–9, 301–3, 320–3; racial obstacles, 257–66; administrative and legal problems, 267–88; social obstacles, 289–303; defensive weakness, 304–16; strategic weakness of, 310–14; improbability of, 317–23; bibliography of, 457–9

Pan-Germanism, importance of sea-power for, 90; economic motives behind, 111–23, 137–8; finds best solution of problems in South America, 138–50; application of economics of, to United States, 351–66

Patriotism, varieties of, 12–3, 14–6

Peace, nature of, 439–42

Philippines, 96; importance of, to Japan, 189–91, 195–6; importance of, to United States, 330–1

Population, modern problems of, 117–23

Prosperity, economic, present conception of, 111–23

Race problem in Latin America, 229, 257–66, 281, 289–303

Revolution, American, showed strength of American position, 28–9, 35–7; influence of sea-power on, 46–8; effect upon our commercial position, 50–1, 65–7; caused by determination to reach West India markets, 64–6

Sea-power, nature of, 41–4; limitations of, 44–53; moderation of England in use of, 55–6, 89; influence on United States, 39, 56–8, 80–97; necessity of cordial relations of United States with, 67–9; part of, in Monroe Doctrine, 70; English possession of, challenged by Germany, 90–1; use of, in time of war, 166–83; prerequisites of independence from, by United States, 333–50; changed conditions of, 334–6

Social equality between citizens of United States and Latin America, 289–303

South America, lure to entice the victor to Western Hemisphere, 4; not able to replace West India market, 84; rediscovery of, 124–34; conditions in, 126–34, 138–42, 240–1; most favorable solution of German problems, 135–50; strategic position of, 146, 310–14; most favorable solution of English problems, 157–65; geographical relation to North America and Europe compared, 218–24

Spanish in America, 32, 34, 71, 125–6, 272

Strategic position of United States, 21–58, 90–108

Sugar trade, 32, 61–5, 83–4

Supremacy of England in the Western Hemisphere, 71–4, 80–97; true basis of, 80–1;

INDEX

Supremacy of England—*Con'd* loss of, by building of German navy, 90-7; will be regained by victory in the war, 152-3
—— of United States in the Western Hemisphere, origin and basis of the idea, 59-60, 65-7, 70, 78-9, 84; attained by the building of German navy, 90-7; will be lost by English victory, 152-3; denied by Latin Americans, 320-3

Transportation, conditions of, in past and its influence on United States, 21-4; improvements in 19th century and influence on United States, 98-102, 120-3, 356; on South America, 127-34, 218-25; influence of, on international interests of the United States, 364-6

United States, effect of war upon position of, 3-4; alternatives before, 3-18; use of term, 28, note; noble part in past history, 7-8; strategic position of, 21-38, 98-108; effect of supremacy of sea upon, 39-58; merchant marine of, 56-7; influence of West Indies upon, 59-79; early relations of, with Latin America, 75-9, 81-2; made supreme in Western Hemisphere by German navy, 90-7; economic structure complementary to England's, 94; probabilities of clash with Germany, 135-50; possibilities of clash with England, 151-83; possibilities of clash with Japan, 184- 200; position on neutral trade, 166-83; attitude of Latin America toward, 226-33; economic relationship of, to Latin America, 232-49; likely to be assailed by Europe in name of Latin America, 316; bibliography of, 448-54

Victor, of European war, only two possible for United States, 5; power of, 5, 415-6; economic motives and problems of, 111-23; probable personnel of, 135, 151; improbability of defense of Western Hemisphere against, by Pan-Americanism, 310

War, nature of, 369, 439-42
—— of 1812, 50-4, 69-70
Warfare, modern, character of, and influence on international politics, 102-7, 344
Western Hemisphere, relation of Monroe Doctrine to, 5; relation of Europe to, 31-2; place of West Indies in history of, 59-79; origin of idea of supremacy of United States in, 59-60, 65-7, 70, 78-9, 84; English supremacy of, 71-4, 80-93; supremacy of United States of, 94-7; strategic points in English hands still, 153; close connection of, with Europe, 218-31; Pan-Americanism not able to protect, from Europe, 308-10

West India Islands, influence of, upon American development, 32-3, 59-79; necessity of freedom of trade with, 54, 60-7, 70, 78; prosperity of, destroyed, 83-4